THE INDIVIDUAL AND
THE COSMOS
IN RENAISSANCE PHILOSOPHY

DATE DUE

ERNST CASSIRER

The Individual and the Cosmos in Renaissance Philosophy

Translated with an Introduction by
MARIO DOMANDI

University of Pennsylvania Press

Philadelphia

THE INDIVIDUAL AND THE COSMOS
IN RENAISSANCE PHILOSOPHY

This English translation copyright © 1963 by Mario Domandi.

Printed in the United States of America.

This book was originally published in German under the
title *Individuum und Kosmos in der Philosophie der
Renaissance* in 1927, as Volume X
in *Studien der Bibliothek Warburg,* published by
B. G. Teubner, Leipzig and Berlin. This translation, published
by arrangement with the author's estate, omits the
Appendices to the German edition.

First Pennsylvania Paperback edition 1972
Reprinted by arrangement with Harper & Row Publishers

Library of Congress Catalog Card Number: 63-17717

ISBN: 0-8122-1036-0

CONTENTS

v

TRANSLATOR'S INTRODUCTION

For more than thirty years, scholars concerned with Renaissance thought have looked upon Ernst Cassirer's *Individuum und Kosmos in der Philosophie der Renaissance* as one of the classics in the field. Outside the narrow circle of Renaissance scholarship, the book has attracted little attention, not only because copies have been scarce, but even more because of a lack of sympathy with Cassirer's intellectual-historical presuppositions and with his method. These presuppositions he makes explicit at the very beginning of this work. He follows Burckhardt in looking upon the Renaissance as an epoch characterized, among other ways, by the discovery of the individual in intellectual, personal, and social life. But Cassirer makes a major modification of Burckhardt's thesis. Burckhardt saw a radical separation between the theory and the practice of the Renaissance. The former, as expressed in its philosophical and religious thought, he called 'mere survivals of a tradition already dead', whereas the latter contained the vital and innovating tendencies of the age—the tendencies towards individuation. And for Burckhardt, these tendencies were to be found in the practice of such Renaissance figures as the tyrants, the humanists, and the artists. Cassirer, on the other hand, sees no separation between the theory and the practice. Here he follows Hegel, in that he considers philosophy to contain 'the full consciousness and spiritual essence of an epoch', reflecting, 'as the proper focus of the period, the entire manifold of the age'.

Having begun with premises drawn from Burckhardt and Hegel, Cassirer proceeds to state his own case. He sets out to show that the thought and practice of the Renaissance, though marked by the greatest diversity and conflict in content, are nevertheless at one in what Cassirer calls the systematic tendency, the common orientation of thought even

vii

in the most divergent fields. He identifies the common orientation as the attempt to give a new formulation of the universal and the particular, and of the relation between them. And with the achievement of such a formulation, the Renaissance comes to represent the first stage in the triumphal march of modern scientific thought.

Cassirer demonstrates carefully how Renaissance thinkers arrived at their vision of the orderliness of nature—an orderliness reducible to and definable through mathematical principles. He shows how the hierarchical, Neo-Platonic view of the cosmos, with its qualitative differences between the various strata that constitute the spiritual and physical universe, gave way to the ideas of the homogeneity of nature and the essential similarity of historical phenomena, making it possible to deal with both scientifically. He traces the idea of a *vera causa* to Pico della Mirandola's 'Treatise Against Astrology', and links that abstruse piece of Italian Humanism to the evolution of scientific method. Seen from this vantage point, the great achievements of the seventeenth and eighteenth centuries do not represent a new age of scientific innovation, but rather the resolution of problems and the elaboration of methods and principles already defined by thinkers from Nicholas Cusanus to Galileo.

Cassirer tells us that he 'does not intend to enter the dispute concerning the content and legitimacy of those historical concepts "Renaissance" and "Middle Ages" ' (p. vi). But in another work, in connection with historical method, he does describe what they are intended to signify. For him, they are not merely chronologically descriptive terms, nor even generic concepts based on empirical facts. Rather, they are ideal 'types', ultimately derived, to be sure, from the 'facts', but not through simple induction. Here lies one of the major differences between the method of the natural scientist and that of the cultural historian. Understood as the logic of quantitative concepts, science requires that an abstraction cover every particular case it subsumes. But in the logic of the *Kulturwissenschaften*, as Cassirer points out apropos of defining the term Renaissance, the abstraction expresses 'a unity of *direction*, not a unity of *actualization* [or, of *actual particulars*]. The particular individuals *belong together*, not because they are alike or resemble each other, but because they are *co-operating* in a *common task*, which, in contrast to the Middle Ages, we perceive to be new and to be the distinctive "meaning" of the Renaissance. . . . We perceive them [i.e., the individuals] to be not only different, but even opposed. What we are asserting of them is that in spite of this opposition, perhaps just because of it, they stand to each other in a specific ideal connection: each in his own way is contributing to the making of what we call the "spirit" of the Renaissance or the civilization of the Renaissance.'[1]

Cassirer's genius lay in the marvellous combination of astounding erudition and artistic insight he brought to the problem of seeing precisely how each thinker he deals with is co-operating in the new and common task. Not only in Leonardo and Galileo, where it is obvious, but even in such thinkers as Pico della Mirandola, Francesco Patrizzi, and Giordano Bruno, Cassirer unerringly distinguishes the old from the new, the 'mere survival of dead tradition' from the quick and fertile. And what seem at first to be a series of unconnected intellectual portraits come to form a subsequent unity, a brilliant tapestry within which each thread contributes to the whole.

Nothing is easier than to point to the very gradual nature of historical transition, and to deny that any given moment can with any accuracy be labelled medieval or Renaissance. Cassirer would have been the last to deny that, and indeed, he speaks of the 'absurdity' of looking for an 'end' to the medieval world and a 'beginning' of the modern world. 'But that does not do away with the necessity of looking for an *intellectual* line of demarcation between the two ages.'[2] For Cassirer, this boundary line exists, and it separates the metaphysical world of transcendence from the scientific world of immanence. Medieval thought is characterized by its notion of a universal hierarchy leading up to God; and together with that goes the acceptance of a transcendent standard for the evaluation and understanding of the things of this world. 'In order to find an unchangeable, an absolute truth, man has to go beyond the limit of his own consciousness and his own existence. He has to surpass himself. . . . By this transcendence, the whole method of the dialectic, the Socratic and Platonic method, is completely changed. Reason gives up its independence and autonomy. It has no longer a light of its own; it shines only in a borrowed and reflected light. If this light fails, human reason becomes ineffective and impotent.'[3] To this Cassirer contrasts the ideal of Renaissance thought, which is to understand the intelligible in and through the sensible—the universal in and through the particular. Whether it be Machiavelli observing the

---

[1] *The Logic of the Humanities*, translated by Clarence Smith Howe, Yale University Press, 1961, pp. 139–40.
[2] *The Myth of the State*, Doubleday Anchor Books, 1955, p. 163.
[3] Ibid., p. 101.

realm of politics, or Leonardo studying nature, the Renaissance mind is seeking to formulate the *ragioni* embodied in things and events.

Although Cassirer did not concern himself primarily with the role of reason in the great Scholastic systems, and in medieval life generally, his distinction nevertheless proves to be as apt as it is fruitful for the study not only of medieval and Renaissance philosophy and religion, but art and literature as well. St. Francis of Assisi's *Cantico delle creature* may serve as a convenient example of the literary applicability of Cassirer's ideas. For philosophical reasons, he dismisses as indefensible Henry Thode's attempt to trace the origins of the Italian Renaissance to the Franciscan doctrine contained in the poem. A strictly literary analysis provides further evidence for Cassirer's argument. In this poem, St. Francis praises God and His creation, and he addresses the various elements as the family of man. These natural objects and phenomena have since been poetically described so often that their attributes have become cliches. But consider the qualities St. Francis attaches to them: our sisters the stars are clear, precious, and beautiful; brother sun illuminates the day, and is beautiful and radiant, with great splendour; sister water is very useful, humble, precious, and chaste; mother earth nourishes and sustains us, and produces various fruit, and colourful flowers and grass. The qualities attributed to each phenomenon in nature are either general and abstract or, if particular, could just as easily be used to describe some other form of being. They derive their value and applicability not from being intimately connected with or immanent in the things they describe, but rather from their association with another, usually a higher realm. The utilitarian qualities ascribed to God's creation are completely consistent with this; the things in nature serve man, who is God's highest creature on earth, and thence they derive their value. Clearly, this exquisite poem is couched in a medieval, hierarchical, Neo-Platonic conception of the cosmos.

It would be a fascinating task to go through the Italian literature of the late Middle Ages and the Renaissance with Cassirer's *kulturwissenschaftlichen* methods and conclusions as guides. Such an excursion might show why Galileo, the man who, like Leonardo, sought the *ragioni* in things, the immanent laws by which they functioned, should be far more attracted to the limpid, precise prose and poetry of Ariosto than by the delicate, sensuous haze that pervades the works of Tasso. Such an excursion might even cause us to modify slightly some of Cassirer's judgments. He looks upon Petrarch's thought, for example, as the embodiment of the transition from the Middle Ages to the Renaissance; and upon Petrarch's mind as the arena for the conflict between the old and the new. And yet, if we look at the poetry of the *Canzoniere*—at the sonnet 'Pentimento', for instance, we see clearly that Petrarch's view of himself and his relation to God have completely broken away from medieval moorings. At the end of his life, Petrarch stands alone. And if he still needs God, it is only because he has experienced what life has to offer and found it wanting. The meaning of his life and experience is not defined by his relation to God, nor is it rendered nugatory in the face of God's omnipotence. On the contrary, the very need for God seems dependent upon the character of that experience. In Petrarch's mind, God's place is determined through and related to the entirety of Petrarch's own experience. And that is precisely the kind of consciousness of individual self and its value that Cassirer considers a Renaissance trait.

Cassirer published his first studies of Renaissance thought in the first volume of the *Erkenntnisproblem* (1906), at a time when the field was largely virgin land. It was still fairly uncultivated in 1927, when the *Individuum und Kosmos* appeared; but since then, Renaissance thought and culture have been the subject of acute and careful scholarship both here and abroad. Cassirer himself never stopped studying the sources, and always kept fully abreast of the results of his fellow scholars' research. Inevitably, some of the details in his original presentation had to be corrected. In his later essays on the Renaissance, several of which are contained in the early volumes of the *Journal of the History of Ideas*, Cassirer never hesitates to make these corrections himself. He admits freely, for instance, that in the *Individuum und Kosmos* he probably overestimated the influence of Cusanus' doctrine on Italian thinkers, especially on Ficino, and that the Italians may very well have come to the same conclusions independently. But such an error does not affect the substance of Cassirer's argument. What he seeks to show in this work is that Renaissance thought constitutes a self-contained unity, and that philosophy is 'related to the entire intellectual movement and its vital forces not as something extraneous and apart, . . . but that it actively affects and determines those forces'. This thesis Cassirer proves with remarkable clarity and skill. No other writer before or since has so convincingly portrayed the originality of Renaissance philosophy—an originality that goes far beyond the high refinement and elaboration of traditional Scholastic problems. And no other writer has described as perceptively as Cassirer the interdependence of philosophy, language, art, science—in a phrase, all the symbolic forms.

The interdependence of philosophy and language is attested by the problems that present themselves when translating a German philosophical text into English. There is a deceptive similarity in the grammatical structure of the two languages. Often, even a simple German sentence sounds awkward when converted into English, whereas the original may have been not only grammatical but elegant. An example of language reflecting the form of philosophical thought is to be found in the German use of an abstract idea as the subject of a sentence, having it act upon or through a man or a school. Such form is certainly consistent with the Idealist conception of philosophy and history and, I suspect, can even be derived from the fact that a good part of the German philosophical vocabulary was created by German mysticism. In English, such grammatical constructions are feasible, but they sound 'Germanic', and that adjective is unquestionably considered pejorative when applied to prose style. For the translator, the question is whether to try to keep the original form of the thought, thus preserving some of its movement and flavour; or to re-form it in the interests of style. I generally chose the latter alternative, whenever it was possible without violence to the thought. To use the same example: whenever an abstraction was used as subject, and the thinker connected to it either as object, through a preposition, or by the passive voice, I made the person the subject and used the active voice. If this be translator's treason, I hope I have made the most of it.

In the preparation of this translation, I incurred only a few obligations, but those are deep. I want to express my sincerest thanks to my friends Eugene Gadol, of the New School for Social Research, and his wife Joan Gadol, of the City College of New York. Their detailed knowledge of the whole range of Cassirer's thought helped me to understand some of the more elusive passages in this work. For the thoughtfulness and accuracy of their criticism, I am deeply grateful.

I am also indebted to my colleague James Hoffman Day of the Classics Department of Vassar College for his expert, meticulous review of the copious Greek and Latin quotations contained in this work.

For all errors I am, of course, solely responsible.

Vassar College, February 1962   Mario Domandi

To A. WARBURG
on his sixtieth birthday
13 June 1926

My dear and esteemed friend,

The work I am presenting to you on your sixtieth birthday was to have been a purely personal expression of my deep friendship and devotion. But I could not have completed the work, had I not been able to enjoy the constant stimulation and encouragement of that group of scholars whose intellectual centre is your library. Therefore, I am speaking today not in my name alone, but in the name of this group of scholars, and in the name of all those who have long honoured you as a leader in the field of intellectual history. For the past three decades, the Warburg Library has quietly and consistently endeavoured to gather materials for research in intellectual and cultural history. And it has done much more besides. With a forcefulness that is rare, it has held up before us the principles which must govern such research. In its organization and in its intellectual structure, the Library embodies the idea of the methodological unity of all fields and all currents of intellectual history. Today, the Library is entering a new phase in its development. With the construction of a new building, it will broaden its field of activity. On this occasion, we members want to express publicly how much the Library means to us and how much we owe to it. We hope, and we are sure, that above and beyond the new tasks which the Library must fulfil, the old tradition of our common, friendly collaboration will not be forgotten, and that the intellectual and personal bond that has hitherto held us together will become ever stronger. May the organon of intellectual-historical studies which you have created with your Library continue to ask us questions for a long time. And may you continue to show us new ways to answer them, as you have in the past.

Ernst Cassirer

Hamburg
13 June 1926

INTRODUCTION

THE philosophy of the early Renaissance does not seem to bear out Hegel's presupposition that the full consciousness and spiritual essence of an epoch is contained in its philosophy; that philosophy, as self-conscious awareness of consciousness itself, reflects—as the proper focus of the period—the entire manifold of the age. At the end of the thirteenth and the beginning of the fourteenth century, a new life begins to stir in poetry, in the visual arts, in politics, and in historical life, becoming ever stronger and ever more conscious of itself as a movement of spiritual renewal. But, at first glance, the new spirit seems to find neither expression nor echo in the philosophical thought of the time. For, even at those points where it seems to be freeing itself from the findings of Scholasticism, the philosophy of the early Renaissance remains bound to the general *forms* of Scholastic thought.

The attack Petrarch ventures in his *De sui ipsius et multorum ignorantia* against the philosophy of the Schools is in fact only a witness to the unbroken force which that philosophy still exercises upon the time. Indeed, the principle that Petrarch opposes to the Scholastic and Aristotelian doctrine has neither philosophical origin nor content. It is not a new method of thought; rather, it is the new cultural ideal of 'eloquence'. Henceforth, Aristotle will and may no longer be considered the master of knowledge, the representative of 'culture' pure and simple, for his works—those that have come down to us—contain 'not the slightest trace of eloquence'. Humanist criticism, then, turns against the style, not against the content of Aristotle's works. But this criticism gradually annihilates its own premises. For, as the scope of humanist knowledge broadens, and as its scholarly instruments become sharper and finer, the picture of the Scholastic Aristotle must necessarily give way to the picture of the true Aristotle, which can now be drawn from the sources themselves. Leonardo Bruni, the first translator of the

Politics and the *Nicomachean Ethics,* asserted that Aristotle himself would not have recognized his own works in the transformations they had undergone at the hands of the Scholastics, just as Actaeon was not recognized by his own dogs after he had been changed into a deer.[1]

With this judgment, the new intellectual movement of Humanism came to terms with Aristotle. Instead of fighting him, Humanism now required that his language and spirit be assimilated. But the problems that grew out of this were of a philological rather than a philosophical nature. A hot debate was fought over the question whether the Aristotelian concept τ'αγαθόν ought to be translated as *summum bonum,* as Leonardo Bruni had done, or as *bonum ipsum.* The dispute concerning the spelling of the Aristotelian term *entelechy* (whether it ought to be *entelechia* or *endelechia*), and the various possibilities of interpretation contingent upon the spelling, attracted such famous humanists as Filelfo, Angelo Poliziano, and others.[2]

Even outside the narrow circle of Humanism, even in circles that recognized the primacy of philosophy over its new ally philology, no real innovation was made in philosophical method. The struggle for pre-eminence between Platonists and Aristotelians, as it is conducted in the second half of the fifteenth century, never penetrates deeply enough to reach ultimate presuppositions. The standard whose applicability both sides accept lies beyond the realm of systematic thought; it lies in religious assumptions and dogmatic decisions. And so this struggle too yields no results for the history of philosophical thought. Instead of a sharp distinction between the actual content and principles of the Platonic and Aristotelian doctrines, we find an attempt at a syncretistic fusion of the two. It was precisely the Florentine Academy, the avowed custodian of the true Platonic inheritance, that went farthest in this attempt. In this undertaking, Ficino was seconded by Pico della Mirandola, the 'Princeps Concordiae', as his friends called him. Pico considered the main purpose of philosophical thought to be the reconciliation of Scholasticism and Platonism. In a letter to Ermolao Barbaro, he explains that he came to the Florentine Academy not as a deserter, but as an explorer; and that as a result of his findings, it became

---

[1] Cf. Georg Voigt, *Die Wiederbelebung des klassischen Altertums* (2 vols., 3rd ed.; Berlin, 1893), II, 169; and Francesco Fiorentino, *Il risorgimento filosofico nel Quattrocento* (Napoli, 1885), pp. 183f.

[2] For a more detailed discussion of this point, see the chapter entitled 'L'umanesimo nella filosofia' in Fiorentino, op. cit., pp. 184ff.

clear to him that Plato and Aristotle, much as they seem to oppose each other verbally, are actually in agreement on everything.[3] In such attempts at unification, the great philosophical systems lose their own distinctive features; they dissolve in the mist of a primordial Christian-philosophical revelation, as witnesses to which Ficino cites Moses and Plato, Zoroaster and Hermes Trismegistos, Orpheus and Pythagoras, Virgil and Plotinus.[4] The fundamental drive of the age, which is the impulse to clear delimitation and articulation, to distinction and in-dividuation, seems to be not yet active in philosophy—or to founder in the first attempt.

With this in mind, it is easy to see why the historian of culture ignores the philosophical documents of this period. To arrive at a comprehensive view, he must take as his point of departure clearly drawn, sharply delineated individuals; but these the philosophical documents of the period do not seem to provide. Jacob Burckhardt, for one, in his great portrayal of Renaissance civilization, granted no place to philosophy. He does not even consider it as a constitutive moment of the entire intellectual* movement, let alone look at it in the Hegelian sense of 'proper focus' or 'spiritual essence of the time'. One might pass over this difficulty by saying that in any conflict between those who do historical research and those who write the philosophy of history, the decision must always go to the historian, since every speculative construction must submit to the 'facts' and recognize in them its limits. But this truism regarding method does not even come to grips with the difficulty, much less resolve it. If one looks below the surface, it becomes evident that by excluding the philosophy of the Renaissance from his presentation. Burckhardt implicitly placed upon himself another limitation, necessarily bound to the first. It was precisely the Scholastic character of Renaissance philosophy that made it impossible to distinguish between philosophical and religious issues. The most

[3] 'Diverti nuper ab Aristotele in Academiam, sed non transfuga . . . verum explorator. Videor tamen (dicam tibi Hermolae quod sentio) duo in Platone agnoscere et Homericam illam eloquendi facultatem supra prosam orationem sese attolentem et sensuum si quis eos altius introspiciat, cum Aristotele omnino communionem, ita ut si verba spectes, nihil pugnantius, si res nihil concordius.' *Ioann. Pici Mirandolae Opera* (Basle, n.d.), i. 368f. For Pico's scholastic studies, cf. ibid., 351f.

[4] Cf. Ficino's letters, in *Opera* (Basle, n.d.), 866, 871. Cf. especially Ficino *De christiana religione* 22 (*Opera* 25).

* The word 'intellectual', as it is used throughout this translation, refers not to theoretical ratiocination, but to conscious mental life in all its forms. It is meant to render the sense of the German word *geistig*, which when translated as 'spiritual', as is often done, carries with it too many overtones alien to the notion itself. I have translated *Geist* as 'spirit' whenever that seemed to be the meaning of the author Cassirer is dealing with. [M.D.]

significant and far-reaching works of philosophy in the Quattrocento are and remain essentially theology. Their entire content is concentrated in the three great problems: God, freedom, and immortality. The disputes between Alexandrists and Averroists at the University of Padua revolve around these problems. And they also form the core of the speculations of the Florentine Platonists.

In his great, comprehensive presentation of the morality and religion of the Renaissance, Burckhardt deliberately omitted this evidence. It seemed to him to be a continuation of a tradition already dead, a theoretical work of secondary importance which no longer stood in any vital relation to the religious forces that in fact animated the time. In keeping with his whole point of view, he had to grasp these forces not through their theoretical formulations, not through philosophical speculations concerning religion, but rather through the direct activity of man, i.e., through man's practical attitude towards the world, and towards moral and spiritual reality. But one may well ask if this sharp distinction between 'theory' and 'practice' in religion corresponds to the historical reality itself, or if it is not rather a work of Burckhardt *the philosopher*? Is it not in fact true that for the 'spirit of the Renaissance', as Burckhardt called it, this separation did not exist; and that these two moments which in the picture of the cultural historian are held apart, in the actual life of the epoch are constantly coalescing and interpenetrating? Is it not true that the ingenuousness of faith is at the same time dogmatic, just as theoretical dogmatism is highly ingenuous, including as plainly as it does the most various elements of faith and superstition? The criticism to which Burkchardt's classic has been subjected by ever-progressing empirical research has aimed mainly at this point.

The history of art, the history of politics, and the general history of culture all seemed to point in the same direction. In opposition to Burckhardt's interpretation, the boundaries regarding both the time and the content of 'the Middle Ages' and 'the Renaissance' began to shift more and more.[5] We may ignore Henry Thode's attempt to place the beginning of the Italian Renaissance in art back in the early thirteenth century, and to see in Francis of Assisi not only the initiator of a new

---

[5] For the details of this development, the individual stages of which cannot be dealt with here, I refer the reader to the excellent work by Konrad Burdach, *Vom Mittelalter zur Reformation: Forschungen zur Geschichte der deutschen Bildung* (Berlin, 1912ff.). Also see Burdach's other works: *Deutsche Renaissance* (2nd ed.; Berlin, 1918); and *Reformation, Renaissance, Humanismus* (Berlin, 1918).

ideal of piety, but also of a movement in art that will find its fulfilment in the painting and poetry of the fifteenth century. Today, practically no scholar would represent or defend Thode's thesis as he formulated it.[6] One thing, however, seems unmistakable: the more one tried to demonstrate *in concreto* the antithesis 'man of the Middle Ages' and 'man of the Renaissance', the more fleeting and fluid did the antithesis threaten to become—especially as *specialized biographical research* on the artists, thinkers, scholars, and statesmen progressed further. According to the recent judgment of a well-known scholar in this field, 'If one tries to view the lives of the leading personalities of the fifteenth century—of Coluccio Salutati, Poggio Bracciolini, Leonardo Bruni, Lorenzo Valla, Lorenzo the Magnificent, or Luigi Pulci—in a purely inductive way, one invariably arrives at the conclusion that the established characteristics of the period (such as individualism and paganism, sensualism and scepticism) oddly enough do not apply to the person being studied. If one tries to understand these . . . characteristics in their vital connections with the life of the man being portrayed, and even more, in connection with the broad currents of the age, they invariably take on a completely different aspect. And if one puts together the results of empirical research, there gradually emerges a new picture of the Renaissance, in which piety and impiety, good and evil, yearning for heaven and love of this earth are intertwined to no lesser extent, but in an infinitely more complex manner.'[7]

The history of philosophy will do well to heed the lesson and the warning contained in these sentences. For although it can never cease trying to achieve the general, and even the most abstract universality, the history of philosophy must never forget that it can only make responsible generalizations by immersing itself in the most concrete particulars and in the most subtle nuances of historical detail. What is needed is the universality of a systematic point of view and of a systematic orientation which in no way coincides with the universality of merely empirical concepts used in the periodization of history for convenient classification. To supply just this will be the aim of the following study. It does not intend to enter the dispute concerning the content and the legitimacy of those historical concepts 'Renaissance' and 'Middle Ages', which is now being waged in the writing of political history, in

---

[6] Cf. Henry Thode, *Franz von Assisi und die Anfänge der Kunst der Renaissance in Italien* (Berlin, 1885).

[7] Ernst Walser, *Studien zur Weltanschauung der Renaissance* (Basle, 1920), pp. 5f.

the history of art, and of literature.[8] Rather, it intends to remain within the realm of the history of philosophical problems, and to seek, on that basis, to answer the question: whether and to what extent the movement of thought in the fifteenth and sixteenth centuries constitutes a self-contained unity despite the multiplicity of starting points and the divergence of solutions to the various problems posed.

If this unity can be successfully demonstrated, if the profusion of problems with which the philosophy of the Renaissance presents us can be successfully related to certain pivotal questions, then the question, 'in what connection does the theoretical thought of the Renaissance stand to the other vital forces which determine the intellectual constitution of the time' will answer itself. It will also become clear that the work of philosophical thought is related to the entire intellectual movement and its vital forces not as something extraneous and apart, and that it does not follow that movement as some 'abstract' shadow, but that it actively affects and determines those forces. It is not simply a part tied on to other parts. Rather, it represents the whole, giving it a conceptual-symbolic form of expression. The following pages will show how the new universal life sought by the Renaissance leads to the demand for a new cosmos of *thought*, and how the new life reflects and finds itself only in this thought.

[8] For the origins of this dispute and for a description of its present state, I refer the reader to the works by Burdach already cited, and especially to Walter Goetz, 'Renaissance und Antike', *Historische Zeitschrift*, CXIII, 237 ff.; and by the same author, 'Renaissance und Mittelalter', ibid., XCVIII, 30 ff. There is also a wealth of material to be found in Karl Borinski, *Die Weltwiedergeburtsidee in den neueren Zeiten, I. Der Streit um die Renaissance und die Entstehungsgeschichte der historischen Beziehungsbegriffe Renaissance und Mittelalter* (*Sitzungsberichte der Bayrischen Akademie der Wissenschaften, Philosophisch-philologische Klasse*, 1919).

CHAPTER ONE

NICHOLAS CUSANUS

I

ANY study that seeks to view the philosophy of the Renaissance as a *systematic* unity must take as its point of departure the doctrines of Nicholas Cusanus. Of all the philosophical movements and efforts of the Quattrocento, only his doctrines fulfil Hegel's demand; only they represent a 'simple focal point' in which the most diverse rays are gathered. Cusanus is the only thinker of the period to look at all of the fundamental problems of his time from the point of view of *one* principle through which he masters them all. His thought knows no barriers that separate disciplines. In keeping with the medieval ideal of the whole, it includes the totality of the spiritual and physical cosmos. He is both a speculative theologian and a speculative mathematician; he is as interested in statics and in general theories of movement as he is in questions of astronomy and cosmography; he is as concerned with problems of church history as he is with problems of political history, history of law, and general intellectual history. And although, as a scholar and investigator, he enriches each of these fields with his own contributions, there is never any danger of specialization or of fragmentation in his work. When Cusanus takes up and elaborates anything, it comes to fit into an intellectual whole, and combines with his other efforts to form a subsequent unity. Indeed, all his thought is simply the unfolding and extension of that fundamental first principle he developed in his first philosophical work, *De docta ignorantia*. We can apply to Cusanus' thought the antithesis *complicatio* and *explicatio*, which he uses to illuminate the relationship of God to the world and of the world to the human mind. His thought blossoms out of *one* intellectual seed that progressively unfolds and, in this process of unfolding, absorbs the entire range and the entire *Problematik* of knowledge in the Quattrocento.

The principle upon which Cusanus' philosophy is based presented

7

itself to him as a new, fundamental truth, born not of syllogistic reasoning, but as a sudden vision that took hold of him with all the power of a great intuition. Cusanus himself has described how this principle, a 'gift of God', first appeared to him during the crossing from Constantinople.[1] If we attempt to give abstract expression to the content of this principle, or to systematically define and historically order what to Cusanus appeared as something incomparable and unique, we shall run the risk of failing to recognize the originality and depth of the new thought. To be sure, the concept of *docta ignorantia*, and the doctrine of the 'coincidence of opposites' based upon it, seem to do nothing more than to repeat thoughts that belong to the solid patrimony of medieval mysticism. Cusanus constantly refers to the sources of this mysticism, especially to the writings of Meister Eckhart and the Pseudo-Dionysius. And so it would seem difficult, if not impossible, to draw a definite line of separation between them. But the kernel of Cusanus' work is not contained in the thought that God, the Absolute Being, is beyond any positive determination, that He is only to be described through negative predications, or that He can be conceived of only by going beyond, by transcending all finite measures, proportions, and comparisons. Had that been the case, no new way, no new objective would have been indicated. In its ultimate foundations, such an orientation of 'mystical' theology might seem to conflict with Scholasticism; but in fact, this conflict itself forms one of the characteristic features of the whole intellectual physiognomy of Scholasticism itself. The great leaders of Scholasticism had long since appropriated the doctrines of the Pseudo-Dionysius. John Erigena referred to the writings of the Areopagite; and the treatment of them in commentaries by Albertus Magnus and Thomas Aquinas gave them a solid place in the medieval system of life and learning. On this score, then, the system was unshakable. If the old thought was to be driven beyond its own boundaries, it had to receive a new imprint and, so to speak, a new accent.

We can describe this new imprint only if we first recall the whole literary and intellectual structure of the work of the Areopagite. The very titles of his works suggest this structure. And they also suggest the

---

[1] *De docta ignorantia* iii. 12: 'Accipe nunc Pater metuende quaejamdudum attingere variis doctrinarum viis concupivi, sed prius non potui, quousque in mari ex Graecia rediens (credo superno dono a patre luminum, a quo omne datum optimum) ad hoc ductus sum, ut incompraehensibilia incompraehensibiliter amplecterer, in docta ignorantia, per transcensum veritatum incorruptibilium humaniter scibilium.'

place these works occupy within the whole medieval conception of God and the world. In these works, for the first time, the problem of *hierarchy* is presented in all its sharpness and metaphysical breadth, in its assumptions and in its manifold transformations. In addition to the work on divine names (περὶ θείων ὀνομάτων), the works on the hierarchy of heaven and the church (περὶ τῆς οὐρανίας Ἱεραρχίας, περὶ τῆς ἐκκλησιαστικῆς Ἱεραρχίας) were especially influential in the succeeding epochs. In these works the two basic intellectual forces and motifs that form the basis of medieval faith and knowledge meet for the first time and become one; we have here the actual fusion of the Christian doctrine of salvation and Hellenistic speculation. Therein lies the significance of these works.

The most important bequest of this speculation (especially of Neo-Platonism) to Christianity was the concept and the general picture of a *graduated cosmos*. The world separates itself into a lower and a higher, into a sensible and an intelligible world. Not only do these worlds stand opposed to each other; their essences, in fact, consist precisely in their mutual negation, in their polar antithesis. But across this abyss of negation a spiritual bond extends between the two worlds. From one pole to the other, from the super-being and super-one, the domain of absolute form, reaching down to matter as the absolute-formless, there is an unbroken path of mediation. The infinite passes over to the finite on this path and the finite returns on it back to the infinite. The whole process of *redemption* is included in it: it is the Incarnation of God, just as it is the deification of man. In this conception, there is always a 'between' to be bridged; there is always a separating medium that cannot be jumped over but must be traversed step by step in strictly ordered succession. This stepladder leading from the celestial to the earthly, and from here back up again, is systematically described and depicted in the works of Dionysius. Between God and man there is the world of pure intelligences and heavenly powers. It consists of three circles, each of which is, in turn, divided into three parts. In the first circle belong the Seraphim, the Cherubim, and the Thrones; in the second, the Dominations, Virtues, and Powers; in the third, the Principalities, the Archangels, and the Angels. Thus, all being emanates from God in determined degrees of radiation, only to gather up again in Him and to re-concentrate in Him. Just as all radii of a circle come from its centre, so God is the beginning and the end of all things. Just as these radii come closer together the closer they get to the centre, so the union of essences prevails over their separation the less distant they are from the common centre, the source of being and of life. And with that we also have the justification, the actual theodicy of ecclesiastical order, which is essentially nothing but the complete reproduction of the spiritual-cosmic order. The ecclesiastical reflects the heavenly hierarchy, and in this reflection becomes conscious of its own inviolable necessity. Medieval cosmology and faith, the idea of universal order, and the idea of the moral-religious order of salvation here flow together into a single fundamental view, into a picture that is at once of the highest significance and of the highest inner consequence.

Nicholas Cusanus never criticized this picture. Indeed, his whole speculation, especially that of the early period, seems rather to presuppose it. Nevertheless, the first sentences of the work *De docta ignorantia* give birth to a new thought, and point to a completely new *total intellectual orientation*. Here, too, the starting point is the opposition between the being of the absolute and the being of the empirical-conditioned, i.e., between the being of the infinite and of the finite. But now the opposition is no longer merely dogmatically posited; rather it must be understood in its ultimate depth and conceived of through the conditions of human knowledge. This position towards the problem of knowledge makes of Cusanus the first modern thinker.[2] His first step consists in asking not about God, but about the possibility of knowledge about God. And of the answers hitherto given to this fundamental question by philosophy or by speculative theology, none satisfies him. They all fail as soon as one calls to mind the simple concept of knowledge and the assumptions included within it. All knowledge presupposes comparison, which, in turn, more precisely understood, is nothing but measurement. But if any contents are to be measured by and through each other, the first, inevitable assumption must be the condition of *homogeneity*. They must be reduced to one and the same unit of measure; they must be capable of being thought of as belonging to the same quantitative order. But precisely this condition becomes unfulfillable as soon as the goal, the object of knowledge is no longer something finite, conditioned, singular, but rather an absolute object.

[2] For a more detailed discussion of this point, see my work, *Das Erkenntnisproblem in der Philosophie und Wissenschaft der neueren Zeit* (3 vols., Berlin, 1906–20), I, 21ff., to which I refer the reader generally for further elucidation of what follows. For a recent, very penetrating investigation that confirms this connection between Cusanus' theology and his epistemology, see: Edmond Vansteenberghe, *Le Cardinal Nicolas de Cues* (Paris, 1920). 'La clef,' he writes, 'de voûte du système philosophique de Nicolas de Cues, et en cela il est bien moderne, est sa théorie de la connaissance' p. 279.

By its essence and by definition, the absolute object lies beyond every possibility of comparison and measurement and therefore beyond the possibility of knowledge. If the characteristic feature of all empirical knowing and measuring consists in reducing one quantity to another, one element to another through a definite series of operations, i.e., *through a finite series of mental steps*, every such reduction must fail when it comes to the infinite. 'Finiti et infiniti nulla proportio.' The distance between the finite and the infinite remains the same no matter how many intermediate terms we may place between them. There is no rational method of thought, no discursive procedure that, adding element to element and passing from one element to another, can close the gap between the two extremes and lead from the one to the other.[3]

In these terse and simple propositions at the beginning of the *De docta ignorantia* a decisive turn has been taken. For now, with a single, sharp incision the bond has been severed that had hitherto joined Scholastic theology and Scholastic logic. Logic, in the form it had till now, has ceased to be an organ of speculative theology. To be sure, the development of Scholasticism itself had prepared the way for these conclusions reached by Cusanus. William of Occam's terminism, and the 'modern' movement in Scholasticism attached to it, had already loosened the connection that, in the classical systems of realism, subsisted between logic and grammar on the one hand and theology and metaphysics on the other.[4] Now, however, a far more radical separation

---

[3] Cf. *De docta ignorantia* i. 1: 'Omnes . . . investigantes in comparatione praesuppositi certi proportionabiliter incertum judicant. Comparativa igitur est omnis inquisitio, medio proportionis utens, ut dum haec quae inquiruntur propinqua proportionali reductione praesupposito possint comparari, facile est apprehensionis judicium; dum multis mediis opus habemus, difficultas et labor exoritur. Uti haec in Mathematicis nota sunt, ubi ad prima notissima principia priores propositiones facile reducuntur et posteriores, quoniam non nisi per medium priorum, difficilius. Omnis igitur inquisitio in comparativa proportione facili vel difficili existit, propter quid infinitum, ut infinitum, cum omnem proportionem aufugiat, ignotum est.'

[4] Cf. Gerhard Ritter's exhaustive studies of the battle between the 'via antiqua' and the 'via moderna' in the fourteenth and fifteenth centuries, in his *Studien zur Spätscholastik: I. Marsilius von Inghen und die Okkamistische Schule in Deutschland. II. Via antiqua und via moderna auf den deutschen Universitäten des 15. Jahrhunderts (Sitzungsberichte der Heidelberger Akademie der Wissenschaften, Philosophisch-historische Klasse*, 1921–2). Ritter has shown that this loosening of the connection between logic and grammar on one hand, and theology and metaphysics on the other, was postulated and, within limits, brought about by Occam's doctrines; but a complete separation of the two moments was never achieved. Indeed, as Ritter has further shown, the boundaries Occam has tried to draw soon begin to blur. This was true even in the camp of the 'moderni', the dominant movement of the university schools. Summarizing the results of his studies, Ritter writes: 'We have followed, step by step, the gradual softening of Occam's radical epistemological propositions by his students. John Gerson was on the verge of understanding one of the most powerful of Occam's original thoughts: viz., that religious knowledge has its roots in

takes place. To Cusanus, Aristotle's logic, based on the principle of the excluded middle, seems precisely for that reason to be merely a logic of the finite, one which must always and necessarily be found wanting when it comes to contemplating the infinite.[5] All its concepts are concepts of comparison; they rest upon the union of the equal and the similar and upon the separation of the unequal and the different. By such a process of comparing and distinguishing, of separating and delimiting, all empirical being splits up into definite genuses and species that stand in a definite relationship of super- or sub-ordination to each other. The whole art of logical thought consists in making this interlocking of the conceptual spheres visible and clear. To define one concept through another, we must traverse the whole series of middle terms that stand between them. Whenever these middle terms do not offer themselves immediately to natural thought, we must discover them by means of syllogistic reasoning. Thus we can join the abstract with the concrete and the general with the particular in a definitely determined order of thought. This order corresponds to the order of being: it reproduces the hierarchy of being in the hierarchical arrangement of concepts. But—objects Cusanus—even if similarities and differences, agreements and oppositions of the finite can be conceived of in this fashion, the absolute and unconditioned, which as such is beyond comparison, will never be caught in this net of logical genus concepts. The content of Scholastic thought contradicts its form; they are mutually exclusive. If the possibility of *thinking* the absolute and infinite is to exist, this thought cannot and may not lean on the crutches of traditional 'logic', which can lead us only from one finite and con-

completely different ground from the natural intellect, and that theological-metaphysical speculation, therefore, would do more harm than good to religious knowledge. If the implications of this idea had been energetically explored, it would have, indeed, meant the end of Scholasticism. But that did not even nearly happen. Gerson was only able to half free himself from the tightly knit web of religious–dogmatic and metaphysical-logical ideas that were the essence of Scholastic thought. . . . He did not doubt the reality of logical concepts formed through abstraction. Furthermore, a study of the philosophical and theological writings of Marsilius of Inghen shows us that a completely closed scientific system could be built on the foundations of Nominalism and still affirm all the essential positions of the late Scholastic metaphysics and theology.' II, 86ff. Keeping in mind these results of Ritter's studies, we will understand that Cusanus, even in his earliest work, had progressed far beyond anything his Occamist teachers in Heidelberg could offer him.

[5] Cf. especially Cusanus' remark against his Scholastic adversary Johann Wenck of Heidelberg: 'Cum nunc Aristotelis secta praevaleat, quae haeresim putat esse oppositorum coincidentiam, in cujus admissione est initium ascensus in mysticam Theologiam, in ea secta enutritis haec via ut penitus insipida quasi proposito contraria ab eis procul pellitur, ut sit miraculo simile, sicuti sectae mutatio, rejecto Aristotele eos altius transsilire.' *Apol. doct. ign.* fol. 64f.

ditioned to another, but never take us beyond the domain of finiteness and conditionality.

With this, every kind of 'rational' theology is refuted—and in its place steps 'mystical theology'. But just as Cusanus went beyond the traditional conception of logic, so now he also goes beyond the traditional conception of mysticism. With the same assurance with which he denies the possibility of conceiving of the infinite by means of logical abstractions and generic concepts, he also denies the possibility of its conception through mere feeling. In the mystical theology of the fifteenth century two fundamental tendencies stand sharply opposed to each other; the one bases itself on the intellect; the other considers the will to be the basic force and organ of union with God. In this dispute, Cusanus sides emphatically with the former. True love of God is *amor Dei intellectualis*: it includes knowledge as a necessary element and a necessary condition. No one can love what he has not, in some sense, known. Love by itself, without any admixture of knowledge, would be an impossibility. Whatever is loved is, by that very act, considered good; it is conceived of *sub ratione boni*. This knowledge of the good must spur on and give wings to the will, even though the What, i.e., the simple essence of the good in itself, remains inaccessible to knowledge. Here too, then, knowing and not knowing coincide. The principle of *docta ignorantia* as 'knowing ignorance' re-affirms itself once again.[6]

At the same time, the moment that distinguishes this principle from every sort of 'scepticism' is also evident. To be sure, the *docta ignorantia*, considered negatively, emphasizes the opposition of the absolute to every form of rational, logical-conceptual knowledge; but this also implies a positive requirement. Unconditioned divine being, inaccessible to discursive knowledge through the mere concept, requires a new mode and a new form of knowledge. The true organ of its apprehension is the intellectual vision, the *visio intellectualis*, wherein all the

---

[6] On this point, cf. especially Cusanus' letter of 22 September 1452, to Gaspar Aindorffer: 'In sermone meo primo de spiritu sancto . . . reperietis quomodo scilicet in dilectione coincidit cognitio. Impossibile est enim affectum moveri nisi per dilectionem, et quicquid diligitur non potest nisi sub ratione boni diligi. . . . Omne enim quod sub ratione boni diligitur seu eligitur, non diligitur sine omni cognitione boni, quoniam sub ratione boni diligitur. Inest igitur in omni tali dilectione, qua quis vehitur in Deum, cognitio, licet quid sit id quod diligit ignoret. Est igitur coincidentia scientiae et ignorantiae, seu doctae ignorantiae.' The opposite point of view, based on a mysticism of pure emotion and will, was represented in a very typical fashion by Cusanus' opponent Vincent von Aggsbach. For more details on this dispute, cf. Edmond Vansteenberghe, *Autour de la docte ignorance. Une controverse sur la théologie mystique au XVe siècle* (Münster, 1915), in which work the individual documents of the controversy are collected. (For the text of Cusanus' letter cf. ibid., pp. 111f.)

oppositions of logical genuses and species are resolved. For in this vision, we see ourselves taken beyond all empirical differences of being and beyond all merely conceptual distinctions, to the simple origin, i.e., to the point that lies beyond all divisions and antitheses. In this kind of vision, and only in it, the true *filiatio Dei* is attained which Scholastic theology had sought in vain to reach, even believing itself able, so to speak, to extort it by means of the discursive concept.[7] Cusanus links this idea of *filiatio* to many of the basic themes of medieval mysticism; but again, quite characteristically, he modifies these themes in accordance with his new total view of the relationship between the absolute and the finite. For Dionysius the Areopagite, 'deification', the θέωσις, takes place according to the hierarchical principle, i.e., in a completely determined *series of steps*—movement, illumination, and finally union; for Cusanus it is a single act, one in which man puts himself into an immediate relationship to God. To be sure, man does not attain this relationship through mere ecstacy, through rapture; rather, the *visio intellectualis* presupposes self-movement of the mind as well as an original force in the mind itself that unfolds in a continuous process of thought. To explain the meaning and the purpose of the *visio intellectualis*, Cusanus relies not on the mystical form of passive contemplation, but on *mathematics*, which he considers the only true, genuine, and precise symbol of speculative thought and of the speculative vision that resolves contraries. *Nihil certi habemus in nostra scientia nisi nostram mathematicam.* Where the language of mathematics fails, nothing remains graspable or knowable by the human mind.[8] Cusanus' theology abandons Scholastic logic, the logic of generic concepts, dominated by the principle of contradiction and of the excluded middle; but it demands in its place a new type of mathematical logic, one that does not exclude but, in fact, requires the possibility of the coincidence of opposites, and requires the convergence of the Absolute-Greatest with the Absolute-Smallest as the firm principle and the necessary vehicle of progressing knowledge.

---

[7] Cf. especially the opus *De filiatione Dei, Opera* fol. 119: 'Ego autem . . . non aliud filiationem Dei quam Deificationem quae et θέωσις graece dicitur, aestimandum judico. Theosin vero tu ipse nosti ultimitatem perfectionis existere, quae et notitia Dei et verbi seu visio intuitiva vocitatur.'

[8] *Dial. de possest, Opera* 259: 'Omnium operum Dei nulla est praecisa cognitio, nisi apud eum, qui ipsa operatur et si quam de ipsis habemus notitiam, illam ex aenigmate et speculo cognito mathematicae elicimus . . . Si igitur recte consideraverimus, nihil certi habemus in nostra scientia, nisi nostram mathematicam, et illa est aenigma ad venationem operum Dei.' Cf. especially *De mathematica perfectione, Opera* 1120ff.

With this, indeed, a new path was taken in theo-logy—a path destined to pass beyond the limits of the medieval *mode of thought* and
beyond the boundaries of the medieval view of the world. The truth
of this emerges clearly if we try to grasp the pecularities of Cusanus'
method not only systematically, but by trying to determine its place in
the entire complex of the history of thought, in the whole of the history of philosophy, and in intellectual history generally. Like the whole
Quattrocento, Cusanus stands at a historical turning point. Intellectual
history finds itself before a great decision—the decision between Plato
and Aristotle. To be sure, it might seem as though the older humanism
had also faced this decision. In his *Triumph of Fame*, Petrarch represents
Plato as the greatest of the philosophers, whom Aristotle follows at a
respectful distance.[9] But he was led to make this decision by literary-
artistic reasons, not by reasons of principle. For Petrarch, the surest
guarantee of Plato's superiority is his 'divine torrent of eloquence', of
which he knew through the testimony of Cicero and Augustine.[10]
Cusanus, instead, was perhaps the first Western thinker to attain an
independent insight into the fundamental and essential sources of
Platonic doctrine. The very physical course of his life set him on this
path. He was chief of the embassy that went from the Council of Basle
to Greece and returned to Italy with the leading Greek scholars and
theologians. It is legitimate to surmise that Cusanus, who had mastered
Greek during his early studies at Padua, must have gained an immediate,
vital view of the Platonic sources from his association with such men
as Georgios Gemistos Plethon, Bessarion, *et al.* From then on, his works
show that he was in constant touch with these sources, conducting a
constant intellectual exchange with them.

His work *De mente*, the third book of *Idiota*, informs us that he was
influenced most of all by the middle books of the *Republic*,[11] which are
methodologically so important. If we recall, moreover, that this influence was exerted upon a mind that had begun very early to steep
itself in Neo-Platonic thought and had been nourished on the writings

[9] Petrarca, *Trionfo della fama*, chapter iii.
   'Volsimi da man manca; e vidi Plato,
   Che in quella schiera andò più presso al segno
   Al quale aggiunge, cui dal cielo è dato.
   Aristotele, poi, pien d'alto ingegno.'
[10] For a detailed discussion of Petrarch's relation to Plato, cf. Voigt, op. cit., I, 81ff.
[11] In Cusanus' library, which has remained intact, we find the *Republic, Phaedo, Apology,
Crito, Meno,* and *Phaedrus*. In addition, Cusanus appears to be especially indebted to the
Parmenides, which he knew in the commentary of Proclus. For details, cf. Vansteenberghe,
loc. cit., pp. 429ff.

of the Pseudo-Dionysius, on the Hermetic Books, and on Proclus, we can understand the problem that had necessarily to arise and that would now press unrelentingly for a solution. That murky mixture of Platonic and Neo-Platonic thoughts which permeated the knowledge and thought of the Middle Ages could no longer suffice. Cusanus had been trained not only in philosophy and mathematics but in humanistic philological criticism as well. Indeed, in his own work, he had attained and consolidated important conclusions through this criticism. For such a thinker there could no longer be any mere *juxtaposition* of Platonic and Neo-Platonic ideas. Everything in him pressed for a clear distinction between them. Cusanus did not give his analysis an explicit literary form, just as he did not personally take part in the famous literary polemic born of Plethon's work περὶ ὧν' Ἀριστοτέλης πρὸς Πλάτωνα διαφέρεται. Instead of philological criticism, he exercised a deeper and much more effective criticism. The speculations of Cusanus became an arena in which elements of thought that had indiscriminately commingled in medieval philosophy now met, recognized each other, and measured themselves against each other. Out of *this* battle—and not out of the literary disputes of Plethon and Bessarion, or of Theodorus Gaza and George of Trebizond—grew a new methodological clarification of the original meaning of Platonism, as well as a new intellectual line of demarcation between Plato and Aristotle on the one hand and between Plato and Neo-Platonism on the other.

Plato's vision of the world is characterized by the sharp division he makes between the sensible and the intelligible world, i.e., between the world of appearances and the world of ideas. The two worlds, that of the 'visible' and that of the 'invisible', that of the ὁρατόν, and that of the νοητόν, do not lie on the same plane and, therefore, admit of no immediate comparison. Rather, each is the complete opposite, the ἕτερον, of the other. Everything predicated of the one must be denied to the other. All the characteristics of the 'idea' may therefore be deduced antithetically from those of appearance. If continuous flux is characteristic of appearance, abiding permanence is proper to the idea. If appearance, by its very nature, is never *one*, but rather dissolves under the very glance that tries to fix it into a multiplicity different from one moment to the next, the idea remains in pure identity with itself. If the idea is characterized and completely determined by the necessary constancy of its significance, the world of sensory phenomena eludes every such determination—indeed, even the possibility of it. Nothing in that world of appearances is a true-being, a true-one, a something or some-how-consistent. Knowledge and opinion, ἐπιστήμη and δόξα, are distinguished on this basis: the one aims at that which is constant being, always acting in the same fashion; and the other at the mere succession of perceptions, of representations, of images. All philosophy, theoretical as well as practical, dialectics as well as ethics, consists in *knowledge* of this opposition. To resolve it, to seek to reconcile the opposites, would mean the dissolution of philosophy itself. Whoever ignores this dualism destroys the presuppositions of knowledge, the sense and meaning of judgment, and therewith all the force of scientific 'dialogue' (διαφθερεῖ πᾶσαν τὴν τοῦ διαλέγεσθαι δύναμιν). Appearance and Idea, the world of phenomena and noumena, can be related through thought; the one can and must be measured by the other. But never does any kind of 'mixture' take place; never does the nature and essence of the one go over into the other in such a way that there could be some kind of boundary line at which the one fades into the other. The separation, the χωρισμός, of both worlds is irrevocable. The ὄντως ὄν and the ὄντα, the λόγοι and the πράγματα can never be joined; the pure 'meaning' of the idea cannot be given as a particular 'existent', and simple existence does not in itself possess an ideal significance, a per-manent sense, or a value content.[12]

Aristotle's criticism of the Platonic doctrine begins with his objec-tion to this separation of the realm of existence and the realm of ideal 'meaning'. Reality is one. How is it possible to grasp it in two different ways of knowing, each the exact opposite of the other? We can em-phasize the opposition between 'matter' and 'form', between 'becom-ing' and 'being', between 'sensible' and 'super-sensible' as much as we like; the fact remains that it can only be understood as opposition if there is some means for going from the one pole to the other. Thus, for Aristotle, the concept of development becomes the basic category and the general principle for the explanation of the world. What we call reality is nothing but the unity of one and the same complex of activities, within which all diversity is contained as a definite phase or step in the process of development. Be they ever so 'heterogeneous', wherever two different kinds or modes of being are given, we need only look at this unitary dynamic process, and within it we shall find the diversity contained and reconciled. The barrier between 'appearance'

---

[12] For further details, see my presentation of Greek philosophy in *Lehrbuch der Philoso-phie*, ed. Max Dessoir (2 vols., Berlin, 1925), esp. I, 89ff.

and 'idea' in the Platonic sense disappears. The 'sensible' and the 'intelligible', the 'lower' and the 'higher', the 'divine' and the 'earthly' are joined by a single, steady nexus of activity. The world is a self-enclosed sphere, within which there are only differences of degree. Force flows from the divine unmoved mover of the universe to the remotest celestial circles, there to be distributed, in a steady and regulated sequence, to the whole of being; to be communicated, by means of the concentric celestial spheres, to the sublunar world. No matter how great the distance between the beginning and the end, there is no break, no absolute 'starting' or 'stopping' point in the path from the one to the other. It is a finite and continuous space, measurable in distinct, determinable stages, separating the beginning from the end, only to connect them again.

Plotinus and Neo-Platonism tried to unite the fundamental ideas of Platonic and Aristotelian thought; but in fact, they succeeded only in producing an eclectic mixture. The Neo-Platonic system is dominated by the Platonic idea of 'transcendence', i.e., by the absolute opposition between the intelligible and the sensible. The opposition is described completely in Platonic fashion and, indeed, in language even more emphatic than Plato had used. But by adopting the Aristotelian concept of development, the Neo-Platonists resolved the dialectical tension indispensable to the Platonic system. The Platonic category of transcendence and the Aristotelian category of development mate to produce the bastard concept of 'emanation'. The absolute remains as the super-finite, the super-one, and the super-being, pure in itself. Nevertheless, because of the super-abundance in it, the absolute overflows, and from this super-abundance it produces the multiformity of the universe, down to formless matter as the extreme limit of non-being. A look at the Pseudo-Dionysian writings has shown us that the Christian Middle Ages adopted this premise and re-shaped it to suit its own ends. It gained thereby the fundamental category of graduated mediation, which on the one hand allowed the integral existence of divine transcendence, and on the other hand mastered it, both theoretically and practically, with a hierarchy of concepts and of spiritual forces. Through the miracle of the ecclesiastical order of life and salvation, transcendence was now both recognized and conquered. In this miracle, the invisible had become visible, the inconceivable had become conceivable to man.

All the thoughts and works of Nicholas Cusanus were still very deeply rooted in this general vision of the medieval mind and of medieval life.

The bond established by the intellectual labours of centuries between the content of Christian faith and the content of the Aristotelian and the Neo-Platonic theoretical systems was much too strong to be rent with one blow by a thinker who stood so firmly and so surely with the content of that faith. Besides, there is another point that makes his attachment to the great Scholastic systems of the past appear not only understandable but, indeed, almost inevitable. These systems had given philosophical thought not only its content but also its form. They had created the only and the peculiar language in which philosophical thought could be expressed. Humanism had, to be sure, tried to attack Scholasticism on this point. It had believed it could conquer Scholasticism by exposing the mistakes and the lack of taste in 'barbaric' Scholastic Latin. But although Cusanus was sympathetic to the basic tendencies of Humanism, he did not follow it on this path. Even if only because he was German, he felt far removed from the great stylists and masters of humanistic eloquence. He felt, and admitted, that he could not compete with Aeneas Sylvius Piccolomini, with Lorenzo Valla, and with all those men who were 'by nature Latinists'. But he was not ashamed of this deficiency, for the purest and clearest meaning could be expressed precisely in the more modest and simple language (*humiliori eloquio*).[13]

This strong attachment of Cusanus to the 'style' of Scholasticism resulted in an inner, technical difficulty and placed him before a new technical task. For what was now required of him was that he express, within the limits of the dominant philosophical-conceptual language, i.e., within the limits of Scholastic terminology, thoughts which in their actual content and tendency pointed far beyond the boundaries of Scholasticism. On the one hand, Cusanus' curious Latin seems murky, enigmatic, and heavy; on the other, it contains a wealth of peculiar and novel turns of phrase; indeed, very often, with *one word*, with a single happily coined term, it illuminates in a flash the whole speculative depth of the fundamental problems with which he is concerned. This Latin is only understandable within the context of his entire intellectual

---

[13] 'Verum et eloquio et stilo ac forma litterarum antiqua videmus omnes delectari, maxime quidem Italos, qui non satiatuntur disertissimo (ut natura Latini sunt) huius generis latiali eloquio, sed primorum vestigia repetentes Graecis litteris maximum etiam studium impendunt. Nos vero Alemanni, etsi non longe aliis ingenio minores ex discrepanti stellarum situ essemus effecti: tamen in ipso suavissimo eloquii usu, aliis plerumque non nostro cedimus vitio, cum non nisi labore maximo, tamquam resistenti naturae vim facientes, Latinum recte fari valeamus.' From the introduction to Cusanus' *De concordantia catholica, Opera* fol. 683f.

relationship to the Middle Ages. That constant wrestling with an expression, so characteristic of his writings, is only a symptom of how the powerful *thought-mass* of Scholastic philosophy in him is beginning to free itself from dogmatic petrification—not to be thrown aside, but to be drawn into a completely new *movement* of thought. At times, the writings of Cusanus only hint at the true objective of this movement; at other times, they reveal it with astounding clarity. This objective may be said to be the establishment of a new relationship between the 'sensible' and the 'super-sensible', between the 'empirical' and the 'intellectual'. The systematic consideration and conception of this relationship leads us back to the genuine Platonic basic concepts, i.e., to the concepts of separation and participation (the μέθεξις and the χωρισμός).[14]

The first sentences of the *De docta ignorantia* already indicate that the division imposed by thought upon the world is going to be made in a manner and from a standpoint different from the classical Scholastic systems. Cusanus takes the Platonic dictum that the Good lies 'beyond being' (ἐπέκεινα τῆς οὐσίας) very seriously. The Good cannot be reached by any series of inferences that begins with the empirically given and that, in a steady progression, places and relates one empirical datum to the other. Such thought moves by simply comparing, which is to say, in the realm of the 'more' and 'less'. But how can something that is beyond all comparison, something that is not just relatively large, or larger, but simply the Greatest, the 'Maximum' be conceived of through such comparisons? The term Maximum must not be misleading: it is not a question of creating a superlative related to a previous comparative. On the contrary, it must be understood as the complete *antithesis* to every possible comparison, to every merely quantitative-gradual procedure. The Maximum is not a quantitative, but a purely qualitative concept. It is the absolute foundation of being as well as the absolute foundation of knowledge.[15] No procedure that deals with

[14] In an excellent essay, Ernst Hoffmann has demonstrated the fact that and the reason why this concept, in its original, Platonic meaning, was and had to be foreign to the thought of the whole Middle Ages. I shall do no more here than refer the reader to this recently published essay, entitled, 'Platonismus und Mittelalter', *Vortraege der Bibliothek Warburg*, III, 17ff.

[15] It may be recalled here, incidentally, that Plato also gave the name 'Maximum' to the idea of the Good, which is at once the highest foundation of reality and of knowledge. The Good is μέγιστον μάθημα (Plato *Republic* vi. 505A). It is hard to determine whether Cusanus took his description of empirical being as the realm of 'more and less' (μᾶλλόν ′τε καὶ ἧττον) directly from Plato. There is no definite evidence in his works to show that he was acquainted with Plato's *Philebus*, wherein this definition is systematically formulated.

quantities, no gradual movement by degrees can fill the gap that separates this original principle of being from empirical existence. All measurement, comparison, and syllogizing that runs along the thread of empirical existence must also end within that realm. Within the empirical world this movement can go on indefinitely; but this limitless progression *going on indefinitely* does not embrace the infinite which is in fact the absolute Maximum of determination. Cusanus clearly differentiates between the 'indefinite' and the 'infinite'. The only relationship that exists between the conditioned, endlessly conditionable world and the world of the unconditioned is that of complete mutual exclusion. The only valid predications of the unconditioned arise out of the negation of all empirical predicates.

Here we see in all its force the idea of 'otherness', the Platonic idea of ἕτερον. It is useless to try to see any kind of 'similarity' between the sensible and the intelligible. A physical circle or sphere never corresponds to the pure concept of either but rather must necessarily remain far behind it. We can refer the physical to the ideal; we can determine that a given, visible being corresponds with greater or less exactitude to the concept of the sphere or of the circle which is invisible *per se*. But the essential difference between archetype and copy can never be overcome. For what characterizes the pure truth of the archetype is precisely that it can never be 'more' or 'less'. To take away or to think away even the tiniest part of it is to destroy it in its essence. The sensible, on the other hand, not only suffers indeterminateness, but possesses therein its very nature. Insofar as being is attributable to it, the sensible 'is' only within this limitlessness of becoming, in this oscillating between being this-way and being that-way. 'Because it is evident that between the infinite and the finite no relationship exists, it is also completely clear that wherever there is something that surpasses and something that is surpassed, one can never attain the absolute Maximum, for that which surpasses, like that which is surpassed, is finite, whereas the absolute Maximum is necessarily infinite. If, therefore, there is

---

The assumption that both the idea and the expression are the independent work of Cusanus throws even more light on the methodological issues that we are investigating here. In any case, Cusanus lauds Plato as the only thinker who ever found the right path to follow for knowledge of God, i.e., the path of *docta ignorantia*. 'Nemo ad cognitionem veritatis magis propinquat, quam qui intelligit in rebus divinis, etiam si multum proficiat, semper sibi superesse, quod quaerat. Vides nunc venatores Philosophos . . . fecisse labores inutiles: quoniam campum doctae ignorantiae non intrarunt. Solus autem Plato, aliquid plus aliis Philosophis videns, dicebat, se mirari, si Deus inveniri et plus mirari, si inventus posset propalari.' *De venatione sapientiae* 12. 307.

something which is not the absolute Maximum, something greater can obviously always be found. Thus there cannot be two or more things so similar that something even more similar could not be found, and so on *ad infinitum*. There always remains a difference between the measure and the thing measured, no matter how close together they may come. The finite intellect, therefore, cannot know the truth of things with any exactitude by means of similarity, no matter how great. For the truth is neither more nor less, since it is something indivisible.... The intellect is to truth as the polygon is to the circle: just as the polygon, the more sides and angles it has, approximates but never becomes a circle, even if one lets the sides and angles multiply infinitely, so we know of the truth no more than that we cannot grasp it as it is with any true precision. For the truth is absolute necessity, which can never be more nor less than it is; whereas our intellect is only possibility.'[16]

We have already seen, in keeping with these few, powerful sentences, that there can be no simple and steady climb from the conditioned to the unconditioned, no progression from empirical or rational 'truths' to the absolute truth; and that therewith the form of Scholastic logic and the purpose of Scholastic ontology are denied. But at the same time this conclusion brings with it a peculiar reversal. The division that separates the sensible from the intelligible, sense experience and logic from metaphysics, does not cut through the vital nerve of experience itself; indeed, precisely this division guarantees the validity of experience. With the same decisiveness and acuteness that he applied to the idea of 'separation', Cusanus now works out the idea of 'participation'. Far from excluding each other, separation and participation, χωρισμός and μέθεξις, can only be thought of *through* and *in relation* to each other. In the definition of empirical knowledge, *both* elements are necessarily posited and connected with each other. For no empirical knowledge is possible that is not related to an ideal being and to an ideal being-thus. But empirical knowledge does not simply contain the truth of the ideal, nor does it comprehend that truth as one of its constituent elements. The character of empirical knowledge is, as we have seen, its limitless determinability; the character of the ideal is its delimitation, its necessary and unequivocal *determinateness* which gives to determinability a definite form and direction. Thus, everything conditioned and finite aims at the unconditioned, without ever being able to attain it.

---

[16] *De docta ignorantia* i. 3. fol. 2f.

That is the second basic thought in the *docta ignorantia*. In relation to theology, this concept affirms the idea of knowing ignorance; with relation to experience and empirical knowledge, it affirms the idea of ignorant *knowledge*. Experience contains genuine knowledge; but certainly this knowledge must recognize that, although it may go far, it can only reach a relative aim and end, never an absolute. And it must further recognize that in this realm of the relative there can be no exactness, no *praecisio*: rather, every pronouncement and every measurement, be it ever so precise, can and will be superseded by another, more precise. In this sense, all of our empirical knowledge remains a 'probability', an attempt, a hypothesis which, from the very beginning, is reconciled to being superseded by better, more exact attempts. Through this concept of probability, of *conjecture*, the notion of the eternal 'otherness' of idea and appearance is joined with the notion of the participation of the appearance in the idea. Only this union renders possible Cusanus' definition of empirical knowledge: 'conjectura est positiva assertio in alteritate veritatem uti est participans.'[17]

Now we have a negative theology together with a positive theory of experience. Neither contradicts the other; rather, each represents one and the same theory of knowledge seen from two aspects. The one truth, ungraspable in its absolute being, can present itself to us only in the realm of otherness; on the other hand, there is no otherness for us that does not in some way point to the unity and participate in it.[18] We must renounce any attempt at identifying the two, any thought of resolving the dualism or of letting the one realm overlap into the other. But it is just this renunciation that gives our knowledge its relative right and its relative truth. In Kantian language, it shows that our knowledge, to be sure, is bounded by insurmountable limits; but that within the domain assigned to knowledge there are no limits placed upon it. Even in otherness, knowledge can and should extend in all directions. By denying any overlapping of the two realms and by teaching us to see the One *in* the other, and the other *in* the One, the

---

[17] *De conjecturis* i. 13.

[18] Ibid. 'Identitas igitur inexplicabilis varie differenter in alteritate explicatur atque ipsa varietas concordanter in unitate identitatis complicatur . . . Potius igitur omnis nostra intelligentia ex participatione actualitatis divinae in potentiali varietate consistit. Posse enim intelligere actu veritatem ipsam uti est, ita creatis convenit mentibus sicut Deo proprium est, actum illum esse varie in creatis ipsis mentibus in potentia participatum. . . . Nec est inaccessibilis illa summitas ita aggredienda, quasi in ipsam accedi non possit, nec aggressa credi debet actu apprehensa, sed potius, ut accedi possit semper quidem propinquius, ipsa semper uti est inattingibili remanente.'

separation itself guarantees the possibility of true participation of the sensible in the ideal.

2

Up to now, we have only described the most general principle of method in Cusanus' philosophy. But this principle implies a series of conclusions which are of decisive importance for the *concrete* view of the world and for the conception of the physical as well as the intellectual cosmos. Immediately related to the propositions of the *De docta ignorantia* and the *De conjecturis* cited above are the principle of the *relativity of movement* and the theory of the *motion of the earth*.

The context of his writings clearly teaches us that Cusanus arrived at these principles not on the basis of physics but through speculative and general epistemological considerations. He speaks not as a physicist but as the theoretician of the method of *docta ignorantia*. Thus, the historian of empirical natural science may find these principles somewhat astonishing and strange. Their form and the way in which they are deduced seem to have the character not so much of empirical research as of a simple 'aperçu'. But the historian of *philosophy* must not be disconcerted. His task is to show that what seems to be an 'aperçu' presupposes the *whole* of Cusanus' doctrine, and to show how this whole proves its validity in the face of a very special task.

To clearly understand the peculiar character of Cusanus' statements and the highly original motifs of his thought, we must begin with his opposition to medieval physics. The medieval conception of physics is based on Aristotle's theory of the four elements, to each of which is allotted a specific place in the structure of the cosmos. Fire, water, air, and earth stand in a rigidly determined spatial relationship to one another, in a definite order of 'above' and 'below'. The nature of every element determines its distance from the central point of the universe. Closest to that point is the earth. Whenever any part of the earth is taken away from its natural place, i.e., from its immediate proximity to the universal central point, it strives to move back there in a straight line. Opposed to this is the movement of fire, which is 'in itself' directed upwards, so that it constantly tries to flee from the central point. Between the locus of the earth and that of fire lies the region to which belong air and water. The general form of physical action is determined by this order of location. Every physical activity takes place in such a way that one element is transformed into one of its neighbouring elements, so that fire becomes air, air becomes water, water becomes earth. This principle of mutual transmutability, this law of birth and decay leaves its stamp on all earthly occurrences. Above the earthly world, however, there is a sphere which is not subject to these laws; it is not born nor does it decay. The matter of the heavenly bodies has its own being, a *quinta essentia*, essentially different from the nature of the four earthly elements. It cannot undergo any qualitative transformation. It is only capable of *one* kind of change: pure change of place. And since, of all possible kinds of movement, the most perfect kind must be proper to the most perfect body, it is clear that the heavenly bodies must describe perfect circles around the centre of the earth.

Throughout the Middle Ages, this system enjoyed almost undisputed dominance. Of course, the question of the 'substance of the heavens' now and then raised some new doubts and even caused some modifications of details; but the basic view itself was never essentially affected by these changes. Duns Scotus and William of Occam, for example, dealt with the question. They maintained the thesis that the heavenly bodies consist of a matter that, like earthly matter, contains the possibility of becoming, i.e., of change into another, different form; but that no natural powers exist capable of bringing about such a change. Thus the heavens lie beyond birth and decay, if not by logical, then by factual necessity; if not conceptually, then actually. Such birth and decay could only be brought about by a direct intervention of God in nature, and not by forces that lie within nature.[19]

This 'classical' Aristotelian and Scholastic conception of the cosmos contradicts in two ways the basic speculative principle developed by Cusanus in his *De docta ignorantia*. On the one hand, it orders the element of the heavens and the four elements of the earth in a spatial relationship that also implies a gradation of values. The higher an element stands in the cosmic stepladder, the closer it is to the unmoved mover of the world, and the purer and more complete is its nature. But Cusanus no longer recognizes any such relationship of proximity and distance between the sensible and the supersensible. If the distance as such is infinite, all relative, finite differences are annihilated. When compared to the divine origin of being, every element, every natural

---

[19] For a discussion of this point and of the further Scholastic transformations of the doctrine of the substance of the heavens, cf. Pierre Duhem, *Études sur Léonard de Vinci* (2nd series, Paris, 1909), pp. 255ff.

being is equally far and equally near to that origin. There is no longer any 'above' and 'below', but a single universe, homogeneous within itself. As empirical cosmos, it stands opposed to Absolute Being, just as, on the other hand, it participates as a whole in the Absolute to the extent that the nature of the empirical allows of such participation. Since this kind of participation is in principle valid for all existence, it cannot be attributed to one of its constituent elements in a higher, to another in a lower degree.

Thus, with one blow, the whole difference in value between the lower sub-lunar world and the higher celestial world is eliminated. Instead of the stepladder of elements that Peripatetic physics had accepted, we have Anaxagoras' proposition that in corporeal nature, 'everything is in every thing'. The difference we perceive in the various bodies of the world is not a specific difference of *substance*, but rather is due to the different proportion in the mixture of basic elements that are everywhere the same and are disseminated throughout the entire world. If we could raise ourselves to the sun, we would find there, too, a layer of water, of air, and of earth besides the element of fire; and the earth, observed from a point above and beyond it, would look like a shining star.[20]

Connected with this is a second consideration which, so far as Cusanus is concerned, robs the cosmological system of Aristotle and the Scholastics of all truth. A closer view of that system reveals that it consists of two dissimilar and ultimately incompatible components. Ideal is mixed with empirical, empirical with ideal. Perfect movement, movement in a perfectly circular orbit is supposed to correspond to the perfect substance of the heavens. But we learned from the principle of the *docta ignorantia* that the truly perfect can never be encountered as something actually existing, i.e., as something present and demonstrable in the reality of things. It is and remains an ideal to which we must indeed refer bodies and physical movements for the sake of knowledge, but which is never present in the things themselves as a perceptible characteristic.[21] The cosmos, therefore, presents neither a

---

[20] *De docta ignorantia* ii. 12. fol. 39f.: 'In Sole si quis esset, non appareret illa claritas quae nobis: considerato enim corpore Solis, tunc habet quandam quasi terram centraliorem et quandam luciditatem quasi ignilem circumferentialem et in medio quasi aqueam nubem et aerem clariorem. . . . Unde si quis esset extra regionem ignis, terra. . . . in circumferentia suae regionis per medium ignis lucida stella appareret, sicut nobis, qui sumus circa circumferentiam regionis Solis, Sol lucidissimus apparet.'

[21] This consideration, on the strength of which Cusanus, so to speak, lifts the Aristotelian edifice from its foundations, had already been expressed clearly and exactly by

perfect sphere nor a perfectly exact circular orbit. It remains, like everything perceptible to the senses, in the realm of imprecision, of the merely 'more and less'.

From these *methodological* premises Cusanus arrives at the essential principles of a new cosmology. The earth is mobile and of spherical shape. Neither its shape nor its movement is such, however, that it can be determined with absolute mathematical precision. But since it shares this inability to attain the unconditional perfection of a geometric concept with everything else that exists in visible nature, the earth may no longer be considered something base or detestable within nature. Rather, it is a noble star, to which is given light and warmth, and an activity of its own different from that of all other stars. Indeed, no part in the whole cosmos is dispensable; each has its own special kind of activity and, correspondingly, its own incomparable value.[22] With this in mind, we can see clearly why, from Cusanus' viewpoint, the new orientation in astronomy that led to the supersession of the geocentric vision of the world was only the result and the expression of a totally new intellectual orientation. This intimate connection between the two was already visible in the formulation of his basic cosmological ideas in *De docta ignorantia*. It is useless to seek a *physical* central point for the world. Just as it has no sharply delineated geometric form but rather extends spatially into the indeterminate, so it also has no locally determined centre. Thus, if the question of its central point can be asked at all, it can no longer be answered by physics but by metaphysics. God

Plato. Οὐκοῦν, εἶπον, τῇ περὶ τὸν οὐρανὸν ποικιλίᾳ παραδείγμασι χρηστέον τῆς πρὸς ἐκεῖνα μαθήσεως ἕνεκα, ὁμοίως ὥσπερ ἂν εἴ τις ἐντύχοι ὑπὸ Δαιδάλου ἤ τινος ἄλλου δημιουργοῦ ἤ γραφέως διαφερόντως γεγραμμένοις καὶ ἐκπεπονημένοις διαγράμμασιν, ἡγήσαιτο γὰρ ἄν πού τις ἔμπειρος γεωμετρίας ἰδὼν τὰ τοιαῦτα, κάλλιστα μὲν ἔχειν ἀπεργασίᾳ, γελοῖον μὴν ἐπισκοπεῖν ταῦτα σπουδῇ ὡς τὴν ἀλήθειαν ἐν αὐτοῖς ληψόμενον ἴσων καὶ διπλασίων ἤ ἄλλης τινὸς συμμετρίας. — τί δ' οὐ μέλλει γελοῖον εἶναι; ἔφη. — τῷ ὄντι δὴ ἀστρονομικόν, ἤν δ' ἐγώ, ὄντα οὐκ οἴει ταὐτὸν πείσεσθαι εἰς τὰς τῶν ἄστρων φορὰς ἀποβλέποντα; νομιεῖν μὲν, ὡς οἷόν τε κάλλιστα τὰ τοιαῦτα ἔργα συστήσασθαι, οὕτω ξυνεστάναι τῷ τοῦ οὐρανοῦ δημιουργῷ αὐτόν τε καὶ τὰ ἐν αὐτῷ. τὴν δὲ νυκτὸς πρὸς ἡμέραν ξυμμετρίαν καὶ τούτων πρὸς μῆνα καὶ μηνὸς πρὸς ἐνιαυτὸν καὶ τῶν ἄλλων ἄστρων πρός τε ταῦτα καὶ πρὸς ἄλληλα, οὐκ ἄτοπον, οἴει, ἡγήσεται τὸν νομίζοντα γίγνεσθαί τε ταῦτα δεὶ ὡσαύτως καὶ οὐδαμῇ οὐδὲν παραλλάττειν, σῶμά τε ἔχοντα καὶ ὁρώμενα, καὶ ζητεῖν παντὶ τρόπῳ τὴν ἀλήθειαν αὐτῶν λαβεῖν; *Republic* 529 D.

[22] *De docta ignorantia* ii. 12: 'Terrae igitur figura est mobilis et sphaerica et ejus motus circularis, sed perfectior esse posset. Et quia maximum in perfectionibus, motibus et figuris in mundo non est, ut ex jam dictis patet, tunc non est verum, quod terra ista sit vilissima et infima. . . . Est igitur terra stella nobilis, quae lumen et calorem et influentiam habet aliam et diversam ab omnibus aliis stellis. . . . Ita quidem Deus benedictus omnia creavit, ut dum quodlibet studet esse suum conservare, quasi quoddam munus divinum, hoc agat in communione cum aliis, ut sicut pes non sibi tantum, sed oculo ac manibus ac corpori et homini toti servit, per hoc quod est tantum ad ambulandum, et ita de oculo et reliquis membris: pariformiter de mundi partibus. Plato enim mundum animal dixit, cujus animam absque immersione Deum si concipis, multa horum, quae diximus tibi clara erunt.'

is the centre of the world, of all the heavenly spheres, and, in fact, of everything there is in the world. And He must be considered not only the central point of the universe but its infinite circumference as well, since his essence includes within itself all others.[23]

For Cusanus, this basic insight has at once a natural and an intellectual sense, a physical and a 'spiritual' sense. The new form of cosmology teaches us that in the cosmic order there is no absolute above and below, and that no body is closer or farther from the divine, original source of being than any other; rather, each is 'immediate to God'. And now a new form of *religion* and a new religious attitude emerge, consistent with the new form of cosmology. From this standpoint, we may bring together the cosmological propositions in *De docta ignorantia* and the religious-philosophical views developed by Cusanus in his *De pace fidei* (1454). From the point of view of content, the works are concerned with entirely different matters. Nevertheless, they are only different reflections of one and the same fundamental, systematic point of view. Earlier, the principle of *docta ignorantia* yielded conclusions for a knowledge of the world; now it yields them for a knowledge of God. In the cosmology of Cusanus the universe dissolved into an infinite multiplicity of infinitely different movements, each circling around its own centre, and all held together both by their relationship to a common cause and by their participation in one and the same universal order. The same is true of spiritual being. Every spiritual being has its centre within itself. And its participation in the divine consists precisely in this centring, in this indissoluble individuality. Individuality is not simply a *limitation*; rather, it represents a particular *value* that may not be eliminated or extinguished. The One that is 'beyond being' can only be grasped *through* this value. According to Cusanus, a *theodicy of religious forms and practices* is attainable only by means of this thought. For only by virtue of this thought do the multiplicity, the difference, and the heterogeneity of these forms cease to appear to be a contradiction of the

---

[23] *De docta ignorantia* ii. 2. fol. 38: 'Non est igitur centrum terra, neque octavae aut alterius sphaerae, neque apparentia sex signorum super horizontem terram concludit in centro esse octavae sphaerae. . . . Neque etiam est ipsum mundi centrum plus intra terram quam extra. Neque etiam terra ista, neque aliqua sphaera habet centrum, nam cum centrum sit punctum aequedistans circumferentiae et non sit possibile verissimam sphaeram aut circulum esse, quin verior dari possit: manifestum est non posse dari centrum, quin verius etiam dari possit atque praecisius. Aequidistantia praecisa ad diversa extra Deum reperibilis non est, quia ipse solus est infinita aequalitas. Qui igitur est centrum mundi, scilicet Deus benedictus, ille est centrum terrae et omnium sphaerarum atque omnium quae in mundo sunt, qui est simul omnium circumferentia infinita.'

unity and universality of religion and become instead a necessary expression of that universality itself.

The work *De pace fidei* places this fundamental conception before us *in concreto*. Representatives of all peoples and of all religious parties appear before God to implore Him to finally settle the controversy that divides them. Since all religions strive towards the same, single goal, and towards the same, simple Being of God, what can be the sense of this controversy? 'What do the living ask, but to live? What does he who is ask, but to be? You, therefore, who are the giver of life and of being, are also the One who seems to be sought in the various rites and in various fashions, who is called by various names, and who yet remains unknown and ineffable. You, who are infinite power, are nothing of that which you have created; nor can the creature grasp the idea of your infinity, for there is no relationship between finity and infinity. But you, almighty God, who are invisible to all intellects, can make yourself visible in such form as you can be grasped. Therefore, hide yourself no longer, oh Lord. Have mercy, reveal your face, and all peoples shall be saved. For no one can shun you, unless it be he who does not know you. If you deign to heed our plea, the sword, hate, envy, and all evil shall disappear, and all shall know that in the multiplicity of rites, there is only one religion. If this multiplicity of rites cannot be given up, or if it seem not good to do away with it, since the differences themselves may become a spur to piety, bringing each land to cultivate its own customs with even greater zeal as those most pleasing to God—let there at least be one religion, even as you are One, and one worship of God.'[24] Here we have the demand for one universal religion, for one world-embracing 'catholicity'. But contrasted with the medieval conception of the church, it now contains a completely new sense and a new foundation. The content of the faith itself, inasmuch as it is always and necessarily a content of human representations, has become 'conjecture'. It is subject to the condition of always having to express the One Being and the One Truth in the form of 'otherness'.[25] No single, specific form of faith can avoid *this* otherness, which is rooted in the nature and in the essence of human knowledge. We no longer have a multitude of mere 'heterodoxies' opposed to a universally valid, universally binding 'orthodoxy'. Rather, the otherness, the ἕτερον, is recognized as the fundamental moment of the δόξα itself. The Truth, ungraspable and inconceivable in itself, can only be known

[24] *De pace fidei* i. fol. 862f.   [25] Cf. *De conjecturis* i. 13. (See above, n. 18.)

in its otherness: 'cognoscitur inattingibilis veritatis unitas in alteritate conjecturali'.[26]

From this basic point of view Cusanus infers a truly grand 'tolerance' which is anything but indifference. The multiplicity of forms of faith is not tolerated as a mere empirical juxtaposition, but rather is speculatively required and epistemologically founded. In the dialogue *De pace fidei*, one of the ambassadors of the peoples, a Tartar, raises an objection to the planned unification of faiths. Because of the radical differences not only of basic theoretical views, but also of customs and usages, unification cannot be achieved, he says. Can there be a greater contradiction than that one religion allows, even requires polygamy whereas the other considers it a crime? Or that in the Christian sacrifice of the mass, the body and blood of Christ is consumed, whereas to every non-Christian, this swallowing and devouring of the Holiest must appear execrable and monstrous? 'Thus I cannot conceive how there can be any unification of things that are different according to time and place. And, as long as this does not take place, persecution will not cease. For differences generate divisions and enmities, hate and war.' But the Divine Word calls upon Paul to reply to this objection. It must be shown, Paul answers, that salvation is given to souls not by virtue of their *works* but of their *faith*. For Abraham, the father of all the faithful, be they Christians or Jews or Arabs, believed in God, and that served as his justification. With this, every external barrier falls. *Anima justi haereditabit vitam aeternam.* If one accepts this, even the diversity of rites no longer constitutes an obstacle, for all institutions and all customs are merely sensible signs for the truth of faith; and whereas the signs are subject to change and to modification, what they signify is not.[27] There is no form of faith so low, so abominable, that it cannot find its relative justification from this point of view. Even polytheism is not excluded. For wherever *gods* are honoured, the thought, the idea of the divine must be presupposed.[28] It is evident that for Cusanus the cosmos

[26] Ibid., i.2. fol. 76.

[27] *De pace fidei* 15: 'Oportet ut ostendatur non ex operibus, sed ex fide salvationem animae praesentari. Nam Abraham, pater fidei omnium credentium, sive Christianorum, sive Arabum, sive Judaeorum credidit Deo et reputatum est ei ad justitiam: anima justi haereditabit vitam aeternam. Quo admisso, non turbabunt varietates illae rituum, nam ut signa sensibilia veritatis fidei sunt instituta et recepta: signa autem mutationem capiunt, non signatum.'

[28] Ibid., 6: 'Omnes qui unquam plures Deos coluerunt divinitatem esse praesupposuerunt. Illam enim in omnibus Diis tanquam in participantibus eandem adorant. Sicut enim albedine non existente non sunt alba: ita divinitate non existente, non sunt Dii. Cultus igitur Deorum confitetur Divinitatem.'

of religions is equally near and far from God, and that it shows the same inviolable identity and the same inevitable otherness, the same unity and the same particularization that we encountered earlier in the depiction of the physical cosmos.

This thought reaches even further. It proceeds from the particularization we find in nature and in the historical forms of the intellect, all the way to the last particular, to the simply individual. From the religious viewpoint, the individual is not the opposite of the universal, but rather its true fulfilment. Cusanus gave the clearest definition and elaboration of this point of view in the *De visione Dei*, which he dedicated to the monks of Tegernsee. Here again, he uses that symbolic form of instruction so characteristic of him. Goethe sees the essence of the symbol in its concrete and living revelation of the inscrutable; Cusanus thought and felt the same. Time and again, he seeks to connect the general and the universal to the particular, to the immediate sensible. At the beginning of the work, he recalls the self-portrait of Rogier van der Weyden, which he had seen in the town hall at Brussels. The portrait possessed a peculiar property: it seemed to look directly at the viewer, no matter where he stood.[29] Imagine a portrait of this kind in the sacristy of a cloister, hung perhaps on the north wall, and the monks standing in a semi-circle around it. Each of them will believe that the eye in the picture is looking directly at him. Not only must we attribute to the picture the ability simultaneously to face south, west, and east, but also a triple simultaneous movement; for while it is still for the stationary observer, it follows the moving one with its glance, so that if one of the brothers walks from east to west and another from west to east, it participates in both these opposite movements. We see, therefore, that this one and the same immobile face can move in such a way towards the east, that it simultaneously moves towards the west, and similarly, moves to the north and simultaneously to the south; a face that, standing fixed in one place, is simultaneously in all other places and which, while it is involved in one movement, is simultaneously involved in all the others.

This represents for us, in a sensible parable, the nature of the basic relationship between God, the all-encompassing being, and the being

---

[29] Erwin Panofsky has very kindly written to inform me that the self-portrait of Roger van der Weyden no longer exists. What has survived is an old Gobelin copy, which is now in the Berne Museum. On the basis of the passage in *De visione Dei*, H. Kauffmann was able to turn up this copy. Cf. *Repertorium für Kunstgeschichte* (1916). Cusanus also referred to another portrait, in the Nürnberg Rathaus, but it can no longer be reconstructed.

of the finite, the ultimate particular. Each particular and individual being has an immediate relationship to God; it stands, as it were, face to face with Him. But the true sense of the divine first discloses itself when the mind no longer remains standing at *one* of these relationships, nor even at their simple total, but rather collects them all in the unity of a vision, a *visio intellectualis*. Then we can understand that it is absurd for us even to want to think the absolute in itself without such a determination through an individual point of view. But we also understand that none of these points of view has any priority, because only the concrete totality of them can mediate a true picture of the Whole for us. In this whole every single viewpoint is included and recognized both in its accidentality and its necessity. And of course, every view of God is as much conditioned by the nature of the 'object' as by the nature of the 'subject'; every view includes the *thing seen* as well as the manner and the direction of the *seeing*. Each man can see himself only in God; just as he can see God only in himself. This pure *interpenetration* cannot be adequately characterized by any quantitative expression, or by any expression that is tied to the opposition of the 'part' to the 'whole'. 'Your true face is free of all limitations. It is neither of this size, nor of this shape, neither spatial nor temporal, for it is itself the absolute form, the face of faces. And when I consider how this face is the truth and the most adequate measure of all faces, I am astounded. For this face, that is the truth of all faces, is not this or that large, has no "more" or "less", nor is it like any other; as the absolute, it transcends all measure. So I see, oh Lord, that your face precedes every visible face, that it is the truth and the model of all faces. Therefore, any face that looks into yours sees nothing different from itself, because it sees its own truth. When I look at this picture from the east, it seems to me that I am not looking at it but it at me; the same is true when I look at it from the south or the west. Likewise, your face is turned to all who look at you. Whoever looks at you with love feels you looking lovingly at him—and the more he tries to look upon you with love, the more lovingly does your face look back at him. Whoever looks at you in anger finds your look angry; whoever looks at you joyfully finds you joyful. For as everything appears red to the physical eye when it looks through a red glass, so the spiritual eye, in its limitedness, sees you, the goal and object of the mind's observation, according to the nature of its own limitation. Man is capable only of human judgment. . . . If the lion attributed a face to you, he would attribute that of a lion, the ox that of an ox, and the eagle that of an eagle. Ah, God, how wonderful is your face: the youth, if he would conceive of it, must imagine it as young, the man as male, the old man as old. In all faces the face of faces appears, veiled, as in an enigma—but it cannot be seen uncovered unless it be when we go beyond all faces to that secret, dark silence, wherein nothing remains of the knowledge and the concept of face.'[30]

With these sentences of the *De visione Dei* we are at the focal point of Cusanus' speculation. And from this point we can see most clearly the connection of this speculation to the fundamental intellectual forces of the epoch. Three forces influenced Cusanus' early education and decisively determined the development of his doctrine. He received his earliest education from the Brothers of the Common Life at Deventer, that community in which was born a new type of personal piety——the ideal of the *devotio moderna*.[31] There, for the first time, Cusanus was touched by the spirit of German mysticism in all its speculative depth and in its moral and religious force. The historical threads that join the form of religious life in Deventer with German mysticism are easily traceable. Gerard Groote, the founder of the Brotherhood of the Common Life, was in close touch with Ruysbroeck,[32] whose basic point of view goes back to Eckhart. Cusanus' own writings continually reveal the strong and lasting influence of Eckhart's doctrines; and they also reveal the directions in which this influence moved.[33] In Eckhart's doctrines he saw the dogmatic content of Christianity remoulded into the individual content of the soul—and this was accomplished with a force of religious sentiment and of verbal expression such as had never before been achieved. The mystery of the Incarnation cannot be explained, nor even merely described, by any analogy taken from the world of nature or the world of history. The place where this miracle of the Incarnation occurs is the soul of man *as such*, i.e., as single, individual soul. This miracle does not belong to the past, it did not

---

[30] *De visione Dei* 6. fol. 185f.

[31] For details on the Brothers of the Common Life and on the religious movement known as the *devotio moderna*, cf. Paul Mestwerdt, *Die Anfänge des Erasmus. Humanismus und devotio moderna* (Leipzig, 1917), pp. 86ff. Also, Albert Hyma, *The Christian Renaissance. A History of the Devotio Moderna* (2 vols.; Grand Rapids, Michigan, 1924).

[32] On Gerard Groote and his relationship to Ruysbroeck, cf. especially Hyma, op. cit., I, 11f. See also Gabriele Dolezich, *Die Mystik Jan van Ruysbroecks des Wunderbaren* (*Breslauer Studien zur historischen Theologie*, IV; Breslau, 1926), 1ff.

[33] Of the many references to Eckhart, the one in the *Apologia doctae ignorantiae, Opera* fol. 69ff., is particularly important. For more details on his relationship to Eckhart, cf. Vansteenberghe, op. cit., pp. 426ff.; also, Fiorentino, op. cit., pp. 108ff

happen in, nor is it confined to a single moment of objective historical time; rather, it can and must renew itself in every Ego, in every time. This divinity must generate itself in the depths, in the very last foundation of the soul: there is the true "child-bed" of divinity.' Later, whenever Cusanus speaks as a mystic, we hear this basic note of Eckhart's faith and piety.

Cusanus' development did not end at this point. His schooling in the *devotio moderna* was followed by schooling in the principles of Scholastic science and Scholastic theology at the university of Heidelberg. There, he followed the 'new way', the *via moderna*, which had been introduced to Heidelberg shortly before by Marsilius of Inghen, the disciple of Occam, and which reigned there nearly uncontested throughout the first decades of the fifteenth century.[34] At Heidelberg, Cusanus received strong and lasting stimulation. Later, his contemporaries very rightly recognized him as one of the best 'connoisseurs of the Middle Ages'.[35] The really decisive intellectual development, however, took place not here, but in Cusanus' Italian period. Cusanus really became himself only after contact with antiquity and with its renaissance in the Italy of the Quattrocento. In the life and thought of the first of the German systematic philosophers, Italy manifested that same power which she later exercised over the lives of the great German artists. And how much greater must this power be over Cusanus, who touched Italian soil when he was only seventeen years old, than, say, over Goethe, who was almost forty when he arrived there. When Cusanus enrolled at the University of Padua in October 1417, he was surrounded for the first time by the new, worldly culture of the time. He had escaped from the closeness and loneliness of mystical sentiment and from the narrowness of medieval German scholarly life; now a wide world and a free life

[34] For a more detailed discussion of the philosophical currents at the University of Heidelberg, cf. especially Ritter, op. cit. (see above, 11, n. 4). It is curious and interesting that later the Heidelberg 'moderns' believed they could count Cusanus on their side in their fight against the 'via antiqua'. Cf. the Schöffer Edition of 1499, in which Cusanus is listed as a 'modern' authority, together with Occam, Albert of Saxony, John Gerson, et. al. (cf. Ritter, op. cit., II, 77, n. 2).

[35] In *Vom Mittelalter und von der lateinischen Philologie des Mittelalters* (Munich, 1914), Paul Lehmann cites the obituary written by John Andreas, Bishop of Aleria, for his friend Cusanus in 1469, and states that in it we have the first recorded instance of the use of the expression 'Middle Ages'. 'Vir ipse quod rarum est in Germanis supra opinionem eloquens et Latinus, historias idem omnes non priscas modo, sed medie tempestatis tum veteres tum recentiores usque ad nostra tempora memoria retinebat.' 6. Cusanus was also praised as a 'connoisseur of the Middle Ages' by Hartmann Schedel, in his chronicle of the world (1493), and by Faber Stapulensis in the preface to his edition of the works of Cusanus (1514).

beckoned him. At Padua he dips into the stream of humanistic culture. He learns Greek, enabling him later to study Plato more deeply and also to study Archimedes and the basic problems of Greek mathematics. Indeed, it is typical of Cusanus, and it distinguishes him from such genuine humanists as Poggio and Valla, that his interest in antiquity moved him towards the study not of the poetry and rhetoric, but of the philosophy and mathematics of antiquity. And in Padua, Cusanus also established what was to become a life-long friendship with *Paolo Toscanelli*, one of the most important among the Italian mathematicians and physicists.[36] Toscanelli introduced him to the geographical, cosmographical, and physical problems of the period. Furthermore, he received from Toscanelli an impulse that he later passed on to the German mathematicians and astronomers *Georg Peurbach* and *Regiomontanus*, and which influenced even *Copernicus*. Now, these three great, fundamental elements in Cusanus' education demand an intellectual reconciliation. They press towards a synthesis which, at first glance, might seem to be a real *coincidentia oppositorum* but which, observed more closely, is nothing but the specific expression of the central intellectual problem of the Renaissance.

There can be no doubt that the Renaissance directed all its intellectually productive forces towards a profound examination of the problem of the *individual*. In this respect, Burckhardt's fundamental thesis remains unshakable. But Burckhardt, in fact, portrayed only *one* aspect of the great process of liberation by which modern man matured towards a consciousness of himself. 'In the Middle Ages', he writes, 'both sides of human consciousness—that which was turned within and that which was turned without—lay dreaming or half awake beneath a common veil. The veil was woven of faith, illusion, and child-like prepossession, through which the world and history were seen clad in strange hues. Man was conscious of himself only as a member of race, people, party, family, or corporation—only through some general category. In Italy this veil first melted into thin air; an *objective* treatment and consideration of the state and of all the things of this world became possible. The subjective side, at the same time, asserted itself with corresponding

---

[36] On Toscanelli, cf. Gustavo Uzielli, *Paolo dal Pozzo Toscanelli* (Florence, 1892). For Cusanus' relationship to him, the dedication of his work, *De transmutationibus Geometricis*, is especially relevant. 'Sed quanto me ab annis juventutis atque adolescentiae nostrae strictiori amicitiae nodo atque cordiali quodam amplexu indesinenter constrinxisti: tanto nunc accuratius emendationi animum adhibe et in communionem aliorum (nisi correctum) prodire non sinas.'

emphasis; man became a spiritual individual, and he recognized himself as such.'[37] Cusanus played an important role both in the re-awakening of objectivity and in the deepening of subjectivity. His greatness and his historical singularity consist in his having brought about this change not in opposition to the religious ideas of the Middle Ages, but from the standpoint of these ideas themselves. His 'discovery of nature and of man' was accomplished from the very heart of religion, where he sought to base and to anchor that discovery.

Cusanus is and remains a mystic and a theologian; as such, he considers himself adequate to deal with the world and with nature, with history and with the new and worldly human culture. Far from rejecting these, he moves ever deeper into them, always relating them to his own realm of thought. We can easily trace this process. It begins with his early works, which are dominated by the Platonic theme of *chorismos*. In the later works, *methexis* gradually becomes the dominant theme. And in them, Cusanus considers 'the apex of the theory' to be the insight that the truth which he had sought earlier in the darkness of mysticism and which he had determined to be the antithesis of all multiplicity and change, reveals itself, in fact, in the very realm of empirical multiplicity; indeed, it is a common, everyday matter.[38] This new feeling about the world emerges ever more clearly in the works of Cusanus, and together with it comes his characteristic religious optimism. The term Pantheism is not applicable to this new sentiment. The antithesis between the being of God and the being of the world is never blurred; indeed, it is maintained in all its rigour. The *De visione Dei* taught us that the truth of the universal and the particularity of the individual interpenetrate each other, so that the Divine Being can only be grasped and seen from the infinitely multiple individual points of view. In like manner, we can see the being that is prior to any limita-

[37] Jakob Burckhardt, *Kultur der Renaissance*; translated by C. G. C. Middlemore, *The Civilization of the Renaissance in Italy* (London and New York, n.d.), p. 143.
[38] *De apice theorie* fol. 332f. 'Quidditas quae semper quaesita est et quaeritur et quaeretur, si esset penitus ignota, quomodo quaereretur? . . . Cum igitur annis multis viderim ipsam ultra omnem potentiam' cognitivam, ante omnem varietatem et oppositionem, quaeri oportere: non attendi, quidditatem in se subsistentem esse omnium substantiarum invariabilem subsistentiam, ideo nec multiplicabilem nec pluralificabilem, et hinc non aliam et aliam aliorum entium quidditatem, sed eandem omnium hypostasin. Deinde vidi necessario fatendum ipsam rerum hypostasin seu subsistentiam posse esse. Et quia potest esse: utique sine posse ipso non potest esse, quomodo enim sine posse potest. . . . Veritas quanto clarior tanto facilior. Putabam ego aliquando ipsam in obscuro melius reperiri. Magnae potentiae veritas est, in qua posse ipsum valde lucet: clamitat enim in plateis, sicut in libello de Idiota legisti, valde certe se undique facile repertum ostendit.' Cf. especially *Idiota* i. fol. 137f.

tion, prior to any 'contraction', only *through* the limitation itself. The ideal towards which our knowledge must strive, then, does not lie in denying and rejecting particularity, but in allowing it to unfold in all its richness. For only the *totality* of faces gives us the One view of the Divine. The world becomes the symbol of God, not in that we pick out one part of it and provide it with some singular mark of value, but rather in that we pass through it in all of its forms, freely submitting ourselves to its multiplicity, to its antitheses.

In the development of his own thought, Cusanus was able to fulfil this speculative requirement and still remain within the church. And precisely this accounts for his unique place in both church history and general intellectual history. Later, when the attacks of Protestantism forced the Catholic Church to retreat into itself and into the traditional content of its dogma, it had to throw out the new thoughts and the new tendencies which Cusanus had still been able to conceive of and master through religion. Giordano Bruno suffered death and Galileo suffered ecclesiastical persecution and did penance for the same cosmological theories proposed by Cusanus in 1440 in *De docta ignorantia*. Cusanus' philosophy stands at the narrow border between the times and between ways of thinking. This becomes clear not only when one compares his doctrines with those of the coming century but also when one compares them to those of the past. We can clearly see worldly individualism and the ideal of the new culture and the new humanity encountered and dealt with in a singular way by a religious individualism rooted in mysticism, especially in the German mysticism of Eckhart and Tauler. The origins of this encounter reach back to the Trecento. Petrarch's life and philosophy revolve around these two points, always struggling to achieve a balance between the requirements of ancient humanism and of medieval religiosity. But he never reaches a resolution, an inner balance between the conflicting forces. Petrarch's dialogues place us in the midst of the battle itself. They show the Ego, harassed and unsteady, at the mercy of the opposed intellectual forces. Therein lies the excitement and liveliness of these dialogues. Petrarch's inner world is divided between Cicero and Augustine. He must reject on the one hand what he seeks on the other. From the religious viewpoint he belittles what he otherwise considers to be the intellectual content and the intellectual value of life. This duality applies to all the worldly human ideals—fame, beauty, love—to which he was attached with every fibre of his Ego. From this is born that schism within his mind, that sickness of the soul which Petrarch depicted in his most personal and most profound work, the dialogue *De secreto conflictu curarum suarum*. The only result of this conflict is resignation, surfeit with the world, *acedia*. In Petrarch's own depiction of this mood, life becomes a dream, a phantasm;[39] it sees its own nullity without being able to escape it. In Cusanus there is not a trace of the inner conflict, pessimism, and asceticism that emerge at the end of Petrarch's thought.

To be sure, in the midst of the hardest battles, Cusanus did sometimes long to be relieved of the burden of worldly woes; at times he did yearn for a cell in the monastery of his friends, the brothers of Tegernsee.[40] That was especially true at the time of his conflict with the Archduke Sigismund of Austria, which finally led to the imprisonment of Cusanus. Nevertheless, his life as a whole is completely oriented towards activity. From beginning to end it is filled with great world-political plans and tasks, with practical reforms, and with philosophical and scientific research. And the basic idea of his speculation emerges precisely out of this enormous activity. The apparent diversity in his activity will become united through this idea; for the essence of the idea is that it sets up antitheses only to reconcile them, to resolve and master them through the principle of the *coincidentia oppositorum*.

When Cusanus reaches the point at which he must make a final decision between religious assumptions and the worldly ideals and cultural forces that affect him, he has recourse to a thesis which must perhaps be called the oddest and most difficult in his philosophy. He considers that the decision can be made by simply deepening the basic content of Christianity itself. The *idea of Christ* is invoked as the justification, the religious legitimation, and sanction of the *idea of humanity*. The idea is presented in the third book of the *De docta ignorantia*. At times it has been so little understood that the attempt has been made to sever it from the whole of Cusanus' *philosophy*, considering it an arbitrary 'theological' appendix rooted in a purely dogmatic interest.[41] But excisions of this sort, with which we are well acquainted, cannot be made in Cusanus' doctrine without tearing apart its whole inner constitution, without destroying its characteristic intellectual structure. Far from being a mere external appendage, the introduction

---

[39] *Epistolae rerum familiarium* ii. 9., to Giacomo Colonna. (Cf. Voigt, op. cit., I, 135.)

[40] Cf. the letter of 16 September 1454, to Gaspar Aindorffer, reproduced in Vansteenberghe, op. cit., p. 139.

[41] This opinion was repeated again recently by T. Whittaker in his essay 'Nicholas of Cusa', *Mind*, XXXIV (1925), 439ff.

and the speculative treatment of the Christ-idea in the *De docta ignorantia* is, in fact, responsible for the complete unfolding and expression of the driving force in Cusanus' thought. We now have before us the actual point of transition, the dialectical transformation of his basic idea. This idea had been concerned with drawing a sharp distinction between the conditioned and the unconditioned, the human and the divine, the finite and the infinite. None of these terms can be reduced to its antithesis, nor even measured by it. When faced with the Absolute, nothing is left to human knowledge but resignation and complete humility. But this resignation contains a positive element. If human knowledge can reach non-knowledge of the absolute, it thereby gains knowledge of this non-knowledge itself. It does not grasp absolute unity in its pure 'whatness'; but it does grasp itself as something different from that unity; that is to say, it does grasp itself in its complete 'otherness'. And precisely this otherness implies a *relation* to this negative pole of knowledge. Without such a relation, knowledge could not even recognize its own nullity; to speak with Hegel, whose basic thought Cusanus anticipates with remarkable clarity—knowledge could not set up the limit if it had not already transgressed it in some sense. The consciousness of difference implies the mediation of difference. But this mediation cannot, in turn, mean that the infinite, the absolute being stands in some relation to the finite, empirical consciousness of self—we still cannot jump over that abyss. In place of the empirical there must be a general self; in place of the human being as an individual, particular existence, there must be the spiritual content of all humanity. This spiritual, universal content of humanity Cusanus sees in Christ.

Christ alone is the genuine *natura media* that embraces the finite and the infinite in one. And this unity is not accidental, but essential. It does not designate a merely actual 'conjunction' of things in themselves separate; rather, it signifies that an original and necessary connection of the two opposed moments is required. The required *natura media* must be so constituted that it includes both the higher and the lower in their totality. As the maximum of the lower and the minimum of the higher world, it must be capable of embracing the whole universe with all its possible forms, so that it may—to use Cusanus' term—'complicate' them within itself. Thus this nature becomes the actual connecting link of the universe, the 'bracket of the world'.[42]

---

[42] *Excitat.* ix. fol. 639: 'Et in hoc passu mediatio Christi intelligitur, quae est copula hujus coincidentiae, ascensus hominis interioris in Deum, et Dei in Hominem.'

Just as Christ is the expression of *all* humanity, just as He signifies nothing but its simple idea and essence, so does man, too, viewed in his essence, include within himself all things. In man as a microcosm all lines of the macrocosm run together.[43] One sees how the microcosm motif, which Cusanus explicitly called an *ancient* motif,[44] intertwines in a peculiar way with the basic religious idea of Christianity. In medieval thought, redemption signified above all liberation from the world, i.e., the uplifting of men above their sensible, earthly existence. But Cusanus no longer recognizes such a separation between man and nature. If man as a microcosm includes the natures of all things within himself, then *his* redemption, his rising up to the divinity, must include the ascension of all things. Nothing is isolated, cut off, or in any way rejected; nothing falls outside this fundamental religious process of redemption. Not only man rises up to God through Christ; the universe is redeemed within man and through him. The *regnum gratiae* and the *regnum naturae* no longer stand opposed to each other, strangers and enemies; now, they are related to each other and to their common, divine goal. The union has been completed not only between God and man, but between God and all creation. The gap between them is closed; between the creative principle and the created, between God and creature, stands the spirit of humanity, *humanitas*, as something at once creator and created.[45]

Cusanus borrows the *terminology* of the old 'division of the world', the *divisio naturae* made by Johannes Scotus Erigena. Scotus Erigena

---

[43] *De docta ignorantia* iii. 3: 'Maximo autem, cui minimum coincidit, conveniet ita unum amplecti, quod et aliud non dimittat, sed simul omnia. Quapropter natura media, quae est medium connexionis inferioris et superioris, est solum illa, quae ad maximum convenienter elevabilis est potentia maximi infiniti Dei: nam cum ipsa intra se complicet omnes naturas, ut supremum inferioris et infimum superioris, si ipsa secundum omnia sui ad unionem maximitatis ascenderit, omnes naturas ac totum universum omni possibili modo ad summum gradum in ipsa pervenisse constat.'

[44] Ibid. 'Humana vero natura est illa, quae est supra omnia Dei opera elevata et paulominus Angelis minorata, intellectualem et sensibilem naturam complicans ac universa intra se constringens, ut μικρόκοσμος aut parvus mundus a veteribus rationabiliter vocitetur.'

[45] Ibid., iii. 2: 'Oportet igitur ipsum tale ita Deum esse mente concipere, ut sit et creatura, ita creaturam ut sit et creator, creatorem et creaturam absque confusione et compositione. Quis itaque excelsum adeo elevarie possit, ut in unitate diversitatem et in diversitate unitatem concipiat, supra omnem igitur intellectum haec unio esset.' Cf. especially *De visione Dei*, chap. xx: 'Video in te Jesu filiationem divinam, quae est veritas omnis filiationis, et pariter altissimam humanam filiationem, quae est propinquissima imago absolutae filiationis. . . . Omnia igitur in natura humana tua video, quae et video in divina, sed humaniter illa esse video in natura humana, quae sunt ipsa divina veritas in natura divina. . . . Video, Jesu bone, te intra murum Paradisi quoniam intellectus tuus est veritas pariter et imago, et tu es Deus pariter et creatura, infinitus pariter et finitus, . . . es enim copulatio divinae creantis naturae et humanae creatae naturae.'

distinguished the nature which creates and is not created from (a) that which is created and creates, (b) that which is created and does not create, and finally, (c) that which neither creates nor is created. But this terminology now has an essentially new meaning. When Erigena speaks of the created and at the same time creating being, he is referring to the non-temporal emergence of things from their Ideas, i.e., from their eternal prototypes and archetypes.[46] But Cusanus does not consider ideas to be creative forces in the Neo-Platonic sense. Instead, he requires a *concrete* subject as the central point and as the point of departure for all truly creative activity. And this subject, according to him, can exist nowhere but in the mind of man. The first and foremost result of this point of view is a new version of the *theory of knowledge*. Genuine and true knowledge is not merely directed towards a simple reproduction of reality; rather, it always represents a specific direction of intellectual activity. The necessity we recognize in science, and especially in mathematics, is due to this free activity. The mind attains genuine insight not when it reproduces external existence, but only when it 'explicates' itself and its own nature. Within itself, the mind finds the simple concept and 'principle' of the point; and from this, after continuously repeated movements, it produces the line, the surface, and the entire world of extension. Within itself, the mind finds the simple idea of 'now', out of which unfolds the infinity of temporal series. And just as the basic forms of intuition—space and time—are in this sense 'implied' by the mind, so too are the concepts of number and of size, as well as all logical and mathematical categories. In the development of these categories the mind creates arithmetic, geometry, music, and astronomy. In fact, everything logical—the ten predicates, the five universals, etc.—is included in this basic power of the mind. It is the necessary prerequisite to all 'discretion', i.e., all categorization of multiplicity according to species and classes; and it is the necessary prerequisite to the possibility of tracing the empirical-mutable back to strictly defined laws.[47] In this foundation of the sciences the creative

---

[46] Cf. especially Johannes Scotus Erigena, *De divisione naturae* ii. 2.

[47] More details on this basic principle of Cusanus' epistemology may be found in my *Erkenntnisproblem*, I, 33ff. Cf. *De ludo globi* ii. fol. 231f.: 'Anima rationalis est vis complicativa omnium notionalium complicationum. Complicat enim complicationem multitudinis et complicationem magnitudinis, scilicet unius et puncti. Nam sine illis, scilicet multitudine et magnitudine, nulla fit discretio. Complicat complicationem motuum, quae complicatio quies dicitur: nihil enim in motu nisi quies videtur. Motus enim est de quiete in quietem. Complicat etiam complicationem temporis, quae Nunc seu praesentia dicitur. Nihil enim in tempore nisi Nunc reperitur. Et ita de omnibus complicationibus dicendum,

power of the rational soul reveals itself in both its basic aspects; by virtue of this power the human mind enters into time and yet remains above time understood as mere succession. For, as the origin and creator of science, the human mind is not so much in time, as time is in it. The mind itself, by virtue of its power of discretion, creates definite time intervals and time divisions and draws the boundaries between the hours, months, and years. Just as all essential differences come from God, so all conceptual differences emerge from the human intellect. And thus it is the primary source of that harmony which is always the resolution of *opposites*. In Ptolemy, the human intellect created the astrolabe; in Orpheus, the lyre. Invention does not come from without; it is simply the material and sensible realization of the concept.

Time is to the soul as the eye is to vision. Time is the organ the soul uses to fulfil its basic function, which is to order and sift the multiplicity, i.e., that which is variously dispersed.[48] With this idealist conception, Cusanus lays the groundwork for the modern concept of time in mathematics and physics—a concept that will later emerge in the works of Kepler and in Leibniz.[49] Furthermore, Cusanus initiates therewith a new view and a new evaluation of *history*. The interpretation of historical existence will now also be subjected to the fundamental anti-

scilicet quod anima rationalis est simplicitas omnium complicationum notionalium. Complicat enim vis subtilissima animae rationalis in sua simplicitate omnem complicitatem, sine qua perfecta discretio fieri non potest. Quapropter ut multitudinem discernat, unitati seu complicationi numeri se assimilat et ex se notionalem multitudinis numerum explicat. Sic se puncto assimilat, qui complicat magnitudinem, ut de se notionales lineas superficies et corpora explicet. Et ex complicatione illorum et illarum, scilicet unitate et puncto, mathematicales explicat figuras circulares et polygonias. Sic se assimilat quieti, ut motum discernat. . . . Et cum hae omnes complicationes sint in ipsa unitae, ipsa tanquam complicatio complicationum explicatorie omnia discernit et mensurat, et motum et agros et quaeque quanta. Et invenit disciplinas, scilicet Arithmeticam, Geometricam, Musicam et Astronicam et illas in sua virtute complicari experitur. Sunt enim illae disciplinae per homines inventae et explicatae. . . . Unde et decem praedicamenta in (animae rationalis) vi notionali complicantur; similiter et quinque Universalia et quaeque logicalia et alia ad perfectam notionem necessaria, sive illa habeant esse extra mentem, sive non, quando sine ipsis non potest discretio et notio perfecte per animam haberi.'

[48] Ibid.: 'Annus, mensis, horae sunt instrumenta mensurae temporis per hominem creatae. Sic tempus, cum sit mensura motus, mensurantis animae est instrumentum. Non igitur dependet ratio animae a tempore, sed ratio mensurae motus, quae tempus dicitur, ab anima rationali dependet. Quare anima rationalis non est tempori subdita, sed ad tempus se habet anterioriter, sicut visus ad oculum: qui licet sine oculo non videat, tamen non habet ab oculo, quod est visus, cum oculus sit organum ejus. Ita anima rationalis, licet non mensuret motum sine tempore, non tamen propterea ipse subest tempori, sed potius e converso: cum utatur tempore pro instrumento et organo ad discretionem motuum faciendam.' Cf. especially *Idiota* iii. 'De mente' 15. fol. 171.

[49] Kepler already referred to the doctrines of the 'divine Cusanus' (*divinus mihi Cusanus*) in his first work, *Mysterium Cosmographicum*. Cf. *Opera* ed. Ch. Frisch; i. 2. 122. See also ibid., ii. 490, 595.

thesis of *complicatio* and *explicatio*. This existence, too, is no mere external 'happening', but rather represents the *activity* most appropriate to man. Only in history can man prove himself to be truly creative and free. Here it becomes clear that, despite the course of fortuitous events, and despite the force of external circumstances, man still remains the 'created God'. Man is completely enclosed in time; indeed, he is completely entrapped in the particularity of any given moment and completely enmeshed in the conditions of that moment; and yet, despite all this, man proves to be a *deus occasionatus*. He remains enclosed within his own being, never transgressing the limits of his own specifically human nature. But inasmuch as he develops and expresses every facet of his nature, man represents the divine in the form and within the limits of the human.[50] Like every being, man has the right to fulfil and to realize *his* form.[51] He may, he even must affirm this form, this limitation of his; for only by doing that can he honour and love God within it and give evidence of the purity of his own origin.[52]

Although Cusanus never doubted the doctrine of original sin,[53] it seems to have lost for him the power that it had exerted on the whole of medieval thought and on its sense of life. The Pelagian spirit is re-awakening now, that spirit so bitterly fought by Augustine, whose polemics became the basis of medieval religious doctrine. Cusanus sharply emphasizes the doctrine of man's freedom, for only through freedom can man become God-like; only through freedom can he

---

[50] *De conjecturis* ii. 14.

[51] *De docta ignorantia* ii. 2: 'Quis ista intelligere posset, quomodo omnia illius unicae infinitae formae sunt imago, diversitatem ex contingenti habendo, quasi creatura sit Deus occasionatus . . . quoniam ipsa forma infinita non est nisi finite recepta, ut omnis creatura sit quasi infinitas finita aut Deus creatus, ut sit eo modo quo hoc melius esse possit . . . ex quo subinfertur omnem creaturam ut talem perfectam, etiam si alterius respectu minus perfecta videatur . . . quiescit omne esse creatum in sua perfectione, quam habet ab esse divino liberaliter, nullum aliud creatum esse appetens tanquam perfectus, sed ipsum quod habet a maximo praediligens, quasi quoddam divinum munus, hoc incorruptibiliter perfici et conservari optans.'

[52] This thought was most clearly and sharply expressed in *De dato patris luminum*. Cf., e.g. chap. i: 'Omnis vis illa quae se esse cognoscit ab optimo, optime se esse cognoscit. Cognoscit igitur esse suum, cujus nullam vellet ullo unquam tempore corruptionem aut mutationem in aliud esse extra speciem propriam, sibi datum non quidem ab alio aliquo, quod non est de sursum, super omnia in altitudine omnis optimitatis. Nam non credit intellectus humanus naturam suam sibi potuisse dari ab aliquo, cujus bonitas non sit altissima de sursum, super omne bonum. Neque quiesceret aliquod ens in data natura, si a diminuto et creato bono esset, sed quia ab optimo et maximo magistro, quo nihil altius, sortitum est esse suum, omne id quod est quiescit in specifica natura sua ut in optima ab optimo.'

[53] For Cusanus' doctrine of original sin, cf., e.g., the sermon 'Coelum et terra transibunt' *Excitat.* v. fol. 495.

become the vessel of God (*capax Dei*).[54] And although man's being is completely derived from God, there is nevertheless a sphere in which he functions as a free creator and in which he reigns autonomously. This is the sphere of *value*. Without human nature there would be no such thing as value, i.e., there would be no principle for evaluating things according to their greater or lesser perfection. Imagine human nature removed from the world; with it will disappear every value-preference of one thing above another. God is, of course, the Master who strikes the coins; but the human mind determines how much they are worth. 'For although the human intellect does not give being to the value, there would nevertheless be no distinctions in value without it. Thus, if one leaves the intellect aside, one cannot know whether value exists. Without the power of judgment and of comparison, every evaluation ceases to exist, and with it value would also cease. Wherewith we see how precious is the mind, for without it, everything in creation would be without value. When God wanted to give value to his work, he had to create, besides the other things, the intellectual nature.'[55]

These sentences completely express the religious humanism and the religious optimism of Cusanus. How could that which is the principle and the source of value be worthless? How could it be lost to corruption and to sin? Just as nature was earlier raised up to God through the mediation of humanity, so now human culture has found its true theodicy. Culture confirms the freedom of the human spirit, which is the seal of its divinity. The spirit of asceticism is overcome; mistrust of the world disappears. The mind can come to know itself and to measure its own powers only by devoting itself completely and unconditionally to the world. Even sensible nature and sense-knowledge are no longer merely base things, because, in fact, they provide the first impulse and stimulus for all intellectual activity. The mind is the living illustration of eternal and infinite wisdom; but until it is stimulated to movement by that admiration which arises from contemplation of the sensible, it

[54] Ibid., fol. 498: 'Creavit autem Deus naturam magis suae bonitatis participem, scilicet intellectualem, quae in hoc, quod habet liberum arbitrium est creatori similior et est quasi alius Deus. . . . Ista natura intellectualis capax est Dei, quia est in potentia infinita: potest enim semper plus et plus intelligere. . . . Nulla natura alia potest fieri melior ex se, sed est id quod est sub necessitate, quae ipsam sic tenet. Sola intellectualis natura habet in se principia, per quae potest fieri melior et ita Deo similior et capacior.'

[55] *De ludo globi* ii. fol. 236ff. Cf. in this connection my *Erkenntnisproblem*, I, 57ff.

is, so to speak, asleep within us.[56] This movement, which begins and ends in the mind itself, must pass through the world of the senses. The mind always 'assimilates' itself to the sensible world; mind becomes sight when presented with colour, hearing when presented with sounds.[57] This descent into the world of perception is now no longer considered a decadence, a kind of sinful fall of knowledge; instead, it accomplishes the ascent of the sense-world itself which now raises itself from multiplicity to unity, from limitations to generality, from confusion to clarity.[58]

Cusanus summarizes all of these thoughts in a pregnant metaphor. The human mind, he writes, is a divine seed that comprehends in its simple essence the totality of everything knowable; but in order for this seed to blossom and to bear fruit, it must be planted in the soil of the sensible world.[59] The basic character of that 'copulative theology' sought by Cusanus lies in this reconciliation of mind and nature, of intellect and sense. With complete consciousness of method, he now opposes this to all theology that is merely 'disjunctive', negating, and divisive.[60]

[56] *Idiota* iii. 'De mente' 5: 'Mens est viva descriptio aeternae et infinitae sapientiae. Sed in nostris mentibus ab initio vita illa similis est dormienti, quousque admiratione, quae ex sensibilibus oritur, excitetur, ut moveatur. Tunc motu vitae suae intellectivae in se descriptum reperit, quod quaerit.'

[57] Ibid., 7: 'Mens est adeo assimilativa, quod in visu se assimilat visibilibus et in auditu audibilibus, in gustu gustabilibus, in odoratu odorabilibus, in tactu tangibilibus, et in sensu sensibilibus, in imaginatione imaginabilibus et in ratione rationabilibus.'

[58] *De conjecturis* ii. 16: 'Intellectus autem iste in nostra anima eapropter in sensum descendit, ut sensibile ascendat in ipsum. Ascendit ad intellectum sensibile ut intelligentia ad ipsum descendat. Hoc est enim intellectum descendere ad sensibile quod sensibile ascendere ad intellectum: visibile enim non attingitur per sensum visus absente intentione intellectualis vigori. . . . Intellectus autem qui secundum regionem intellectualem in potentia est, secundum inferiores regiones plus est in actu. Unde insensibili mundo in actu est, nam in visu visibile et in auditu audibile actualiter appraehendit. . . . Unit enim alteritates sensatorum in phantasia, varietatem alteritatem phantasmatum unit in ratione, variam alteritatem rationum in sua unit intellectuali simplici unitate.'

[59] *Idiota* iii. 5. fol. 154: 'Quia mens est quoddam divinum semen sua vi complicans omnium rerum exemplaria notionaliter; tunc a Deo a quo hanc vim habet, eo ipso quod esse recepit est simul et in convenienti terra locatum, ubi fructum facere possit et ex se rerum universitatem notionaliter explicare, alioqui haec vis seminalis frustra data ipsi esset, si non fuisset addita opportunitas in actum prorumpendi.'

[60] Cf. especially his letter of 14 September 1453 to the monks of Tegernsee, reproduced in Vansteenberghe, op. cit., pp. 113ff. Also see *De filiatione Dei* fol. 125: 'Una est . . . Theologia affirmativa, omnia de uno affirmans, et negativa omnia de eodem negans, et dubia neque negans neque affirmans, et disjunctiva, alterum affirmans, alterum negans, et copulativa opposita affirmativa connectens. . . . Oportet ditrende studentem non negligere quomodo in hac schola sensibilis mundi in modorum varietate quaeritur unum, quod omnia, sed parto jam magisterio in caelo intelligentiae pure in uno omnia sciuntur.'

CHAPTER TWO

CUSANUS AND ITALY

I

THE strong influence exercised by the personality and doctrine of Cusanus on Italy and on Italian intellectual life in the Quattrocento is attested by his contemporaries.[1] And yet, up to now, both the history of philosophy and the general cultural history of the Renaissance have failed to recognize this relationship clearly and to examine it carefully. The importance of Cusanus for the history of *Italian philosophy* first becomes clear and unmistakable in the work of Giordano Bruno. Bruno himself never left any doubt as to how much he owed to the two thinkers whom he valued as the true liberators of his mind: the 'divine Cusanus', and Copernicus. Now, nearly one and a half centuries elapsed between the year the *De docta ignorantia* appeared and the time Bruno's main philosophical works were published. Ought we to assume that during this period Cusanus' basic speculative ideas remained in the dark, that they exercised no immediate influence on their own epoch? The assumption almost seems necessary when we consider that the truly representative philosophical systems of the time never even refer to the basic teachings of Cusanus, and that his very *name* seems to have become unfamiliar to them. Nicholas of Cusa is mentioned neither by Pomponazzi and the thinkers of the Paduan school nor in the works of the Florentine Platonists Ficino and Pico.[2] As soon as we try to establish a bond, it threatens to dissolve. Simple observation of the facts seems enough to bar any 'constructive' attempt

[1] Cf. *Apologia doctae ignorantiae* fol. 75: 'Jam dudum audivi per Italiam ex hoc semine per tuam solicitam culturam studiosis ingeniis recepto magnum fructum effluxisse.'

[2] In Pico's works, the name Cusanus never appears. Ficino mentions him only once, in a letter, and—curiously enough—misspells his name. In a list of philosophical works dealing with Platonic thoughts, Ficino mentions, besides Bessarion's defence of the Platonic doctrine, 'certain speculations' of Cusanus (*quaedam speculationes Nicolai Caisii* (sic) *Cardinalis*). Cf. *Epistola* ix. *Opera* fol. 899. That Ficino nevertheless knew Cusanus' works is beyond doubt. Cf., e.g., G. Saitta, *La filosofia di Marsilio Ficino* (Messina, 1923), p. 75, and below, for more evidence.

at establishing a connection between Cusanus and the basic doctrines of Italian philosophy in the fifteenth century.

Italian historians of philosophy in particular have, for the most part, come to this conclusion. National sentiment, nourished especially in the last decade of Italian philosophical literature, plays a role in the formation of this judgment. Renaissance thought, like Renaissance culture generally, must be derived from its own national soil; it must be recognized as an autochthonous creation of the Italian mind. Only by keeping these tendencies in mind can we understand how it is possible for a scholar like Gentile to avoid even the slightest mention of Cuanus' doctrine in his studies on Giordano Bruno and in his treatise on the 'Concept of Man in the Renaissance'.[3] And yet, over forty years ago, one of the leading Italian historians of philosophy formulated clearly and unequivocally the relationship that exists between Cusanus and Italy. At the very beginning of his work, *Il Risorgimento filosofico nel Quattrocento*, which appeared posthumously, Fiorentino writes: 'We would be deceived if we thought that our Renaissance signified a simple return of ancient ideas. Apart from the fact that history never repeats itself, there is also the fact that a new branch had been grafted upon the old Italo-Greek trunk: namely, German thought. If we neglect this new factor in the history of speculative thought, or if we try, out of misconceived national ambition, to lessen its importance, we would come to an inaccurate and unfair judgment, and we would shut ourselves off from a true understanding of the beginning of modern philosophy.' Had Fiorentino, who was one of the best scholars of Renaissance philosophy, been able to document and to demonstrate this thesis in detail, it certainly would have been an extraordinary boon to the knowledge of the intellectual origins and foundations of the Renaissance. But his work remained a fragment; it breaks off precisely at the point at which documentary proof of that basic relationship would have had to be cited. Still, it is incumbent upon objective historiography at least to heed Fiorentino's methodological exhortation and warning. We cannot understand the history of a great intellectual movement, especially of a philosophical movement, by looking at it from a onesidedly national point of view. Every truly great genius, every 'national' genius in the deeper sense of the word, forces us to give up the narrowness of such a point of view at once. This is doubly true of Cusanus. We have already seen how much he owed to Italy—how

[3] Giovanni Gentile, *Giordano Bruno e il pensiero del Rinascimento* (Florence, 1923).

he was first led into the bright and wide world through contact with the Italian culture of the fifteenth century, and how, through that contact, his thoughts gained a stable form and definition. But the force and vigour of Italy's influence upon him are equalled by his counter-influence which, though not immediately apparent, is nevertheless present. To grasp it, we must not judge the philosophy of the Renaissance by its 'school concept', but by its 'world concept'. It is in this 'world concept' that the basic themes of Cusanus' doctrine converge. And the less we look for the adoption of single notions or particular conclusions, the more strongly do the themes of Cusanus' thought prove to be influential. Cusanus gave to the Italian philosophy of his time not specific conclusions but tendencies and impulses. These, in turn, become visible not so much in definite dogmatic teachings as in a new *direction* of the total conception, and in the new *objectives* towards which life and thought now press.

To measure the significance and scope of Cusanus' influence, it will not do to turn to philosophy and to the leaders of philosophical schools; rather, we must look to the *lay* world and its intellectual representatives. Burckhardt pointed to the 'increase in completely educated men' in the fifteenth century as one of the characteristic features of the Renaissance. These 'versatile' and 'universal' men, as he called them, could no longer take the elements of their intellectual education from the philosophy of the time, which had remained more or less bound to the forms of Scholastic thought and of Scholastic erudition. To better emphasize his own style of life and his own ideal of education, Petrarch had felt it necessary to attack vigorously the pretensions of a philosophical and academic training, proudly professing and asserting his ignorance of such matters.[4] And *Leonardo da Vinci*, too, fought constantly against authority and tradition. As a result of this battle, a new idea of knowledge begins to dawn upon him, an idea towards which he has been groping and for which he must lay the methodological foundations. Leonardo divided thinkers into two opposed groups: the original discoverers, and the imitators and 'commentators'. The first great minds—the 'primitives', to use Leonardo's term—recognized only one pattern and one model for their work: experience. And for that, they deserve the name of discoverers. Their followers, on the other hand, abandoned nature and reality and lost themselves in a world of merely conceptual distinctions (*discorsi*). Now only a return

---

[4] Cf. especially *De sui ipsius et aliorum ignorantia*.

to 'natural' human understanding, only a return to the power of the unspoiled mind can set matters aright. 'Le bone lettere son nate da un bono naturale, e perchè si dee più laudare la cagion che l'effetto, più lauderai un bon naturale sanza lettere che un bon letterato sanza naturale.'[5]

This principle, which expresses the entire tenor and orientation of Leonardo's research, was formulated more sharply and grounded more firmly by Cusanus than by any other thinker of the age. From the Brothers of the Common Life, Cusanus had learned and adopted the principle of lay piety, the *devotio moderna*. To this he now adds the new ideal of lay *knowledge*. Cusanus dedicated one of his most important works to the presentation and justification of this ideal. Its very *title* suggests the basic thought: to the three dialogues 'De sapientia', 'De mente', and 'De staticis experimentis', Cusanus gave the title *Idiota*. In all three, the layman, the untutored one, emerges as the teacher of both the orator and the philosopher. It is he who asks those decisive questions, in which the answers are already implicit—in a sense even anticipated. The work opens in the Roman Forum, where the layman meets an orator. The layman tells him that the true nourishment of the mind does not lie in the writings of others, just as true wisdom cannot be found in devotion to any authority. 'You consider yourself wise, without being it, and are proud of your wisdom. I consider myself ignorant, and because I do, I am perhaps wiser than you.' Wisdom needs no scholarly appurtenances; it is to be found everywhere. Those with eyes can perceive it in the hustle and bustle of the marketplace and in the daily transactions of men. It is present in the traffic between buyers and sellers, in the weighing of goods, in the counting of money. For all these things are based on the basic power of the human being, the power of measuring, of weighing, and of counting. In this power lies the foundation of all the activities of reason: it is the distinguishing feature of mind. To grasp the essence and the secret of our intellectual nature, we need only examine its simplest and most ordinary expressions.[6]

[5] *Il codice Atlantico di Leonardo da Vinci* (Milan, 1894ff.) fol. 75.
[6] *Idiota* i. 'De sapientia' fol. 137. 'Idiota (ad Oratorem): "Traxit te opinio auctoritatis, ut sis quasi equus, natura liber, sed arte capistro alligatus praesepi, ubi non aliud comedit, nisi quod illi ministratur. Pascitur enim intellectus tuus, auctoritati scribentium astrictus, pabulo alieno et non naturali." Orator: "Si non in libris sapientium est sapientiae pabulum; ubi tunc est?" Idiota: "Non dico ibi non esse, sed dico naturale ibi non reperiri. Qui enim primo se ad scribendum de sapientia contulerunt, non de librorum pabulo, qui nondum erant, incrementa receperunt, sed naturali alimento in virum perfectum perducebantur et ii caeteros, qui ex libris se putant profecisse, longe sapientia antecedunt. . . . Scribit aliquis verbum illud, cui credis. Ego autem dico tibi, quod sapientia foris clamat in

With this in mind, we can understand the influence Cusanus had precisely on the highly gifted 'laymen'. Now that *Duhem's* penetrating research has uncovered the sources of Leonardo's thought, we know how close the objective relationships were between Nicholas Cusanus and Leonardo. Duhem has reported in detail how Leonardo received a great number of problems immediately from the hands of Cusanus, and how he took them up precisely at the point that Cusanus had left them.[7] The deeper reason for this historical relationship now becomes clearer. Leonardo could, as it were, take direct possession of so much of Cusanus' intellectual estate for the simple reason that both men had the same *attitude towards method*. For Leonardo, Cusanus represents not only a specific philosophical system but, what is more important, a new kind and a new orientation of research. From this we can also understand that the relationship now established will grow beyond the bounds of the merely individual. Cusanus becomes, in a sense, the exponent of that whole intellectual circle to which Leonardo belonged —that circle which, next to the declining Scholastic and the ascendant humanistic education, represents a third, specifically modern form of knowledge and of will to knowledge in the Italian fifteenth century. These men were not concerned with giving scientific determination and definition to fundamentally religious issues. Nor did they demand a return to the great tradition of antiquity, to seek there the regeneration of mankind. Instead, they dealt with concrete, technical and artistic problems, for which they sought a 'theory'. This creative and artistic activity soon feels the need for a deeper understanding of itself; and this need could not be satisfied without going back to the ultimate foundations of knowledge, especially of mathematical knowledge.

Besides Leonardo, the most noteworthy among those concerned with the new form and the new problem of intellectual life is Leon Battista Alberti. He too is connected with Cusanus. Aside from their personal relationship, there are the references in Alberti's main theoretical works to Cusanus' mathematical and philosophical speculation, especially to his studies in method relative to the problem of squaring a

plateis et est clamor ejus, quomodo ipsa habitat in altissimis." Orator: "Ut audio, cum sis Idiota, sapere te putas?" Idiota: "Haec est fortassis inter te et me differentia: tu te scientem putas, cum non sis, hinc superbis; ego vero Idiotam me esse cognosco, hinc humilior, in hoc forte doctior existo" ' etc.

[7] *Études sur Léonard de Vinci, ceux qu'il a lus et ceux qui l'ont lu* (Seconde série; Paris, 1909), pp. 99ff.

circle.[8] This single problem suffices to show that the men of this group were connected with Cusanus by fundamentally important ideas.[9] The *De docta ignorantia* had begun with the proposition that all knowledge is definable as measurement. Accordingly, it had established as the medium of knowledge the concept of *proportion*, which contains within it, as a condition, the possibility of measurement. *Comparativa est omnis inquisitio, medio proportionis utens.*[10] But proportion is not just a logical-mathematical concept: it is also a basic concept of aesthetics. Thus the idea of measurement becomes the connecting link, joining the natural scientist to the artist who creates a second 'nature'. In the words of *Luca Pacioli*, the friend of Leonardo, proportion is not only the mother of knowledge; it is the 'mother and queen of art'. Thus, the speculative-philosophical, the technical-mathematical, and the artistic tendencies of the period converge in the concept of proportion. And this convergence makes the *problem of form* one of the central problems of Renaissance culture.

Here again, we can clearly observe that process of 'secularization' which the religious ideas of the Middle Ages underwent since the beginning of the Renaissance. Even the new concepts of 'nature' and of 'natural truth' that are now beginning to form have their historical origins in these religious ideas. The return to nature—taken in its

---

[8] For more details see Girolamo Mancini, *Vita di Leon Battista Alberti* (2nd ed.; Florence, 1909), and Leonardo Olschki, *Geschichte der neusprachlichen wissenschaftlichen Literatur* (Heidelberg, 1919), I, 81ff.

[9] As further proof of the strong influence that Cusanus' doctrines exercised in Italy, Vansteenberghe, in his biography, cites the 'small Cusanian school' in Italy that held an 'academic reunion' some time toward the end of the century. The fact that Pacioli, in the preface to his work *Divina Proportione*, reports that, in addition to 'a large number of erudite admirers of the great cardinal', Leonardi da Vinci also took part in the gathering, would seem to be a further confirmation of Duhem's thesis. But there is apparently an error here. So far as I can see, the dedication of *Divina proportionae* contains nothing to indicate the existence of such a Cusanian community. It does tell of a meeting that took place on 9 February 1498 in the Castle of Milan, in the presence of the Duke Lodovico Maria Sforza. Among those *present* at this gathering were Ambrogio da Rosate, Marliani, Pirovano, Leonardo da Vinci, Andrea Novarese, and *Niccolò Cusano*. This last is then spoken of as a man admired and honoured by all those present because of his great knowledge of medicine and astronomy. (E dali prefati molto in tutti premesse (discipline) admirato e venerato Nicolo cusano.) Cf. Luca Pacioli, *Divina proportionae* (new ed. in *Quellenschriften für Kunstgeschichte und Kunsttheorie des Mittelalters und der Neuzeit*, N.F., II, Vienna, 1889), p. 32. There is nothing at all here about admiration for the person and for the doctrines of the *philosopher* Nicholas Cusanus. The Niccolò Cusano mentioned was simply a doctor of the same name, who held a professorship at Pavia. For details concerning him and the others mentioned in Pacioli's preface, cf. Gustavo Uzielli, *Ricerche intorno a Leonardo da Vinci* (1st series; Torino, 1896), pp. 368ff. As for the gathering itself, it was a reunion of the so-called 'Academia Leonardo da Vinci'. For further details, see Uzielli, op. cit., pp. 341ff., and Olschki, op. cit., I, 239ff.

[10] *De docta ignorantia* i. 1.

religious, not in its modern aesthetic or scientific sense—was already unmistakably apparent in that great return of *piety* brought about by medieval mysticism. On *this* point, Thode, in his work on Francis of Assisi, was undoubtedly right. With his new, Christian ideal of love, Francis of Assisi broke through and rose above that dogmatic and rigid barrier between 'nature' and 'spirit'. Mystical sentiment tries to permeate the entirety of existence; before it, all barriers of particularity and individualization dissolve. Love no longer turns only to God, the source and the transcendent origin of being; nor does it remain confined to the relationship between man and man, as an immanent ethical relationship. It overflows to all creatures, to the animals and plants, to the sun and the moon, to the elements and the natural forces. No longer mere 'parts' of being, independent and isolated, they are now fused by the glow of mystical love to a unity with man and with God. The category of specific and individual 'thingness', by which life in nature is divided into definitely determined species and into definite degrees, cannot stand up to the mystical category of brotherliness. Like the fish and the birds, the trees and the flowers, so, too, the wind and the water here become 'brothers and sisters' of man for Francis of Assisi.

In Franciscan mysticism the medieval mind begins the great work of redeeming nature and liberating it from the stain of sin and sensuality. But there is still lacking a knowledge corresponding to this love and capable of justifying it. We saw that this knowledge begins with Cusanus, who also began as a mystic, but who now requires and seeks the *speculative* justification of nature. And for this, of course, another path had to be taken. For this, the mystic had to call on the logician for aid. But the old logic of the School, the logic of the 'Aristotelian sect', as Cusanus calls it, will be of no help. The philosopher of the *coincidentia oppositorum* had rejected the very fundamental principles of this logic.[11] In its place, in the place of formal syllogistics, comes the *logic of mathematics*, to provide the means by which we can raise ourselves above the sphere of mystical feeling into that of intellectual *vision*. Only thus does the mystic's love of God attain its fulfilment and its true objective. Cusanus says that all true love is based on an act of *knowledge*.[12] Thus there follows a curious spectacle, unique in the history of philosophy: the *exactness* of mathematics is sought not for its own sake, nor even as a foundation for knowledge of nature, but for

---

[11] *Apologia doctae ignorantiae.* Cf. above, chap. i, n. 5.
[12] Cf. above, p. 14.

the foundation and the deepening of *knowledge of God*. According to the *De docta ignorantia*, all wise men, all the godliest and holiest teachers agree that everything visible is an image of the invisible, which we cannot see except in a mirror or in an enigma. For us, then, the spiritual remains unattainable in itself; we can never grasp it except in a sense-image, a symbol. But we may at least demand that the sense-image itself contain nothing unclear, nothing doubtful; for the road to uncertainty can only lead through certainty.[13] This is the novelty: he requires of the symbols in which the divine becomes graspable by us not only sensible fullness and force but also intellectual precision and certainty. With that, the character of the relationship between the world and God, between the finite and the infinite, undergoes a complete transformation.

For the mystical mode of thought, any point in being may serve as the starting point for this relationship, because in every individual thing there is a 'trace of God'. He reveals himself in the reflected splendour of the finite. Cusanus also maintains this view,[14] but puts it into a new and universal context. For him, nature is not only the reflection of the divine being and the divine force; rather, it becomes the book God has written with his own hand.[15] We are still on religious ground here; but at the same time the breakthrough—to speak with Schelling—into the free, open field of objective science has been accomplished. Neither subjective feeling nor mystical sentiment suffice to understand the meaning of the book of nature. Rather, it must be investigated, it must be deciphered word for word, letter for letter. The world may no longer remain a divine hieroglyph, a holy sign; instead, we must analyse and systematically interpret this sign.

Depending on the direction this analysis takes, it may lead either to a new metaphysic or to an exact science of nature. The natural philosophy of the Renaissance took the first path. It took up the idea that nature is the 'book of God', and then transformed it into a host of new variations. *Campanella* built his entire theory of knowledge and his

---

[13] *De docta ignorantia* i. 11: 'Dicimus, cum ad divina non nisi per symbola accedendi nobis via pateat, quod tunc mathematicalibus signis propter ipsorum incorruptibilem certitudinem convenientius uti poterimus.'

[14] Cf., e.g., *De docta ignorantia* ii. 2: 'Creaturae esse non possit aliud esse quam ipsa resplendentia (Dei), non in aliquo alio positive recepta, sed contingenter diversa.'

[15] Cf. *Idiota* i. 'De sapientia' fol. 137: 'Orator: "Quomodo ductus esse potes ad scientiam ignorantiae tuae, cum sis Idiota?" Idiota: "Non ex tuis, sed ex Dei libris." Orator: "Qui sunt illi?" Idiota: "Quos suo digito scripsit." Orator: "Ubi reperiuntur?" Idiota: Ubique . . ." '

entire metaphysics upon this foundation. For him, 'to know' means simply to read the divine signs that God has written into nature. *Intelligere* means nothing but *intus legere*. 'The world is the statue, the living temple, and the codex of God, into which He wrote and designed those infinitely worthy things He carried in his spirit. Blessed is he who reads in this book and learns from it the way things are and who does not invent things according to his own fancy or according to the opinion of others.'[16] Here, a new and specific feeling for nature is expressed in an old parable that can be traced through Cusanus to medieval philosophy, to Augustine and Thomas. But it is significant that these sentences occur at the end of the work entitled *De sensu rerum et magia*. The bond that holds together the innermost recesses of nature and that joins nature to man is still conceived of completely as a magical-mystical bond. Man can only understand nature by inserting his own *life* into it. The limits of his feeling for life, the barriers to a direct *sympathetic feeling* of nature, are at the same time the limits of his *knowledge* of nature.

The opposite form of interpretation is found in that study of nature that leads from Cusanus through Leonardo to Galileo and Kepler. It is not satisfied with the imagistic and sensible force of the signs in which we read the spiritual structure of the universe; instead, it requires of these signs that they form a system, a thoroughly ordered whole. The *sense* of nature must not be mystically felt; it must be understood as a logical sense. And this requirement can only be fulfilled by means of mathematics. Only mathematics establishes unequivocal and necessary standards against the arbitrariness and uncertainty of opinions. For Leonardo mathematics becomes the dividing line between sophistry and science. Whoever blames the supreme certainty of mathematics feeds his mind with confusion. Whoever relies on individual words falls prey to the uncertainty and ambiguity characteristic of the single word, and finds himself entangled in endless logomachies.[17] Only mathematics can give a purpose to these disputes in that it fixes the meanings of words and subjects their connections to definite rules. Instead of a mere aggregate of words, mathematics gives us a strictly syntactical structure of thoughts and propositions.

Galileo takes this path to its very end. For him, the individual sense

---

[16] Campanella *De sensu rerum et magia*, ed. Tob. Adami (Frankfurt, 1620), 370f. (For more details see *Erkenntnisproblem*, I, 268f., 282.)

[17] Leonardo da Vinci, *Scritti letterari*, ed. Jean Paul Richter (2 vols; London, 1883), II, 289 (No. 1157).

perception, no matter how intense or forceful it may be, is a mere 'name'; it neither 'says' anything nor has any objectively definite meaning.[18] Such meaning is born only when the human mind relates the content of the perception to the basic forms of knowledge, the archetypes of which are in the mind itself. Only through this relationship and this interpenetration does the book of nature become readable and comprehensible. Thus, from Cusanus' basic notion of 'indestructible certitude' (*incorruptibilis certitudo*), which is proper to none of the symbols necessary and possible to the mind except the mathematical signs, we move in a continuous historical line and arrive at those famous fundamental and guiding principles by which Galileo defines the aim and the character of his research. And when the revelation of the 'book of nature' is juxtaposed to the revelation of the bible, the process of secularization is completed. There can be no fundamental opposition between them since both represent the same spiritual sense in different forms, i.e., since the unity of the divine originator of nature is manifested in them. But if a disagreement between them should nevertheless seem to arise for us, it can only be settled in one way: we must prefer the revelation in *works* to that in *words*; for the word is something of the past and of tradition, whereas the work, as something at hand and enduring, stands before us, immediate and present, ready to be questioned.[19]

The development of the concept of nature and its gradual emancipation from the religious and theological assumptions that surrounded it were both brought about by those two forces that were so influential in all the intellectual life of the Renaissance, slowly guiding it in a new

[18] Cf. Galilei, *Il saggiatore*, *Opere*, ed. Albèri, IV, 334: 'Per lo che vo io pensando, che questi sapori, odori, colori, ecc., per la parte del suggetto, nel quale ci par che riseggano, non sieno altro che puri nomi, ma tengano solamente lor residenza nel corpo sensitivo ecc.'

[19] See especially Galilei's letter to Diodati of 15 January 1633 (in Edizione Nazionale XV), 23: 'Se io domanderò al Fromondo di chi sono opera il sole, la luna, la terra, le stelle, le loro disposizioni e movimenti, penso, che mi risponderà essere fattura d'Iddio. E domandato di chi sia dettatura la Scrittura Sacra, so che risponderà essere dello Spirito Santo, cioè parimente d'Iddio. Il mondo dunque sono le opere, e la Scrittura sono le parole del medesimo Iddio. Domandato poi se lo Spirito Santo sia mai usato nel suo parlare di pronunziare parole molto contrarie in aspetto al vero e fatte così per accomodarsi alla capacità del popolo, per lo più assai rozzo e incapace, sono ben certo che mi risponderà, insieme con tutti i sacri scrittori, tale essere il costume della Scrittura. . . . Ma se io gli dimanderò se Iddio per accomodarsi alla capacità e opinione del medesimo volgo ha mai usato di mutare la fattura sua, o . . . ha conservato sempre e continua di mantenere suo stile circa i movimenti, figura e disposizione delle parti dell'universo, son certo che egli risponderà che la luna fu sempre sferica, sebbene l'universale tenne gran tempo ch'ella fosse piana, e in somma dirà nulla mutarsi giammai dalla natura per accomodare la fattura sua alla stima e opinione deli guomini.'

direction. The new intellectual form of the Renaissance is generally determined by the new possibilities of expression now created by *language* and *technics*. In his *Idiota*, Nicholas Cusanus clearly and definitely set up the ideal of a new lay knowledge; but this knowledge lacked an adequate and commensurate form of expression. The 'layman' undertakes to convince both the orator and the philosopher of their ignorance. He attacks the fundamental assumptions of both the Scholastic and the humanistic concepts of knowledge—but he himself still speaks the Latin of the Schools. We have already seen how much this link to the language and terminology of the Middle Ages limited the free unfolding even of Cusanus' original thoughts (cf. above, p. 14). But now, the Italians who take up and develop his thoughts are free of this limitation. They—the mathematicians, the technicians, and the artists—reject not only the content but also the form of traditional knowledge. They want to be discoverers, not commentators. Just as they want to think with their own heads, they want also to speak their own language. 'If I cannot cite authors, as you can'—Leonardo retorts to the Scholastics and the Humanists of his time—'I shall nonetheless cite a much greater and worthier thing, in that I refer myself to experience, the master of your masters. You walk about swollen and pompous, dressed and adorned not by your own efforts, but by the efforts of others, and you will not even grant me mine. But if you despise me, the inventor, how much more are you susceptible to censure, who are only the trumpeters and the reciters of the works of others. . . . You will say that, because I am unlettered (*per non avere lettere*), I cannot speak well or correctly of that which I intend to treat; do you not know that my things are to be treated more through experience than through the words of others? Just as experience was the teacher of all those who have written well, so I, too, will take it for my teacher and will cite it in all cases.'[20]

Nevertheless, this turn towards experience could not have been fruitful and could not have led to a true liberation from Scholasticism if it had not created a new *organ*. In his *Geschichte der neusprachlichen wissenschaftlichen Literatur* Olschki has masterfully demonstrated that the two tasks are interconnected and that they could only be solved through each other. The liberation from medieval Latin, the gradual

[20] *Il codice atlantico di Leonardo da Vinci* fol. 115ʳ. 117ᵛ. A glance at the early passages of the *Idiota* will show just how close Leonardo was to Cusanus in the *formulation* and *foundation* of his methodological principles. See above, n. 6.

construction and development of the *volgare* as an independent scientific
form of expression was the necessary prerequisite for the free development of scientific thought and its methodological ideals. This confirms
the truth and depth of Humboldt's basic view, according to which
language does not merely follow thought but, rather, is one of the
essential moments in its formation. The difference between Scholastic
Latin and modern Italian is not merely a 'difference of sounds and of
signs'; rather, it expresses a 'difference in views of the world'. Here
again, language did not merely serve as the vessel for the new view of
the world; rather, it brought that view forth from within itself, letting
it be born together with the form and shape of the language itself.

The technical thought of the Renaissance moved in the same direction as the linguistic.[21] In this, too, surprising though it may seem,
Cusanus led the way. For in his philosophy, a new meaning and a new
place are given to the technical spirit, the spirit of the 'inventor'.
When Cusanus sets up and defends his basic view of knowledge, when
he explains that all knowledge is nothing but the unfolding and explica-
tion of the complication that lies within the simple essence of the mind,
he is referring not only to the basic concepts of logic, of mathematics,
and of mathematical natural science, but also to the elements of technical knowledge and technical creation. The mind develops space out
of the principle of the point, which is in the mind; it develops time out
of the simple 'now', and number out of unity. In like manner, an ideal
'blueprint' must precede the mind's *working* upon nature. Every art and
every skill is based on such a blueprint. Besides the categories of logic,
the concepts of geometry and arithmetic, music and astronomy,
Cusanus cites such technical accomplishments as the lyre of Orpheus
and the astrolabe of Ptolemy as evidence of the independence and
eternity of the mind.[22] To be sure, in exercising its own creative power,
the mind does not remain within itself but must have recourse to
sensible 'matter', which it forms and transforms. But this does not
indicate a retreat from the purely intellectual nature and essence of the
mind. For here, again, the way up and the way down are one and the

---

[21] For a detailed analysis of this subject, cf. Olschki, op. cit., I, 3ff., 30ff., 53ff., *et passim.*
[22] Cf. especially *De ludo globi* ii. fol. 232: 'Creat anima sua inventione nova instrumenta,
ut discernat et noscat: ut Ptolemaeus astrolabium et Orpheus lyram et ita de multis.
Neque ex aliquo extrinseco inventores crearunt illa, sed ex propria mente. Explicarunt
enim in sensibili materia conceptum.' Cf. especially *Excitat.* v. fol. 498: 'In ista natura
(intellectuali) Deus voluit magis ostendere divitias gloriae suae: videmus enim, quomodo
intellectus omnia ambit et assimilat et artes de se exserit assimilativas, ut est fabrilis et
pictoria.' Cf. above, pp. 41ff.

same; the intellect descends to the sensible only to raise the sense-world up to itself. Its action upon a world made of apparently opposite stuff is the condition for its recognizing and realizing its own form, and for translating this form from potential to actual being.[23]

From this we can understand that a strong 'realistic' influence could stem from the Idealism of Cusanus. And we can also understand that the man who revived the Platonic doctrine of *anamnesis* could become the founder of modern empirical science and the leader of the great 'empiricists'. They also see no contradiction between 'apriorism' and 'empiricism'; because what they seek in experience is necessity—it is reason itself. When Leonardo refers to experience, it is to discover there the eternal and unchangeable order of reason. His true object is not experience itself but the rational principles, the *ragioni* that are hidden and, so to speak, incorporated in experience. And he emphatically states that nature is full of 'rational principles' that have not yet been part of experience: *la natura è piena d'infinite ragioni che non furono mai in isperienza*.[24] Galileo follows the same path. Though he considered himself a champion of experience, he nevertheless emphasized that the mind can only create true, *necessary* knowledge by its own principles (*da per sè*). In view of this attitude on the part of the leading scientific minds, it becomes understandable that while science was freeing itself from Scholasticism, it felt no need to sever the bond that joined it both to ancient philosophy itself, and to the efforts at its restoration. In fact, that bond could now be strengthened.

2

With these last observations we have gone far beyond the epoch to which belong Cusanus' doctrine and its immediate influence. If we now look back, the question that seems most pressing is: what significance did this doctrine have for the development and the formation of the genuinely 'philosophical' problems of the Quattrocento? Here, as we have seen, the historical witnesses are mute. As a *mathematician*, Cusanus immediately gathered about him a wide circle of students, including the Germans Peurbach and Regiomontanus, as well as a large number of Italian mathematicians. At that time, Italy possessed no truly leading

---

[23] *De conjecturis* ii. 16 (see above, chap. i, n. 58).
[24] *Le manuscrits de Léonard de Vinci*, ed. Ravaisson-Mollien (Paris, 1881ff.), J. fol. 18r; cf. especially *Il codice Atlantico* fol. 147ᵛ: 'Nessuno effetto è in natura sanza ragione, intendi la ragione e non ti bisogna esperienzia.'

minds in the field of mathematics, no thinkers comparable with Cusanus in the originality and profundity he showed in *setting up the problem*. According to the judgment of M. Cantor in his work on the mathematicians of the fifteenth century, 'there was only one highly gifted mind with the stamp of the inventor: Cusanus. The weaknesses in his discoveries are perhaps due to the fact that he was not allowed to be exclusively a man of science, a mathematician first and foremost.'[25]

The philosophy of the time, on the other hand, though strongly rooted in the past, was rich in its own peculiar problems. Thanks to the continuous work in source criticism and in translations, the 'true' Aristotle and the 'true' Plato began to be discovered. And now, the two philosophers become more than just great figures of the past. The Platonic theory of love, the doctrine of ideas, and Aristotle's recently re-stated theory of the soul become immediately influential forces in the thought of the epoch. Developments are quick and lively; no sooner is a point reached, a system established, than it is abandoned. Cusanus' doctrine also takes part in this lively movement. But although his influence—as closer investigation will show—is unmistakably present here, it is an influence that stems not from his system as a whole but from particular problems and motifs. Inasmuch as they can be adapted to the complex of new philosophical concerns now emerging, these problems are taken up and these motifs further developed. And if we recall the inner transformation that the spirit of the 'Renaissance' underwent in the period between the middle and the end of the fifteenth century, we shall understand that before this adaptation could be accomplished certain difficulties and obstacles had to be surmounted.

Only one generation separates the philosophical works of Cusanus from those of Ficino and Pico. And yet, as soon as we compare them, we see immediately that a transformation has taken place both in the abstract *Problematik* and in the tone of the thought, that is to say, in the whole intellectual attitude. If we remember this, we shall see the error in the belief that the liberation of the Renaissance from the 'Middle Ages' took place as a steady development, moving in a straight line. No such quiet and even unfolding, no simple growth from within is observable at all. In the conflict of forces that takes place, only a temporary, thoroughly unstable equilibrium is ever achieved. In the great dispute between the religious and the philosophical concepts of truth,

[25] Moritz Cantor, *Vorlesungen über Geschichte der Mathematik* (4 vols.; Leipzig. 1894–1908), II, 211.

between faith and knowledge, religion and worldly culture, the system of Cusanus provided just such an equilibrium. His religious optimism dared to encompass the *whole* world. He tried to embrace and to reconcile man and the cosmos, nature and history. But he underestimated the strength of the contending powers that were to be overcome and bound. This tragic error reveals itself not so much in his philosophy as in his life, i.e., in his political and ecclesiastical career. He begins his career by fighting against the absolute power of the papacy. In *De concordantia catholica*, he maintains the doctrine of the sovereignty of the entire church, which, when embodied in a general council, stands above the bishops and above the pope. The pope represents the unity of the Catholic Church. He is the image of the One Church, as the church is the image of Christ. But the original is always superior to the copy; just as Christ is superior to the church, so the church is superior to the pope.[26]

The quarrels at the Council of Basle made him abandon this basic theoretical conviction. He became convinced that it was necessary to go over to the enemy camp if his ideal of church unity was to be preserved, and if the church was to be protected from schism and degradation. He joined the papal party and remained for ever and completely loyal to it. In fact, he became one of its strongest spokesmen. His whole life, his political as well as his intellectual activity, took place within this ecclesiastical hierarchy. In its name he took up the battle against opposed secular claims and fought to the bitter end, endangering both his freedom and his life.[27] Thus, the opposing forces that Cusanus tried to reconcile *intellectually* diverge in his *life*. What he had tried intellectually to bring together into a systematic unity and harmony fell apart in the immediate reality in which he stood. In the midst of these disappointments Cusanus remained the great optimist and the great irenic spirit, always continuing to believe in the necessary and possible 'coincidence' of opposites. And yet, historical developments seemed to render this faith more and more nugatory. The new forces, now beginning to achieve a clear consciousness of themselves, could neither be limited nor constrained in their development; each of them claimed full independence for itself. Philosophy could take one of two views towards

[26] *De concord. Catholica* ii. 18. fol. 738: 'Unde sicut Christus est veritas cujus figura et significatio est petra sive Ecclesia: ita petra est veritas, cujus significatio et figura est Petrus. Ex quo clare patet, Ecclesiam supra Petrum esse, sicut supra illam est Christus.'
[27] For more details, see A. Jaeger, *Der Streit des Kardinals Nikolaus von Cusa mit dem Herzoge Sigmund von Österreich* (2 vols.; Innsbruck, 1861).

this claim: it could further and support the claim by removing, piece by piece, the foundation of the old structure of thought built by Scholasticism; or it could try to renovate this structure with the tools provided by classical-humanistic culture.

The philosophy of the Quattrocento is divided between these two tendencies; but the retrogressive movement, the attempt at restoring Scholastic forms of thought, gradually gains more and more breadth and strength. This movement reaches its apex in the last decades of the fifteenth century, the epoch characterized by the ascendancy of the Platonic Academy in Florence. Philosophy becomes the defensive bulwark against worldly forces pressing from all sides. But philosophy could not carry out this task without endangering the beginnings Cusanus had made towards creating an independent and specific methodology—without, in other words, becoming more and more transformed into theology again. It is no accident that Marsilio Ficino entitled his main work *Theologia Platonica*; nor that Pico della Mirandola began his philosophical and literary activity with the *Heptaplus*, an allegorical commentary on the Mosaic story of creation. To be sure, in the great idealistic systems of modern times Platonism is considered the foundation of *scientific* philosophy; it could even lead a thinker like Leibniz to demand a *perennis quaedam philosophia*. But *Florentine* Platonism was satisfied with the demand for a *pia quaedam philosophia*.[28] Faith was to be renewed in its completely medieval and ecclesiastical form, as *fides implicita*. In one of his letters, Ficino states: 'ego certe malo divine credere, quam humane scire'.[29] In this epigrammatic formulation we can sense how much the tension between faith and knowledge has again been heightened. With his principle of *docta ignorantia*, Cusanus clearly pointed out such tension; but he was also aware that precisely this principle afforded him the means for resolving the tension speculatively, *philosophically*. In their speculation, Ficino and Pico also try to take the same path. But the beginning and the end of their path, its point of departure and its objective, can no longer be assured by knowledge as such. They can only be assured by revelation—a revelation understood in half mystical, half historical sense.

[28] Ficino *Epistolae* viii. *Opera* (Basel n.d.), fol. 871: 'Non absque divina providentia volente omnes pro singulorum ingenio ad se mirabiliter revocare factum est, ut pia quaedam Philosophia quondam et apud Persas sub Zoroastre et apud Aegyptos sub Mercurio nasceretur, utrobique sibimet consona. Nutriretur deinde apud Thraces sub Orpheo atque Aglaophemo. Adolesceret quoque mox Pythagora apud Graecos et Italos. Tandem vero a divo Platone consummaretur Athenis.'
[29] *Epistolae* v. fol. 73.

If we were to judge the attitude towards life of the Florentine circle mainly by the hymns or by the *canti carnascialeschi* of Lorenzo the Magnificent, we should be badly misled indeed. To be sure, the cult of art and beauty became a cult of this-worldliness and of sensuality; joy in the 'here and now' expressed itself strongly and uninhibitedly. But soon, other notes were added to the expression of this sentiment. The dark shadow of Savonarola was, so to speak, discernible in this circle even before he himself appeared, even before his actual historical influence. The leading minds of the Florentine Academy finally succumbed to Savonarola and bowed before him almost without resistance. That they should do so is understandable only if we pay attention to the ascetic features that were present from the start in the Florentine Academy's view of the world. In the life of Ficino these features played a strong and ever-growing role in determining the form of his mind, as well as his general moral attitude. Ficino himself reported how, during a grave illness that befell him in his forty-fourth year, he vainly sought for consolation in philosophy and in the reading of the profane writers. His recuperation is supposed to have come about after he made a vow to the Virgin Mary, asking her for a sign of recovery. Thereupon he interpreted his illness as a divine sign that philosophy alone does not suffice for the true salvation of the soul. He throws his commentary on Lucretius into the fire, so as not to be guilty of pagan errors. He decides to dedicate all his philosophy and his literary activity completely to the service of religion, to the strengthening and propagating of the faith.[30] Gradually, the deep, dark shadows also begin to fall over Pico della Mirandola, a man who appeared to his contemporaries so light and shining, a true 'phoenix among the minds'. After the first, promising period of his career, filled with a nearly unlimited faith in the power of the human mind and in humanistic ideals of life and culture, Pico's ascetic features start to become more prominent. The notes of negation and contempt of the world resound with particular force and clarity in his correspondence.[31] For no soul did Savonarola fight more stubbornly, more passionately, more fanatically than for Pico's—and he finally won the fight. Shortly before his death, Pico was about to follow Savonarola's constantly repeated admonition to enter the monastery of San Marco. Thus, his life ends with renunciation, with a

---

[30] See Ficino *Epistolae* i. fol. 644; cf. L. Galeotti, 'Saggio intorno alla vita e agli scritti di Marsilio Ficino', *Archivio storico italiano*, N.S., T. IX, pp. 33f.

[31] Cf. especially Pico's letters to his nephew Giovan Francesco, *Opera* 340ff., 344ff.

resigned return to religious dogma, to the sacraments of the church, and to the Christian-medieval forms of life.

If the Platonic Academy had been nothing but a completely retrogressive movement, we could never explain the strong and immediate influence it exerted on all the great Florentines—an influence that even affected the sceptical and cold mind of Machiavelli for a while. It is true that religious and theological interests determined the whole attitude and development of philosophical thought in the Academy. But it is also true that the religious spirit itself entered into a new phase. The intellectual labours of the first half of the Quattrocento, out of which grew a new, 'modern' concept of religion, were not lost on the Florentine Academy. It is certainly difficult to distinguish and follow the individual threads connecting the Platonic Academy to these intellectual labours; but the general, the immediate connection is quite obvious. One important connection between the doctrines of Ficino and Cusanus is apparent in the way they both pose and solve the *problem of knowledge*. But even more clearly than in these basic logical matters, the connection becomes visible in questions concerning metaphysics and the philosophy of religion. The speculations of Cusanus had established a new relationship between *God* and the *world*—a relationship that gave these speculations their distinctive character. Despite all the opposing intellectual currents it encountered there, this relationship remained in force even in Ficino's thought. In fact, it even found itself supported there by a motif that was relatively far from the mind of Cusanus. In his religious 'justification' of the world, Cusanus was concerned essentially with mathematical and cosmological problems. But the Florentine Academy always returns to the miracle of beauty, to the miracle of artistic form and of artistic creation. And upon this miracle it founds its theodicy.

The beauty of the universe indicates its divine origin and affords the ultimate and highest proof of its spiritual value. Beauty always appears as something completely objective—as measure and form, as relationship and harmony within things themselves. But the mind seizes this objective quality as something that belongs to it, i.e., as something that sprang forth from the essence of the *mind*. Since even the common, uneducated intellect distinguishes the beautiful from the ugly, and since it flees from the formless and turns to the formed, it follows that the intellect, independent of all experience and doctrine, carries within it a definite norm of beauty. 'Every mind lauds the round figure when it first encounters it in things and knows not wherefore it lauds it. So, too, in architecture we laud the symmetry of the walls, the disposition of the stones, the forms of windows and doors; and, in the human body, the proportion of its members; or, in a melody, the harmony of tones. If every mind approves of these, and if it must do so even without knowing the reason for this approbation, it can only be because of a natural and necessary instinct. . . . The reasons for these judgments are, therefore, innate in the mind itself.'[32] Thus, harmony becomes the seal God has impressed upon his work; through harmony he has ennobled this work and placed it in an inner and necessary relationship with the human mind. With its *knowledge* of beauty, and with the standard it finds within itself, the human mind places itself between God and the world and thus encompasses both for the first time in a true unity.

Here again, we have the microcosm idea in that characteristic form given to it by Cusanus. Cusanus considers man to be the bond that joins the world—not only because man unifies within himself all the elements of the cosmos, but because the religious destiny of the cosmos is, in a sense, decided within man. Because he is the representative of the universe and the essence of all its powers, man cannot be raised to the divine without simultaneously raising the rest of the universe by virtue of and within the process of man's own ascension. The redemption of man, therefore, does not signify his liberation from a world worthy of being left behind because it is the inferior realm of the senses. Rather, redemption now applies to the whole of being.

The Florentine Academy takes up this thought. Indeed, it becomes one of the most important and fruitful elements in Ficino's philosophy of religion. Ficino also considers the soul as the spiritual 'mid-point' of the world, the 'third realm' between the intelligible and the sensible world. It is above time, because it contains time within itself; but it is also below things which do not participate in time. It is mobile and immobile, simple and multiple.[33] It contains the higher, but in such a manner that it does not abandon the lower; it is never completely exhausted in a *single* movement, but rather contains the possibility of turning and of returning even in the midst of that movement. Thus the soul embraces the universe not only statically but, more important, dynamically. The soul is not made up of the single parts that form the macrocosm; rather, it is directed according to its intention towards all

[32] Ficino *Theologia Platonica sive de immortalitate animae* xi. 5. fol. 255.
[33] Cf. *Theologia Platonica* i. 3 ff.

of these parts, but without ever being completely fixed or exhausted by any one direction.[34] And this direction comes not from without but from within the soul itself. No overpowering fate, no violence of nature draws the soul down to the sensible world; nor does it passively receive divine grace that raises it up to the super-sensible. On this point Ficino differs from Augustine, whom he otherwise nearly always considers, as does Petrarch, the highest religious authority. Again, this departure from Augustine brings Ficino closer to Cusanus. Faithful to the basic attitude that dominates his whole philosophical doctrine, Cusanus had opposed the Pauline-Augustinian dogma of predestination. To be sure, he seeks neither to deny nor to limit the effectiveness of grace. But he nevertheless stoutly maintains the belief that the actual religious impulse derives not from without but from within the soul. For the essence of the soul is the capacity for self-movement and self-determination. In the *De visione Dei*, the soul says to God: 'Whoever does not possess you, cannot see you. No one grasps you to whom you have not given yourself. But how can I possess you, how can my word reach you, who are the unattainable? How can I entreat you? Is there anything more absurd than that you should give yourself to me, you who are all in all? And how could you give yourself to me, without at the same time giving me heaven, earth, and all that is within them?' And the answer the soul receives from God dismisses these doubts. 'Be you yours, and I shall be yours.' Man's freedom allows him to want or not to want himself— and only if he autonomously chooses the former will God be given to him. The choice, the final decision, rests with man.[35]

Ficino's *De christiana religione* also maintains this basic view.[36] It also

---

[34] Ibid., iii. 2. fol. 119: 'In universo Dei opere connexio partium est ponenda, ut unius Dei unum quoque sit opus. Deus et corpus extrema sunt in natura et invicem diversissima. Angelus haec non ligat; nempe in Deum totus erigitur, corpora negligit. . . . Qualitas etiam non connectit extrema nam declinat ad corpus, superiora relinquit, relictis incorporeis fit corporalis. Hucusque extrema sunt omnia seque invicem superna et inferna fugiunt, competentia carentia vinculo. Verum essentiali ista tertia interjecta talis existit, ut superiora teneat, inferiora non deserat. . . . Est enim immobilis, est et mobilis. Illinc cum superioribus, hinc cum inferioribus convenit. Si cum utrisque convenit, appetit utraque. Quapropter naturali quodam instinctu ascendit ad supera, descendit ad infera. Et dum ascendit inferiora non deserit, et dum descendit, sublimia non relinquit. Nam si alterutrum deserat, ad extremum alterum declinabit, neque vera erit ulterius mundi copula.'

[35] *De visione Dei* chap. vii: 'Cum sic in silentio contemplationis quiesco, tu Domine intra praecordia mea respondes, dicens: sis tu tuus, et ego ero tuus. O Domine . . . posuisti in libertate mea ut sim, si voluero, mei ipsius. Hinc nisi sim mei ipsius, tu non es meus. . . . Et quia hoc posuisti in libertate mea, non me necessitas, sed expectas, ut ego eligam mei ipsius esse.'

[36] See, e.g. chap. xxxv, fol. 74: 'Non cogit ad salutem Deus homines quos ab initio liberos procreavit, sed assiduis inspirationibus singulos allicit, quod si qui ad eum accesserint, hos durat laboribus, exercet adversitatibus, et velut igne aurum, sic animum probat

modifies the idea of redemption in such a way that now the universe, including the sense world, seems saved in the religious sense. Not only has man's redemption given him a new being; it has given the universe a new form. This transformation, this *reformatio*, is equivalent to a new spiritual creation. Man's mistrust of the world disappears as soon as he becomes conscious of his own divinity, as soon as he conquers his mistrust of his own nature. In his Incarnation, God declared, and brought it to pass, that there would no longer be anything formless nor anything completely contemptible in the world.[37] He could not raise man without also ennobling the world within man. As man comes to a deeper understanding of his own nature and of the pure spirituality of his origin, he places a correspondingly higher value upon the world. And conversely, if his faith in himself is shaken, the entire cosmos is thrust back into the void, into the sphere of mortality. *This* interpretation of the idea of redemption, Ficino states emphatically, precludes all hierarchical gradation or meditation. God has bound himself to man without any instrument of mediation (*absque medio*). Similarly, we must recognize that our salvation consists in being related to him without mediators.[38] With this thought we are on the way to the *Reformation*: but the transformation has been prepared by a genuine and basic *Renaissance* motif. It is the self-affirmation of man which now also becomes the affirmation of the world. The idea of *humanitas* gives a new content and a new meaning to the macrocosm.

With this in mind, we can completely understand the deep influence exerted by the Platonic Academy on the great *artists* of the Renaissance. According to Ficino, the whole point of religious and philosophical *knowledge* is nothing other than the eradication from the world of everything that seems deformed; and the recognition that even things that seem formless participate in form. But such knowledge cannot

---

difficultate,' etc. Cf. also *Epistolae*, Lib. ii, fol. 683: 'Si quis autem dixerit, mentem ab alienis vel extrinsecis ad intelligentiam non moveri, sed ipsam et propria et mirabili quadam virtute suas sibi species, sua objecta concipere, dicemus ex eo sequi mentem esse incorpoream penitus et aeternam, si nequaquam ab alio, sed a seipsa movetur.'

[37] *De christiana religione* 18. fol. 22: 'Non minus ferme est deformia reformare, quam formare simpliciter ab initio. . . . Decuit igitur Deum omnium effectorem perficere quae defecerant, quemadmodum per insensibile verbum omnia creaverat. . . . Quid sapientius quam universi decorem miram primae et ultimae rationis copulam fieri? . . . Sic ergo et declaravit et fecit ut nihil esset in mundo deforme, nihil penitus contemnendum, cum regi coelorum terrena conjunxit atque ea quodammodo coelestibus adaequavit.'

[38] Ibid., chap. xix. fol. 23: 'Proinde quia Deus homini absque medio se conjunxit, meminisse oportet, nostram felicitatem in eo versari, ut Deo absque medio haereamus. . . . Desinant igitur, jam desinant homines suae divinitati diffidere, ob quam diffidentiam mortalibus se ipsos immergunt.'

content itself with the mere concept; it must be transformed into action, and prove itself through action. Here begins the contribution of the artist. He can fulfil the requirement that speculation can only state. Man can only be certain that the sense world *has* form and shape if he continually *gives* it form. Ultimately, the beauty of the sensible world does not derive from itself; rather, it is founded in the fact that it becomes, in a sense, the medium *through which* the free creative force of man acts and becomes conscious of itself. Seen in this light, however, art no longer lies outside the province of religion but rather becomes a moment of the religious process itself. If redemption is conceived of as a renovation of the *form* of man and of the world, i.e., as a true *reformatio*,[39] then the focal point of intellectual life must lie in the place where the 'idea' is embodied, i.e., where the non-sensible form present in the mind of the artist breaks forth into the world of the visible and becomes realized in it. Thus, speculation will inevitably go astray if it looks only at that which is already formed, instead of concerning itself with the basic act of formation itself. 'Oh investigator of things,' says Leonardo, 'do not praise yourself for your knowledge of things brought forth by nature in its normal course; rather enjoy knowing the aim and the end of those things designed by your mind.'[40] For Leonardo, *this* is science and art. Science is a second creation of nature brought about by reason, and art is a second creation of nature brought about by the imagination.[41] Reason and imagination no longer confront each other as strangers; for each is simply a different manifestation of the same basic power in man, the power to give form.

If we trace the early history of this thought, we are led to the important shift occasioned by Cusanus' doctrine of the 'likeness' between the mind of man and the mind of God. Now, any objective or contentual similarity between them is excluded from the start by the principle of

[39] In his penetrating investigation of the history of words and ideas, Konrad Burdach has shown that the concepts of 'renewal' and 'rebirth', *reformatio* and *renasci*, have their roots in religion. Only gradually were they carried over into the secular sphere. 'Sinn und Ursprung der Worte Renaissance und Reformation', *Sitzungsberichte der Berliner Akademie der Wissenschaften* (1910). Reprinted in *Reformation, Renaissance, Humanismus* (Berlin, 1918). Unfortunately, Burdach did not treat the *philosophical* literature of the Renaissance. And yet, that literature forms one of the most important phases in the process of change he describes. A passage as the one from Ficino's *De christiana religione* quoted earlier (see above, n. 37), puts the transformation of the idea, so to speak, before our very eyes: 'reformare' means the new spiritual creation of being through the process of redemption; and at the same time, it brings that 'discovery of man and the world' that is being accomplished by the new elements of worldly culture now emerging.

[40] *Le manuscrits de Léonard de Vinci*, ed. Ravaisson-Mollien, G fol. 47ʳ.

[41] *Trattato della pittura*, ed. Manzi, 38.

the *docta ignorantia: finiti et infiniti nulla proportio*. God and man, then, are comparable neither in their being nor in their works. For whereas God's creation produces the things themselves, the human mind has to do only with their signs and symbols. The mind sets these symbols before itself, refers to them in its knowledge, and relates them to one another through fixed rules. God creates the reality of things, whereas man constructs the realm of the ideal; the *vis entificativa* belongs to God, the *vis assimilativa* to man.[42] Thus, the divine and the human mind belong, as it were, to different dimensions: they are disparate both in the form of their existence and in the object of their production. Nevertheless, there is a connection between them, and it consists in the manner in which they produce. Here alone lies the real *tertium comparationis*. The relationship cannot at all be understood through any comparison taken from the world of finished things, for it is a dynamic, not a static relationship. We cannot require or seek an essential similarity of substance but rather a correspondence in act, in operation. Indeed, no matter how much of the substantial essence of the archetype we might attribute to the copy, it would never be anything but a dead copy. Only a coincidence in the form of *acting* will give it the form of *life*.

Let us assume that God, who is the power of creation pure and simple, is the 'absolute art'. If this absolute art should decide to embody itself in an image, two ways would be possible. It could create an image that contained as much perfection as a created thing can contain. But then the image could never step beyond the limit of possible perfection because it already stood at that very limit. Or the absolute art could produce a less perfect image, but one which had the power of constantly heightening itself and of making itself more and more similar to the original. There can be no doubt which of these two images is preferable. Imagine the portrait of a man, similar to the model in all features, but standing there mute and dead; then imagine another portrait which, though less similar to the original, nevertheless received from its creator the gift of movement. The two images stand in the same relationship as would these two portraits. Precisely in this sense, our mind is the complete and living image of infinite art. For although the actual mind, at the beginning of creation, is far inferior to this

---

[42] *Idiota*, Lib. iii. 'De mente'; chap. 3: 'Si mentem divinam universalitatem veritatis rerum dixeris: nostram dices universalitatem assimilationis rerum, ut sit notionum universitas. Conceptio divinae mentis est rerum productio, conceptio nostrae mentis est rerum notio. Si mens divina est absoluta entitas, tunc ejus conceptio est entium creatio et nostrae mentis conceptio est entium assimilatio: quae enim divinae menti ut infinitae conveniunt veritati, nostrae conveniunt menti, ut propinquae ejus imagini.' Cf. also chap. 7.

infinite art, it nevertheless possesses an innate *power* through which it can become more and more like it.[43] Thus, the proof of the mind's *specific* perfection consists in its refusal to stand still at any attained goal and in its constant questioning and striving beyond the goal. The eye, as a sense organ, is neither satiated nor limited by anything visible; for the eye can never have too much of seeing; likewise, intellectual vision is never satisfied with a view of the truth. In this thought, perhaps, the basic Faustian attitude of the Renaissance received its clearest philosophical expression and its deepest philosophical justification. The striving for the infinite, the inability to stop at anything given or attained is neither a fault nor a shortcoming of the mind; rather, it is the seal of its divine origin and of its indestructibility.[44] We can easily follow this basic and characteristic Renaissance motif as it penetrates every sphere of intellectual endeavour and is modified in each of them. The same motif is at the centre of Leonardo's theory of art,[45] and at the centre of Ficino's philosophical doctrine of immortality.

Cusanus had distinguished a threefold direction and a threefold significance in the concept of infinity. God is the Absolute-Infinite, the pure Maximum which as such remains unattainable to the human intellect. And opposed to Him are two forms of the relative-infinite. One is present in the world, the other in the human mind. In the first, the infinity of the absolute presents and reflects itself in the image of the universe without spatial limits, stretching to indeterminate distances; in the second, the relation is so expressed that the mind in its progress recognizes no *ne plus ultra*, no limit to its striving. This view exerted a *cosmological* influence only very much later, in the natural philosophy of the sixteenth century, and most especially in the philosophy of Giordano Bruno. But its psychological implications were taken up and developed by the Florentine School. Ficino's main work, the *Theologia Platonica*, is completely based upon it. To be sure, Ficino's work constantly refers to ancient and medieval models and renews all the arguments cited by Plato and Plotinus, by the Neo-Platonists and Augustine

---

[43] Cf. ibid., iii. 'De mente' chap. xiii. fol. 169.

[44] *Excitat.* v. (*Ex sermone*: 'Si quis sermonem meum servaverit.') fol. 488: 'Sicut vis visiva sensibilis est infinibilis per omne visibile (nunquam enim satiatur oculus visu), sic visus intellectualis nunquam satiatur visu veritatis. Semper enim acuitur et fortificatur vis videndi: sicut experimur in nobis, quod quanto proficimus plus in doctrina, tanto capaciores sumus et plus proficere appetimus, et hoc est signum incorruptibilitatis intellectus.'

[45] Cf., e.g. Leonardo, *Trattato della Pittura*, p. 28: 'Li semplici naturali sono finiti e l'opere che l'occhio commanda alle mani sono infinite; come dimostra il pittore nelle finzioni d'infinite forme d'animali et erbe, pianti e siti.'

for the indestructibility of the soul. And yet, all the force of the argumentation and all the pathos born of this knowledge derive from the premise that the mind can have no end in time, because it itself gives birth to all temporal limits; the mind itself partitions the continuous flux of becoming into definite blocks and periods. The mind is raised above time once and for all by its *knowledge* of time, i.e., by its knowledge of the infinite progression and of the definite measurements of time.[46] Indeed, by means of these measurements, time is, in a sense, halted; it is 'fixed' by thought.

We are led to the same conclusion if we consider the *will*. For the will only becomes truly *human* inasmuch as it reaches out beyond all finite goals. All natural existence and life is satisfied to be within a definite sphere and wants to persist in whatever condition it has attained. But to man, everything that is ever attained will seem trivial so long as there is something more to be acquired. For man there is no moment at which to rest, no place to stand still.[47] This thought attains its full significance when it is transferred from the individual nature of man to his specific nature, i.e., when the scope of psychological observation is enlarged to the scope of the philosophy of history. And here again, the basic idea in Ficino's philosophy of religion provides the bridge between the two fields. For Cusanus the whole of humanity is comprehended as a unity in Christ, so that every individual becomes *unus*

---

[46] *Theologia Platonica* viii. 16. fol. 200f.: '(Mens) corpora dividit in partes plurimas partiumque particulas, numeros auget supra numeros absque fine. Figurarum modos mutuasque illarum proportiones atque etiam numerorum comparationes innumerabiles invenit, lineas supra coelum ultra terminum undique protendit. Tempus in praeteritum absque principio, in futurum absque fine producit. Neque solum ultra omne tempus aliquid antiquius cogitat, verum etiam ultra omnem locum alium semper cogitat ampliorem. . . . Illud . . . mihi videtur vim mentis . . . interminatam prae ceteris demonstrare, quod ipsam infinitatem esse invenit, quidve sit et qualis definit. Cum vero cognitio per quandam mentis cum rebus aequationem perficiatur, mens cognitae infinitati aequatur quodammodo. Infinitum vero oportet esse, quia aequatur infinitati. Ac si tempus, quod successione quadam metitur motum, infinitum esse oportet, si modo motus fuerit infinitus, quanto magis infinitam esse oportet mentem, quae non modo motum tempusque stabili notione, sed infinitatem ipsam quoque metiatur? Cum necesse sit mensuram ad id quod ipsa metitur habere proportionem, finiti vero ad infinitum sit nulla proportio.' The last sentences contain a direct quotation from the *De docta ignorantia*; for a connection with Cusanus cf. also *De ludo globi* ii. and *Idiota* iii. 15 (see above, chap. i, n. 48).

[47] *Theologia Platonica* xiv. 7. fol. 315: 'Non certa quaedam rerum aliquarum possessio aut species aliqua voluptatis sufficit homini, quemadmodum caeteris animantibus, sed paulum quid in iis adeptum se putat, donec restat aliquid vel minimum acquirendum. . . . Homo solus in praesenti hoc vivendi habitu quiescit nunquam, solus hoc loco non est contentus.' Cf. ibid. xviii. 8. fol. 411: 'Solemus . . . in nullo cognitionis modo quiescere priusquam, quid sit res ipsa secundum substantiam, cognoverimus. Praeterea rationi naturalis est continua per rationes discursio, quousque ad summam perveniat rationem, quae quoniam infinita sit, ideo sola rationis discursum ex se absque fine frustra pervagaturum sistere possit. Siquidem ultra finitum quodlibet mens semper aliqui dulterius machinatur.'

Christus ex omnibus.[48] In like manner Ficino modifies the idea of Christ, immediately converting it into the idea of humanity in the ancient Stoic sense of the word.[49] With that, a philosophy of history becomes possible which, though bound to Christian dogma, nevertheless gradually overcomes all dogmatic narrowness. For it succeeds in seeing the concept of religion embodied not exclusively in one religious form but in the *totality* of historical religious forms. And with that, the classical form of the Christian philosophy of history created in Augustine's *De civitate Dei* is shattered.

Augustine's work was concerned exclusively with the *goal* of history. In that goal, the meaning of history was supposed to become clearly visible. All specific events received their theological significance through their relation to the two religious poles of original sin and redemption. But now, the broad scope of events themselves becomes the object of historical scrutiny. With this, the idea of development is brought to the field of religion, and the multiplicity of forms and phases of religious worship is justified by the unity of the idea of God itself. True Christinity does not require that the opponents of the faith be destroyed but that they be convinced through reason, converted through instruction, or be peacefully tolerated.[50] For divine providence does not allow that there ever be any part of the earth which does not worship God in some form. It is concerned that God *be* worshipped rather than that He be worshipped through certain rites and gestures. Even the seemingly most base and inane form of faith and cult is acceptable, so long as it is a *human* form and an expression of human nature in its necessary limitations.[51] Despite its attachment to the theological concept of

---

[48] *De docta ignorantia* iii. 12: 'Una (est Christi humanitas in omnibus hominibus et unus Christi spiritus in omnibus spiritibus, ita ut quodlibet in eo sit, ut qui sit unus Christus ex omnibus. Et tunc qui unum ex omnibus, qui Christi sunt, in hac vita recipit, Christum recipit, et quod uni ex minimis fit, Christo fit.' (Cf. above, chap. i, n. 43.)

[49] Ficino *Epistolae* i. fol. 635: 'Singuli namque homines sub una idea et in eadem specie sunt unus homo. Ob hanc ut arbitror rationem sapientes solam illam ex omni virtutum numero hominis ipsius nomine, id est humanitatem appellaverunt, quae omnes homines quoddammodo seu fratres ex uno quodam patre longo ordine natos diligit atque curat.'

[50] *De christiana religione* 8. fol. 11.

[51] Ibid., chap. iv: 'Nihil Deo magis displicet quam contemni, nihil placet magis quam adorari. . . . Idcirco divina providentia non permitit esse aliquo in tempore ullam mundi regionem omnes prorsus religionis expertem, quamvis permitat variis locis atque temporibus ritus adorationis varios observari. Forsitan vero varietas hujus modi, ordinante Deo, decorem quendam parit in universo mirabilem. Regi maximo magis curae est revera honorari, quam aut his aut illis gestibus honorari. . . . Coli mavult quoquo modo, vel inepte, modo humane, quam per superbiam nullo modo coli.' Cf. Cusanus' letter to Aindorffer, 22 September 1452: 'Inexplicabilis divinae scripturae fecunditas per diversos diverse explicatur, ut in varietate tanta ejus infinitas clarescat; unum tamen est divinum verbum in omnibus relucens.' See especially above, pp. 28ff.

revelation, the philosophy of Ficino is clearly preparing a dialectical reversal precisely within that very concept. If *all* spiritual values embraced by the history of humanity can be reduced to and based upon a single revelation, it would also seem to imply conversely that this desired unity of revelation is to be sought in the *whole* of history and in the totality of its forms. Instead of abstract simplicity, such as can be expressed in a generally binding dogmatic formula, we now have the concrete universality of the *form* of religious consciousness; and with it, as a necessary correlate, the diversity of symbols in which this consciousness expresses itself.

CHAPTER THREE

FREEDOM AND NECESSITY IN THE PHILOSOPHY
OF THE RENAISSANCE

I

TOWARD the end of the year 1501, a Ferrarese Embassy appeared in Rome for the purpose of escorting Lucrezia Borgia to Ferrara to marry Alfonso d'Este. Among the pageants performed at the papal palace in honour of this embassy, there was one that depicted a *Battle between Fortune and Hercules*. Against her old enemy Hercules, Juno sends Fortune. But instead of conquering him, she is overpowered, taken, and chained. Upon Juno's insistent request, Hercules does indeed set Fortune free; but only on the condition that neither she nor Juno ever undertake anything inimical to the houses of Borgia and Este; instead, both must henceforth show favour to the matrimonial bond established between the two houses.[1] This is simply a court pageant, clothed completely in the language of courtly convention. Even the choice of the Hercules figure seems at first glance to signify nothing more than a reference to the *name* of the reigning duke of Ferrara, Ercole d'Este, the father of Alfonso. But surprisingly enough, we constantly encounter the same allegorical opposition presented in this play not only in the *literature* of the period but in the philosophy as well. In fact, towards the end of the century we find the same theme in the principal moral-philosophical work of Giordano Bruno. In Bruno's *Spaccio della bestia trionfante* (1584), Fortune comes before Zeus and a gathering of the Olympian gods to request of them the place that Hercules had hitherto occupied in the heavenly constellations. But her claim is declared invalid. Indeed, to her, the roving and inconstant one, no single place is denied; at her pleasure she may show herself anywhere in heaven or on earth. But the place of Hercules is assigned to *Valour*. For where truth, law, and right judgment are to reign, Valour cannot

---

[1] For further details about this pageant, cf., e.g., Ferdinand Gregorovius, *Lucrezia Borgia* (5th ed.; Stuttgart and Berlin, 1911), pp. 183f.

be absent. It is the palladium of every other virtue, the shield of justice and the tower of truth. Valour is unyielding to vice, unconquerable by suffering, constant through danger, severe against cupidity, contemptuous of wealth—and the tamer of Fortune.[2]

We need not hesitate to juxtapose the courtly and the philosophical expressions of the thought. The possibility of such a relationship and of such a juxtaposition is characteristic of the culture of the Renaissance and its whole intellectual attitude. *Burckhardt* has shown us how much the spirit of the Renaissance is revealed in its conviviality and in the form of its feasts and games. Giordano Bruno teaches us that the allegorical masks dominating these games extend their influence far into a field which, according to our habits of thought, should be reserved for abstract, conceptual, image-less thought. This was a time when intellectual forms dominated and filled life; a time when even festival pageants were influenced by the basic thoughts concerning freedom, destiny, and the relationship of man to the world. In such a time, thought does not remain enclosed within itself but rather strives for visible symbols. Giordano Bruno is the clearest exponent of this basic disposition and attitude of Renaissance philosophy. Starting with his earliest works, particularly with the work *De umbris idearum*, he maintained the view that for human knowledge ideas can only be presented and embodied in the form of images. It may be that this kind of presentation will seem hazy when compared to the eternal, transcendent content of the ideas; nevertheless, it is the only one proper to *our* thought and *our* mind. Just as the shadow is not simply darkness but a mixture of light and dark, so, too, the ideas conceived in human forms are not deception and illusion but the truth itself insofar as it is conceivable by a limited and finite being.[3] For such a mode of thought, allegory is no mere external appendage, no casual cloak; instead, it becomes the vehicle of thought itself. Bruno's *ethics* especially, concerned as they are not so much with the form of the universe as with that of man, reach out for this specifically human means of expression. Bruno's *Spaccio* develops in all directions that ethical-allegorical language which seeks to shed light on the relationships of the inner world by using figures of the visible, spatial cosmos. The forces that move the inner man are viewed as cosmic potencies; virtues and vices are viewed as

[2] Giordano Bruno, *Spaccio della bestia trionfante*, Dial. II, terza parte; *Opere italiane*, ed. Paul de Lagarde (Göttingen, 1888), pp. 486ff.
[3] Giordano Bruno, *De umbris idearum*, Intentio secunda, *Opera latina*, ed. Tocco, Imbriani, *et al.*, ii. 21f.

constellations. In this view, *Fortezza* (valour) assumes the place of honour; but it must not be understood only in its ethical signification or in its moral limitation. In keeping with the original etymological sense of *virtus*, whose idea it expresses, *Fortezza* means the strength of virility itself, the strength of the human will which becomes the tamer of destiny, the *domitrice della fortuna*. To use the expression Warburg coined in another field, we can now detect a new and yet ancient *Pathosformel* (formula of pathos); it is a heroic passion, seeking its language and its intellectual justification.

This is the ultimate root, to which we must always return if we would comprehend in their true depth the philosophical doctrines of the Renaissance concerning the relationship between freedom and necessity. The philosophy of the Renaissance has added little to the purely dialectical motifs of this eternal and fundamentally unchanging problem. A work such as Pomponazzi's *De fato, libero arbitrio et prae-destinatione* completely enumerates all these motifs with methodic thoroughness and places them before us again. It follows the question in all its ramifications; it pays careful attention to all the conceptual distinctions through which ancient philosophy and Scholasticism had tried to demonstrate the compatibility of divine foreknowledge with the freedom of human will and action. But the work does not present any new solution, nor does it even appear to be seeking one. To determine clearly Pomponazzi's own position, we must refer to his other philosophical works, especially to his work on the immortality of the soul. In these works, and particularly in the new foundation of ethics contained in *De immortalitate animae*, we can observe a relaxation of the rigidity of the traditional concepts and formulas which Pomponazzi still uses to a great extent. We have here before us a process similar to the one traceable in the transformations undergone by the Fortune symbol in the visual arts. This process has been depicted in the studies by Warburg and Doren. They have shown that the rigidified medieval forms of Fortune were maintained for a long time; but that besides these other motifs emerged with ever increasing force. Though these other motifs had their roots in antiquity, they were now imbued with a new spirit and new life. The same thing occurs in the realm of thought. Here too, new solutions are not immediately achieved. Before that can happen, it is necessary to create, so to speak, a new *state of tension* in thought. There is no real break with the philosophical past; but a new *dynamic* of thought announces itself, a striving—to speak with Warburg

—for a new 'energetic state of equilibrium'. Just as the visual arts seek plastic formulas of balance, so philosophy seeks intellectual formulas of balance between the 'medieval faith in God and the self-confidence of Renaissance man'.[4]

This effort is as clearly visible in these half philosophical, half rhetorical tracts that are the literary trademark of the new humanistic age, as it is in the genuinely 'philosophical' literature of the time. From Petrarch's *De remediis utriusque fortunae* the path leads past *Salutati* to *Poggio* and further to *Pontano*. Poggio attempts a solution by asserting that each of the conflicting forces that mould human life will predominate over a period of human existence. The dangers threatening man from without (the forces of destiny) are strongest so long as man's true self has not yet been completely formed, i.e., so long as he is still in childhood or early youth. They retreat as soon as this self is awakened, and as soon as it is developed to full efficiency through the energy of moral and intellectual effort. Thus, it is *virtus* and *studium* that finally defeat all the inimical forces of the heavens.[5]

Such statements indicate a new orientation of faith; but they also reveal a new discordance within the soul. Gone for ever is the plastic and intellectual unity of *Dante's* image of Fortune. His was an image that forced all opposing themes into one great synthesis, making of Fortune an entity with its own being and character and at the same time fitting it into the spiritual and divine cosmos. Such unity was never achieved again. And yet, when compared with the certainty and comfort of the medieval belief in providence, the new uncertainty signifies a new liberation. In the medieval doctrine of two worlds, and in all the dualisms derived from it, man simply stands apart from the forces that are fighting over him; he is, in a sense, at their mercy. Though he experiences the conflict of these forces, he takes no active part in it. He

---

[4] For further details on the transformations of the *Fortuna* image in Renaissance art, cf. Aby Warburg, 'Francesco Sassetti's letztwillige Verfügung' (*Kunstwissenschaftliche Beiträge, August Schmarsow gewidmet*; Leipzig, 1907), pp. 129ff.; also Alfred Doren, 'Fortuna im Mittelalter und in der Renaissance', *Vorträge der Bibliothek Warburg*, ed. Fritz Saxl, 1922–3; Teil I (Leipzig, 1924), pp. 71ff. Doren's literary evidence was recently complemented by H. R. Patch, 'The Tradition of the Goddess Fortuna in Medieval Philosophy and Literature', *Smith College Studies in Modern Languages* (July, 1922).

[5] Poggio *Epistolae* ii. 195: 'Verissimum quidem est, quod scribis neque sidera neque coelorum cursus praestantes hominum naturas bonarum artium studiis et optimis moribus corroboratas pervertere ac depravare posse: sed ante assumptum robur, ante adeptos optimos mores, antequam bonarum artium institutis homines firmentur . . . plus sidera et coelum valere arbitror ad disponendum animum nostrum quam hominum praecepta et suasiones.' Further details in Ernst Walser, *Poggius Florentinus* (Leipzig and Berlin, 1914), pp. 196, 236ff.

is the stage of this great drama of the world, but he has not yet become a truly independent antagonist. In the Renaissance a different image emerges ever more clearly. The old image of Fortune with a wheel, seizing men and dragging them along, sometimes raising them, sometimes throwing them down into the abyss, now gives way to the depiction of Fortune with a *sailboat*. And this bark is not controlled by Fortune alone—man himself is steering it.[6]

We find that the statements of the theoreticians point in the same direction. This is especially true of those theoreticians concerned with a definite sphere of action or creation rather than with scholastic knowledge. For *Machiavelli*, Fortune rules over half of all human actions. But she gives herself to him who acts, to him who quickly and boldly grasps her, and not to the passive observer. For *Leon Battista Alberti*, the current of Fortune will not drag away a man who, trusting his own strength, makes his way in the current as an able swimmer.[7] 'La fortuna per sè, non dubitare, sempre fu e sempre sarà imbecillissima et debolissima a chi se gli opponga.'[8] Both Machiavelli and Alberti are voicing the sentiments of their Florentine circle. Until their strength and confidence were broken by Savonarola, these sentiments were dominant not only in statesmen and men of action like Lorenzo the Magnificent, but in the speculative thinkers as well. To be sure, in a letter to Rucellai, *Ficino* declares it best to make peace with Fortune and to adapt our will to hers so that she will not violently drag us in some unpleasant direction.[9] But the words of the younger leader of the Platonic Academy sound much bolder and freer. 'The wonders of the mind are greater than the heavens. . . . On earth, nothing is great but man; and nothing is great in man but his mind and his soul. When you rise up to them, you rise up beyond the heavens.'[10] From the midst of the strictly devout, even strictly ecclesiastical world of Florentine Platonism, that 'heroic passion' now breaks forth which will subsequently lead to Giordano Bruno's dialogue *Degli eroici furori*.

Here we are not trying to trace these changes in intellectual attitudes but only to grasp their *systematic* expression in philosophical theory.

---

[6] Cf. the illustrations of Warburg's essay on Sassetti, p. 141; and Doren, op. cit., Plate VI, illustrations 14 and 16.

[7] Machiavelli, *Il Principe*, chap. xxv; L. B. Alberti *Intercoenales*, *Opere ined.*, ed. Mancini, 136ff. For details, cf. especially Doren, op. cit., pp. 117f., 132f.

[8] L. B. Alberti, *Della tranquillità dell'animo libri III*, *Opere volgari*, I, 113f. (Cf. Patch, op. cit., p. 217.)

[9] Cf. the text of Ficino's letter to Rucellai, in Warburg, 'Francesco Sassetti', p. 149.

[10] Pico della Mirandola *In astrologiam* iii. 27, *Opera* fol. 519.

Lorenzo Valla's work *De libero arbitrio* begins the theoretical discussion of the freedom of the will. Far more than the content, it was its *form* that gave significance to this work and immediately raised it far above the host of medieval Scholastic tracts on the same subject. Indeed, this work announces not only a new literary style but a new style of thought. For the first time since antiquity, the problem of freedom is taken before an entirely secular forum, before the bench of 'natural reason'. To be sure, Valla never attacked dogma directly. In the end, he always bowed to the decisions of the 'mother church', partly in good faith, partly with irony. He did just that, for instance, when he was summoned one day to appear before the tribunal of the inquisition in Naples.[11] Nevertheless, we sense in all his writings the presence of that new, modern critical spirit which is beginning to become conscious of its strength and of its intellectual weapons. Valla created that form of dogma-criticism used in the seventeenth century by Bayle and even in the eighteenth century by Lessing. Valla leaves the *decision* to other instances; but he demands that the *investigation* be conducted exclusively from the point of view of reason and with its means. Reason is the 'best author', and cannot be contradicted by any other testimony.[12] The content of the faith was not to be touched. Indeed, Valla assured, as Bayle did later, that he was only concerned with keeping this content pure and with freeing it from any dangerous connection with 'philosophy'. Nevertheless, the traditional *foundations* of this content are now critically examined and, as a result, worn away, layer by layer.

At first, this criticism is directed against the moral and legal bases of the hierarchical system. In his *De concordantia catholica*, Cusanus began the attack on the Donation of Constantine. Now Valla takes up the battle with new weapons and with far greater force, and proves that the legal claim of the church to secular dominion is null and void.[13] In his *De professione religiosorum*, Valla presents the ethical counterpart to this legal contestation of the foundations of the hierarchy. Here again, the religious content as such is never attacked. But Valla violently

---

[11] For Valla's attitude towards the ecclesiastical inquisitors, cf., e.g., the depiction in Voigt, *Weiderbelebung*, I, 476ff.

[12] Cf. Valla *Confutat. prior in Benedictum Morandum Bononiensem, Opera* (Basel, 1543), 445ff.: 'Sed omissis utrinque criminibus inspiciamus civiliter, quid mihi objectas. Nempe quod Livium ausus sum reprehendere, an tu eum nusquam reprehendi posse existimas? . . . Et in Demosthene atque Cicerone summis oratoribus nonnulla desiderantur, et in Platone Aristotele, philosophis maximis, aliqua notantur. . . . Numquid deterius est rationis, quam hominis testimonium? . . . An melior ullus autor est quam ratio?'

[13] See Valla *De falso credita et ementita Constantini donatione declamatio, Opera* fol. 761ff.

assaults the claim that this content is exclusively or especially embodied in one single form of life, or in one special form of society. The monastic ideal and the pre-eminence of the clergy are decisively rejected. The essence of religion and piety consists in the free relationshp that the ego, the subject of faith and will, has with God. We will misunderstand, or even destroy the peculiarity of this relationship if we look upon it as an external, legal obligation; or, if we believe that the value of pure inwardness is enhanced by adding to it a specific, external conduct. There is no conduct, no action or forbearance that can even be compared to the devotion of the individual, or that can heighten the ethical-religious significance of such devotion: *omnia dat, que se ipsum dat*. In a conception such as this, oriented as it is towards the subject rather than the object, and towards faith rather than works, there can no longer be any hierarchical representation of religiosity: *non enim in solid cucullatis vita Christi custoditur*.[14] As a result of this liberation from the straits of hierarchy, both action and thought have a completely new amplitude. To be sure, the claim of Christianity that it contains the truth pure and simple remains unassailed. But more and more, the content of Christian faith must submit to an interpretation that adapts it to the requirements of natural reason.

We can clearly observe this happening in Valla's first work, the dialogue *De voluptate*. Here, pleasure is shown to be not only the highest good, but the good pure and simple, the conserving principle of life, and therefore the basic principle of all value. Now, this renewed hedonism does not present itself as an enemy of the faith—rather, it places itself under the protection of the faith itself. Valla's basic thesis states that Christianity is not inimical to Epicureanism, for it is itself nothing but a more elevated and 'sublimated' Epicureanism. Is the bliss that Christianity promises its followers anything but the highest and most complete form of pleasure?[15] In this early work as in all his philosophical writings, Valla is not so much concerned with the proof of his thesis as he is with the joy in battle. Lessing's dictum applies

---

[14] See Valla *Apologia contra calumniatores ad Eugenium IV, Opera* fol. 799ᵛ: 'Via a Christo tradita nulla est tutior, sicut nec melior, in qua nulla professio nobis injungitur. At vita ipsorum, inquiunt, ab illa Christi non discrepat. Sane vero, sed ne aliorum quidem, nec enim in solis cucullatis vita Christi custoditur.' Cf. especially *De professione religiosorum* (ed. Vahlen, Laurentii Vallae opuscula tria; Vienna, 1869), especially 160ff.

[15] Cf. especially Valla *De voluptate* iii. 9. fol. 977: 'Beatitudinem quis dubitat aut quis melius possit appellare quam voluptatem? . . . Ex quo debet intelligi non honestatem, sed voluptatem propter seipsam esse expetendam, tam ab iis qui in hac vita, quam ab iis qui in futura gaudere volunt.'

completely to Valla: the pleasure of the chase is worth much more than the catch. And it is just this sense that gives Valla's work on the freedom of the will its peculiar literary and intellectual character. The historical influence of this work was still strong in the time of Leibniz. To a great extent, its success was due to the fact that if offered a complete, terse, and highly polished *formulation*, both intellectually and stylistically, of a problem that Scholasticism had broken down into infinite sub-questions and endless dialectical distinctions. And in this undertaking, Valla the humanist is at least the equal of Valla the philosopher. Only a humanist and a highly gifted writer could create the external form with which he now dressed this problem. Instead of discussing the concepts of divine foreknowledge and divine omnipotence, and opposing both to the concept of human freedom of the will, Valla begins with a concrete *embodiment* of the concepts. Ancient myth now receives a new role; it becomes the vehicle of logical thought. Divine foreknowledge is represented in the figure of Apollo, the divine omnipotence in that of Jupiter. There is no conflict between these two powers; for the *knowledge* of a future event does not bring it about, just as the knowledge of something in the present does not produce that thing. The certainty with which a future event is foreseen does not provide a sufficient reason for its coming to pass. And so Apollo, the seer, who predicts to Sextus Tarquinius the crime he will commit, is in no way responsible for the deed. He may summon Sextus before the tribunal of Jupiter, who gave him this tendency, this disposition of the will. And at this point, Valla's investigation breaks off. How is it possible that man, a creature, owes the whole of his being to God and yet is gifted with freedom of the will by virtue of which he is responsible for his decisions? This question, according to Valla, can no longer be answered by philosophy. Only resignation remains, only refuge in mystery.[16] Nor need we see in this resignation a retreat in the face of dangerous theological consequences; for, indeed, it is completely consistent with the whole of Valla's intellectual constitution. Neither here nor elsewhere does he want to present us with final conclusions. He is satisfied with placing the question before us in its sharpest possible formulation; then he leaves us with the question.

A completely different spirit reigns in Pomponazzi's work, *De fato, libero arbitrio et praedestinatione*. Instead of Valla's aphoristic treatment of the problems of free will and predestination, we have here again

---

[16] See *De libero arbitrio Opera* fol. 1004ff.

genuine Scholastic thoroughness and sobriety of analysis. Only Pomponazzi's careful and critical use of sources makes us feel the distance that separates him from Scholasticism. He constantly demands a return to the 'pure' Aristotle, the Aristotle of the sources. And now the Stagirite, whom Valla had expressly refused to follow,[17] is again judged to be the highest authority in secular knowledge. But Pomponazzi no longer expects a reconciliation of this authority, which he considers the embodiment of human reason, with faith. Far from trying to hide the opposition between faith and reason, he intentionally emphasizes and sharpens it. Thus, the doctrine of the 'double truth' is the last word in wisdom. But it also becomes clear that the inner intellectual and spiritual attitude towards this doctrine has changed since the Middle Ages. In Pomponazzi, the dogmatic pronouncements of the church are recognized and the concept of *fides implicita* is never attacked. And yet, comparing this recognition with that, say, of Occamism, we can sense that the centre of gravity has moved very far in the direction of 'reason'. Pomponazzi has been called the 'last Scholastic', but he could just as well be called the first man of the Enlightenment. For, indeed, his work generally represents Enlightenment in Scholastic garb. He conducts all his investigations meticulously and soberly, and with conceptual purity and precision. He lets only science speak—cutting it off, to be sure, before the final results and consequences. He leaves the transcendent world of ecclesiastical faith intact; but he does not conceal that he needs this world neither for ethics nor for the construction of science, i.e., psychology and the theory of knowledge. For Pomponazzi, these are based on their own autonomous foundations; they have become independent of theological forms.

Pomponazzi's work on the freedom of the will also exhibits these characteristic features of his thought. Valla's was a work of intellectual and literary concentration that sought to squeeze the problem into a few pages; Pomponazzi instead lets all the proofs and counter-proofs, the definitions and the distinctions, pass in review once again. The work is in the form of a commentary on the treatise by Alexander of Aphrodisias, περὶ εἱμαρμένης, and it goes over this treatise point by point. Throughout, a searching intellect and a sharp dialectic are at work, seeking to think every proposition through to its final

---

[17] Cf. especially Valla *Dialecticae disputationes*, *Opera* fol. 645ff.; very typical also 'De libero arbitrio', fol. 1004: 'Antonius: "Hic te teneo. An ignoras praeceptum esse philosophorum, quicquid possibile est, id tanquam esse debere concedi?" . . . Laurentius: "Philosophorum mecum formulis agis? quasi eis contradicere non audeam!" '

consequences, and to present every argument with a counter-argument. To be sure, Pomponazzi's own systematic judgment remains suspended. Only *one* point is sharply and definitely emphasized and elaborated; it is the one Valla also stressed, *viz.*, that divine foreknowledge does not necessarily conflict with the freedom of human action. If God knows future actions, He knows them not through their *causes*, which, indeed, would be irreconcilable with the assumption of freedom; rather, He knows them in their simple 'factualness', in their mere 'that-ness'. Man grasps the past and the present according to its 'that', but grasps the future only according to his knowledge of the 'why', because this future is not immediately given to him, but is rather only *deducible* through its causes. But this difference between an immediate and a mediate, between given and deduced knowledge, is not valid for divine knowledge. For in divine knowledge all temporal differences, so necessary for our conception of the world, disappear. To know the future, divine knowledge needs no mediation, no discursive succession of the conditions by virtue of which the future comes to be.[18]

This solution to the problem of the prescience of human action is similar to the one offered by Valla. But Pomponazzi attaches little importance to that other problem, left unsolved by Valla, *viz.*, the problem of the compatibility of divine omnipotence with human freedom and responsibility. Although he does not quite dare to express himself unambiguously on this point, Pomponazzi's judgment tends unmistakably towards a strict determinism. In his work on natural philosophy, *De naturalium effectuum admirandorum causis*, the causality of events is interpreted in a strictly astrological sense. The world of history and the world of nature are both viewed as necessary results of the influence of the heavenly bodies. And elsewhere too, whenever he is speaking freely, Pomponazzi considers Fate in the Stoic sense the relatively most satisfactory and rational solution. What makes the acceptance of this solution difficult are not so much logical as ethical objections. A substantial part of the work is dedicated to the removal of these objections. In his *De voluptate*, Valla had striven to adapt the form of his completely world-oriented ethics to the form of religious metaphysics; now, with an energetic blow, Pomponazzi severs the bond that had hitherto conjoined metaphysics and ethics. In principle, each is completely independent of the other. Our judgment concerning the

[18] On this whole question, cf. Pomponazzi *De fato, libero arbitrio, et de praedestinatione* (Basel, 1567). Cf. especially v. 913ff.

value of human life is not dependent on our ideas concerning the continuation of life or the immortality of the human soul; and similarly, the question of the value or non-value of our actions must be considered from a point of view other than what caused these actions. No matter how we may decide this latter question, the ethical-practical judgment remains free. This freedom is what we need, not some chimerical causelessness.

Pomponazzi's work is separated from Valla's by more than eight decades; the one was composed in 1520, the other seems to have been written in about 1436.[19] It was precisely in these decades that the Platonism of the Florentine Academy transformed the philosophical thought of the Renaissance. And not only temporally, but systematically, too, the doctrines of the Academy stand directly between humanism and that late blossom of Scholasticism represented by the Paduan school. But at the same time, the formation of these doctrines was deeply affected by the influence of Cusanus on Florentine Platonism. Pico's famous oration, which was to serve as the introduction to his defence of the nine hundred theses in Rome, clearly reveals this intellectual filiation. When Pico chooses the 'dignity of man' as his central theme, he is merely taking up certain motifs which the older humanism had again and again treated rhetorically. The treatise *De dignitate et excellentia hominis*, already written in 1452 by Gianozzo Manetti, is constructed according to the same formal and intellectual schema that Pico's oration follows. To the world of nature, the world of that which *has become*, Manetti opposes the intellectual world of *becoming*, the world of culture. The human mind is at home only in this latter world, in which man can demonstrate his dignity and his freedom. *Nostra namque, hoc est humana, sunt, quoniam ab hominibus effecta, quae cernuntur: omnes domus, omnia oppida, omnes urbes, omnia denique orbis terrarum aedificia. Nostrae sunt picturae, nostrae sculpturae, nostrae sunt artes, nostrae scientiae, nostrae . . . sapientiae. Nostrae sunt . . . omnes adinventiones, nostra omnium diversarum linguarum ac variarum litterarum genera, de quarum necessariis usibus quanto magis magisque cogitamus, tanto vehementius admirari et obstupescere cogimur.*[20]

[19] For the date of Valla's dialogue *De libero arbitrio*, cf. M. von Wolff, *Lorenzo Valla* (Leipzig, 1893), pp. 36ff. Pomponazzi's tract was first published in Basel in 1567, as an appendix to the work *De admirandorum effectuum causis*; but a note at the end of it reveals that it had already been written in 1520.

[20] The sentences from Giannozzo Manetti's tract *De dignitate et excellentia hominis* (1452) are thoroughly analysed by Giovanni Gentile, 'Il concetto dell' uomo nel Rinascimento' (reprinted in *Giordano Bruno e il pensiero del rinascimento*, Florence: Vallecchi, 1920), pp. 111ff.

Essentially, these sentences of Manetti hearken back to ancient Stoic thought; but in Pico's oration, a new element is present. His whole view is pervaded by that characteristic microcosm motif developed by Cusanus and by Ficino after him (see above, pp. 64ff.). Through this motif the oration becomes something more than a mere rhetorical showpiece. Its rhetorical pathos contains a specifically modern pathos of thought. The dignity of man cannot reside in his being, i.e., in the place allotted man once and for all in the cosmic order. The hierarchical system subdivides the world into different levels and places each being in one of these levels as its rightful place in the universe. But such a view does not grasp the meaning and the problem of human freedom. For this meaning lies in the *reversal* of the relationship we are accustomed to accepting between *being* and *acting*. The old Scholastic proposition *operari sequitur esse* is valid in the world of things. But it is the nature and the peculiarity of the human world that in it, the opposite is true. It is not being that prescribes once and for all the lasting direction which the mode of action will take; rather, the original direction of action determines and places being. The being of man follows from his doing; and this doing is not only limited to the energy of his will, but rather encompasses the whole of his creative powers. For all true creativity implies more than mere action upon the world. It presupposes that the actor distinguishes himself from that which is acted upon, i.e. that the subject consciously stands opposed to the object. And this opposition is not a process that takes place once and that closes when certain results are achieved, but rather one which must be completed over and over again. Both the being and the value of man are dependent upon this completion. Therefore they can only be described and defined dynamically, not statically. We may ascend the hierarchical ladder of being as high as we like, we may climb to the celestial intelligences, even to the divine source of all being: so long as we remain standing at any rung of this ladder, we shall not be able to find there the specific value of freedom. In the rigid hierarchical system, the value of freedom must always seem something foreign, something incommensurable and 'irrational', because the order of mere *being* does not capture the meaning and the movement of pure *becoming*.

As a whole, Pico's doctrine is determined largely by the Aristotelian-Scholastic and by the Neo-Platonic traditions; but these thoughts indicate that a new advance has been made. For now we see that neither the category of creation nor that of emanation suffices to characterize the relationship that exists between God and man and between man and the world. Creation in the ordinary sense can only be understood as the conferring upon the created of both a definite, limited being and, at the same time, a definite, prescribed sphere of willing and of acting. But man breaks through every such barrier. His activity is not dictated to him by his reality; rather, man's activity contains ever new possibilities which, by their very nature, go beyond any finite circle. This is the secret of his nature, for which he is envied not only by the lower world but by the world of intelligences as well. For man alone constitutes an exception to the rule that governs the rest of creation; man is the only exception to its rigid 'type'. At the end of creation—according to the myth with which Pico's oration begins—the wish was born in the demiurge to create a being able to recognize the reason for this creation and to love it for its beauty. 'But in the eternal archetypes of things there was no model left for the new offspring; nor did the Creator possess among his treasures a gift with which to endow his new son; nor was there a place left in the whole world where the viewer of the universe might seat himself. For the universe was filled, and to every circle, the highest as well as the lowest and the middle, beings of a corresponding order were assigned. . . . Whereupon the Greatest Artisan ordained that the creature to which he could give no special property should, instead, possess the endowments of every individual being in common with it. He formed man according to a general image that contained no particularities, and, setting him in the centre of the world, said to him: "We have given you, Adam, no definite place, no form proper only to you, no special inheritance, so that you may have as your own whatever place, whatever form, whatever gifts you may choose, according to your wish and your judgment. All other beings have received a rigidly determined nature, and will be compelled by us to follow strictly determined laws. You alone are bound by no limit, unless it be one prescribed by your will, which I have given you. I have placed you at the centre of the world, so that you may more easily look around you and see everything that is in it. I created you as a being neither heavenly nor earthly, neither mortal nor immortal, so that you may freely make and master yourself, and take on any form you choose for yourself. You can degenerate to animality or be reborn towards divinity. . . . Animals bring forth . . . from the bodies of their mothers everything they ought to have. The higher spirits are, from the beginning or soon afterwards, everything they will be for eternity.

But on man, the Father conferred, at the moment of birth, the seeds and germs of every form of life. Those which he cultivates will grow in him and bear fruit. If they are the plant seeds, he will vegetate; if he follows the senses, he will become an animal; if he cultivates the power of reason within him, he will become a celestial creature; if he follows intelligence, he will become an angel and a son of God." '21

Burckhardt called Pico's oration one of the most noble bequests of the culture of the Renaissance. And indeed, it summarizes with grand simplicity and in pregnant form the whole intent of the Renaissance and its entire concept of knowledge. In this oration, we can clearly see the polarity upon which is based the moral and intellectual tension so characteristic of the Renaissance. What is required of man's will and knowledge is that they be completely *turned towards* the world and yet completely *distinguish* themselves from it. Will and knowledge may, or rather, must devote themselves to every part of the universe; for only by going through the entire universe can man traverse the circle of his own possibilities. But this complete *openness* towards the world must never signify a *dissolution* in it, a mystical-pantheistic losing of oneself. For the human will possesses itself only inasmuch as it is conscious that no single goal will fulfil it; and human knowledge possesses itself only inasmuch as it knows that no single object of knowledge can suffice for it. Thus, this turning towards the whole of the cosmos always implies the ability not to be bound to any one part. The force of this total conversion is balanced by the force of a total return. The duality of man and the world, 'mind' and 'nature', is strictly observed. But, on the other hand, this duality is not allowed to become an absolute dualism of the Scholastic-medieval variety. For the polarity is not an absolute, but a relative opposition. The difference between the two poles is only possible and conceivable in that it implies a reciprocal relationship between them. Here we have before us one of the basic conceptions of Florentine Platonism, one which was never completely submerged or extinguished by opposing currents of thought or by the tendency towards 'transcendence' and towards asceticism which gradually became stronger and stronger in that school. To be sure, Pico and

---

[21] Pico *Oratio de hominis dignitate*, *Opera* fol. 314ff. The idea that man, as a free being, stands above the demons and the heavenly intelligences, derives from the Hermetic tradition, which was very influential in the Florentine School. Marsilio Ficino translated the old corpus of Hermetic writings into Latin. For details on this point, see Burdach's commentary to the *Ackermann aus Böhmen* in *Vom Mittelalter zur Reformation*, III, part I, 293ff, 325ff.

Ficino are generally under the influence of Neo-Platonic themes; but in this case, the genuine Platonic sense of the concepts *chorismos* and *methexis* is recaptured. 'Transcendence' itself postulates and requires 'participation', just as 'participation' postulates and requires 'transcendence'. Objectively considered, this reciprocal determination may seem enigmatic and paradoxical; nevertheless, it proves to be necessary and singularly clear, if we take as our point of departure the nature of the Ego, i.e., of the willing and knowing subject. In the free *act* of willing and in the free *act* of knowing, those things are conjoined which in simple *existence* seem always to be fleeing from each other. For both the power of distinction and the power of unification are properties of these acts. They alone can distinguish to the highest degree without, at the same time, letting the things distinguished fall into an absolute *separation*.

In this thought, the relationship of the Ego to the world, i.e., the relationship of the subject to the object is understood, in the genuine manner of Cusanus, as a *coincidentia oppositorum*. The connection emerges even more clearly if we trace the historical course of the motifs Pico took up in his *Oration on the Dignity of Man*. In Pico's oration itself we can clearly hear the echo of Cusanus' speculation. In *De conjecturis* Cusanus states: *Humanitatis unitas cum humaniter contracta existat, omnia secundum hanc contractionis naturam complicare videtur. Ambit enim virtus unitatis ejus universa atque ipsa intra suae regionis terminus adeo coercet, ut nihil omnium ejus aufugiat potentiam. . . . Homo enim Deus est, sed non absolute, quoniam homo. Humanus est igitur Deus. Homo etiam mundus est, sed non contracte omnia, quoniam homo. Est igitur Homo μικρόκοδμος aut humanus quidem mundus. Regio igitur ipsa humanitatis Deum atque universum mundum humanali sua potentia ambit. Potest igitur homo esse humanus Deus atque Deus humaniter, potest esse humanus angelus, humana bestia, humanus leo aut ursus, aut aliud quodcumque. Intra enim humanitatis potentiam omnia suo existunt modo. In humanitate igitur omnia humaniter, uti in ipso universo universaliter, explicata sunt, quoniam humanus existit mundus. Omnia denique in ipsa complicata sunt humaniter, quoniam humanus est Deus. Nam humanitas unitas est, quae est et infinitas humaniter contracta. . . . Non ergo activae creationis humanitatis alius extat finis quam humanitas. Non enim pergit extra se dum creat, sed dum eius explicat virtutem ad se ipsam pertingit neque quicquam novi efficit, sed cuncta quae explicando creat, in ipsa fuisse comperit.*[22]

[22] Cusanus *De conjecturis* ii. 14 (cf. above, pp. 40ff.).

Whenever humanism sought to be more than just a scholarly movement, whenever it sought to give itself a philosophical form and a philosophical foundation, it had to go back to these basic propositions. Their influence is not restricted to a single group, but goes beyond national boundaries and beyond the boundaries of philosophical schools. These propositions mark the beginning of an intellectual movement that goes from Italy to France and that moves from a philosophical humanism of Platonic stamp to one of Aristotelian stamp. We can clearly see the objective and systematic connections between the thoughts, and we can distinguish the individual historical threads clearly from one another. Jacobus Faber Stapulensis (Jacques Lefèvre), the true restorer of Aristotelian studies and the creator of the 'Aristotelian Renaissance' in France, is also the publisher of the first complete edition of the works of Nicholas Cusanus. Moreover, he was influenced not only by the ideas of Cusanus, whom he always mentions with the greatest admiration and reverence, but by the Platonic Academy in Florence as well. Both are united in the work of Faber's disciple Carolus Bovillus (Charles de Bouelles), which constitutes the immediate continuation and the systematic development of the basic ideas in Pico's oration.[23]

Bovillus' *De sapiente* (1509) is perhaps the most curious and in some respects the most characteristic creation of Renaissance philosophy. In no other work can we find such an intimate union of old and new ideas, of sterile and fertile ideas. The work is still nearly completely dominated by that basic tendency of medieval thought which tries to spin a thick web of analogies over the entire cosmos and to capture the whole physical and spiritual world in the network of these analogies. One and the same basic schema is constantly repeated and is supposed to decipher and reveal to us the order of the microcosm and the macrocosm; the order of the elements and of the natural and moral forces; and the logical world of syllogisms as well as the metaphysical world of real reasons and consequences. And yet, in the midst of this schematic-

[23] A letter of 1 September 1496 from Gaguin to Ficino reveals that the doctrines of the Platonic Academy very early found favour in France, particularly at the University of Paris. 'Virtus et sapientia tua, Ficine,' he writes, 'tanta in nostra Academia Parisiensi circumfertur, ut cum in doctissimorum virorum collegiis, tum in classibus etiam puerorum tuum nomen ametur atque celebretur.' Rob. Gaguini *Epistolae et Orationes* ed. Thuasne (Paris, 1903/4), ii. 20f., quoted according to Mestwerdt, *Die Anfänge des Erasmus*, p. 165. For the influence of Florentine Platonism on the development of Faber Stapulensis, cf. especially A. Renaudet, *Préréforme et Humanisme à Paris pendant les premières guerres d'Italie (1494–1517)* (Paris, 1916), pp. 138ff.

allegorical presentation of the cosmos, there are thoughts of such pure speculative content and of such peculiarly new stamp that they are immediately reminiscent of the great systems of modern philosophical idealism—of Leibniz or of Hegel. According to Bovillus, the world consists of four different levels which represent, so to speak, the path from the object to the subject, from simple 'being' to 'consciousness of self'.[24] Being, as the most abstract element, is common to everything that exists; consciousness of self, as the most concrete and the most developed, is the property only of the highest creature, man. And between these two extreme poles stands nature as a preliminary level and as a potency of the mind. Nature embodies the various forms of *life*; but it only leads to the threshold of reason, of *reflexive knowledge*, knowledge of self. *Esse, vivere, sentire, intelligere*; these are the various stages through which being runs in order that it may arrive at itself, at its own *concept*. The lowest of these levels, existence as such, belongs to everything that is—to the stone as well as the plant, to the animal as well as to man. But above this foundation of simple substantiality arise the various orders of subjective life.[25]

With these thoughts Bovillus anticipates the Hegelian formula, according to which the meaning and aim of the mental process of development consists in the 'substance' becoming 'subject'. Reason is the power in man by which 'mother nature' returns to herself, i.e., by which she completes her cycle and is led back to herself.[26] But after this return, she finds she no longer has the same form that she had when she started out. Once the first separation in man has been completed, once he has stepped out of the simplicity of his original state, he can never again return to this unbroken simplicity. He must go through the opposite in order to pass beyond it to find the true unity of his being—

[24] Just how closely related the theme of Bovillus' work was to the theme of Pico's oration *De hominis dignitate* can be seen from a passage in chap. xxiv: 'Hominis nichil est peculiare aut proprium, sed ejus omnia sunt communia, quecunque aliorum propria. Quicquid hujus et hujus, illius et alterius et ita singulorum est proprium, unius est hominis. Omnium enim in se naturam transfert, cuncta speculatur, universam naturam imitatur. Sorbens enim hauriensque quicquid est in rerum natura, omnia fit. Nam neque peculiare ens homo est, hoc vel hoc, neque ipsius est hec aut hec natura, sed simul omnia est.' (*De sapiente* was written in 1509 and appeared in Paris in 1510, together with other works by Bovillus. For details on that edition and on Bovillus' theory of knowledge, which cannot be given here, cf. my *Erkenntnisproblem*, I, 66ff.)

[25] See *De sapiente*, 1, 2.

[26] Ibid., chap. 5: 'Fit iterum ut rite diffiniri a nobis possit ipsa ratio adulta esse et consumata nature filia, sive altera quedam natura prima nature speculatrix et que ad prioris nature imitationem omnia in semetipsa effingit cunctaque sapienter (vires supplens matris) moderatur. Rationem quoque eam vim diffinimus, qua mater natura in seipsam redit, qua totius nature circulus absolvitur quave natura sibi ipsi restituitur.'

that unity which does not exclude difference but rather postulates and requires it. For no power resides within simple being as such; it only becomes really fruitful when it divides itself in two and then reconstitutes its unity through this division.[27]

In the development and expression of this thought Bovillus is obviously following the speculative interpretation that Cusanus gave to the doctrine of the trinity. Like Cusanus, he stressed that the true triunity is not to be understood statically but dynamically; that it is not to be conceived of as the simple juxtaposition of three 'natures' within one actually simple substance, but rather as the continuous unity of a development that leads from mere 'possibility' to 'reality', from 'potentiality' to full and complete 'actualization'. Applying this conception of God to man, one sees that the true reality of man is to be found only where he has gone through the individual stages of this process. Only in this becoming can he attain and understand his specific being. What we call 'wisdom', therefore, is not really a knowledge of external objects but a knowledge of our own selves; not nature but *humanitas* is its proper object. The wise man is he who has passed through the contradictions that are contained within man, recognized them, and therewith overcome them. He is *homo in potentia* and *homo in actu, homo ex principio* and *homo ex fine, home existens* and *homo apparens, homo inchoatus* and *homo perfectus, homo a natura* and *homo ab intellectu.*[28] And for Bovillus, this definition of wisdom also contains the formulation and the solution of the problem of freedom. To him, freedom simply means that man does not receive his being ready-made from nature, as do the other entities, nor does he, so to speak, get it as a permanent fief; but rather that he must acquire it, must *form* it through *virtus* and *ars*. His value is dependent upon the greater or lesser power of this formation. Bovillus inserts into his speculative metaphysical system a complete system of ethics, based on the same foundations. Just as being is graduated into *Esse, Vivere, Sentire,* and *Intelligere*, so man can freely choose to pass through the whole series of levels, or to persist and remain standing at one level. If he falls prey to the vice of inertia—the medieval *acedia*—he can sink down to the level at which only naked

---

[27] Ibid., chap. 6 and 7: 'Natura sapienti simplex esse condonavit. Ipse vero sibi ipsi compositum esse: hoc est bene beateque esse progenuit. . . . Accipet enim sapiens a natura substantialis munus hominis, ex cujus fecunditate studiosum hominem parturivit. Insipiens vero parem quoque ac substantialem hominem mutavit a natura, sed nullo virtutis fenore splendescit. Hic igitur homo rite habere et non habere, ille vero habere et habere predicatur.'

[28] Ibid., 6.

existence remains to him, without form and hence without consciousness of existence. On the other hand, he can ascend to the highest level,
where, through the medium of his own self knowledge, he attains a
knowledge of the cosmos.[29] For the one is only attainable through the
other. Self knowledge and knowledge of the world only appear to be
distinct processes that move in opposite directions. Actually, the Ego
only finds itself by turning to the world, by trying to draw the world
into itself completely and then trying to copy it in all its forms, its
'species'. But this copying, which seems to be a merely passive activity,
a function of the memory, in reality contains all the powers of the
intellect, of thoughtful consideration, and of reflection. Thus, the truth
of the *major mundus* can be understood when it passes over into the
minor mundus. The world contains the totality of things; but only man
knows this totality. The world contains man as a part; but man grasps
the world in its *principle*. Thus, compared with the world, man can be
called both the greatest and the smallest; the smallest, if we measure by
the standard of substance; the greatest, if we measure by knowledge.
*Mundus maxima substantia, scientia nullus. Homo scientia amplissimus,
substantia pusillus. Uterque stat in utroque; uterque utriusque capax. Hominis
enim substantia versatur in mundo, mundi vero scientia in homine. Mundus
substantialis mundus est, homo rationalis mundus. Quanta in mundo substantiarum discretio quantaque rerum differitas, tantum in homine rationum
discrimen. In utroque sunt omnia, in quolibet quodlibet et in utroque nihil.
In homine substantia nulla: in mundo ratio itidem et conceptio nulla. Vacuus
uterque est et plenus uterque. Inops rerum homo: rationum dives est. Mundus
vero rerum plenus, inanis rationum.*[30] The opposition between 'substantiality' and 'subjectivity', between 'being in-itself' and 'being for-itself,'
can hardly be expressed more clearly.[31] And, like Hegel, Bovillus
requires that this opposition be resolved in a supreme speculative synthesis. The man of nature, simple *homo*, must become the man of art,

---

[29] Ibid., 1, 2.   [30] Ibid., 19.

[31] Cf. also ibid., 24: 'In omni quippe mundana substantia: aliquid delitescit humanum,
aliqua cuivis substantie indita est hominis atomus, homini propria, qua componendus
est et conflandus studiosus homo, quam sibi vendicare et ingenii vi abstrahere a materia
natus est homo. . . . Qui igitur conflatus est et perfectus a natura homo (homo, inquam,
noster situs in mundi medio) matris imperio per mundum (circumferri iussus): exquirit
a singulis que sua sunt, abstrahit a qualibet mundi substantia proprie speciei atomum.
Illam sibi vendicat atque inserit et ex plurium specierum atomis suam elicit profertque
speciem, que naturalis et primi nostri hominis fructus seu acquisitus studiosusve homo
nuncupatur. Hec itaque hominis est consumatio: cum ad hunc modum ex substantiali
scilicet homine rationalem, ex naturali acquisitum et ex simplici compositum, perfectum,
studiosum.'

the *homo-homo*; but this difference is already overcome, inasmuch as it is recognized in its necessity. Above the first two forms arises now the last and highest; the trinity *homo-homo-homo*, in which the opposition of potency and act, of nature and freedom, of being and consciousness, is at once encompassed and resolved.[32] Man no longer appears therein as a part of the universe but as its eye and mirror; and, indeed, as a mirror that does not receive the images of things from outside but that rather forms and shapes them in itself.[33]

In keeping with its peculiar character, Renaissance philosophy is not satisfied with the abstract expression of these thoughts but rather seeks a pictorial and symbolic expression for them. The ancient Prometheus myth seems to offer itself naturally to this end, and thus it now undergoes a kind of resurrection and intellectual rebirth. The Prometheus myth is one of those primeval mythical motifs with which ancient philosophy itself had already been very much concerned. Plato in *Protagoras*, as well as Plotinus and Neo-Platonism, tried to give an allegorical explanation of it. Now this motif encounters the Christian *Adam* motif either to fuse with it, or to oppose it and, by virtue of this

[32] Ibid., 22: 'Manifestum . . . est sapientiam esse quendam hominis numerum, discrimen, fecunditatem, emanationem eamque consistere in hominis dyade, genita ex priore monade. Primus enim nativus noster et sensibilis homo ipsiusque nature mutuum monas est et totius humane fecunditatis fons atque initium. Artis vero homo, humanave species arte progenita, dyas est et primi quedam hominis emanatio, sapientia, fructus et finis. Cuius habitu qui a natura homo tantum erat, artis fenore et uberrimo proventu reduplicatus homo vocatur et homohomo. Et non modo ad dyadem, sed et ad usque tryadem humane sapientie vis hominis numerum extendit humanitatemque propagat. Sine quippe medio extrema sunt nulla; sine propinquitate nulla distantia; sine concordia dissociatio nulla et sine concurrentia nulla disparata. Sunt autem monas et dyas. Natura item et ars quedam extrema. Similiter et nature homo et artis homo, seu substantialis homo et vera ejus imago virtute progenita; nature mutuum sive naturale donum et hominis acquisitum. Horum igitur extremorum symplegma est aliquod, concordia et concurrentia aliqua. Aliquis amor, pax, vinculum: et medium aliquod amborum, proventus, unio, fructus, emanatio. Juncta etenim invicem monas et dyas tryadem eliciunt proferuntque, suam copulam, unionem et concordiam. Itaque sapientia quedam est trina hominis sumptio, hominis trinitas, humanitas tryas. Est enim trinitas totius perfectionis emula, cum sine trinitate nulla reperiatur perfectio.'

[33] Ibid., 26: 'Homo nichil est omnium et a natura extra omnia factus et creatus est, ut multividus fiat sitque omnium expressio et naturale speculum abjunctum et separatum ab universorum ordine: eminus et a regione omnium collocatum, ut omnium centrum. Speculi etenim natura est, ut adversum et oppositum sit ei, cujus in sese ferre debet imaginem. . . . Et in quocunque loco cuncta mundi statueris entia: in ejus opposito abs te collocandus et recipiendus est homo, ut sit universorum speculum. . . . Verus igitur et speculi et hominis locus est in oppositione, extremitate, distantia et negatione universorum, ubi inquam omnia non sunt, ubi nichil actu est. Extra omnia, in quo tamen fieri omnia nata sunt. . . . Nam consumatis et perfectis omnibus, postquam actus singuli sua loca sortiti sunt, vidit Deus deesse omnium speculatorem et universorum oculum. . . . Viditque nullum supremo huic oculo inter cetera superesse locum. Plena quippe actuum erant omnia; quodlibet suo gradu, loco et ordine constiterat. Et ex actibus diversis disparatisque speciebus aut rerum differentiis et mundi luminaribus (que per se intermisceri, confundi,

opposition, force it to undergo an inner transformation. In his detailed study of the course and the development of the Adam motif, Burdach has shown how fruitful and productive it proved to be during the period of transition from the Middle Ages to the Renaissance. The figure of the first man had been determined by the view of the church, based on the biblical story. In the Renaissance, the figure comes to have a new meaning—a meaning determined in part by Platonic-Augustinian and Neo-Platonic-hermetic thought. The first man becomes an expression of the spiritual man, the *homo spiritualis*, and thus, all the spiritual tendencies of the epoch that are directed towards a renewal, rebirth, and regeneration of man come to be concentrated in his form.[34]

This transformation is observable in English literature in William Langland's *Piers the Plowman*, and in German literature in the dialogue between the peasant and death, written by Johannes von Saaz in about 1400. Burdach called this dialogue the greatest German poetic work of the whole epoch. Through its creative power and the enormous force of its language it reveals to us the new *ideal* forces now pressing to be expressed. We are dealing with poetry, not doctrine; but it is a poetry completely inspired and penetrated by the breath of a new idea. And this idea is not burdened with any Scholastic appendages; it exists, so to speak, in the free space of thought. The problems are not presented and elaborated through abstract philosophical meditations; rather, we see life itself, asking itself the eternal questions concerning its origin and its value. All merely dialectical oppositions now become dramatic oppositions. But the dialogue only presents us with the oppositions themselves, not with their solutions. There is, apparently, no decision in the battle between the peasant and death, between destiny's power of destruction and the spirit of man, which combats this power. The dialogue closes with God's judgment, giving the victory to death; but

concurrere et fas et possibile non est) fieri homo haudquaquam poterat. Extra igitur cunctorum differentias et proprietates in opposito omnium loco, in conflage mundi, in omnium medio coaluit homo: tanquam publica creatura, que quod relictum erat in natura vacuum potentiis, umbris, speciebus, imaginibus et rationibus supplevit.' These sentences are of special historical significance because they show the characteristic 'transformation' which the motif of the microcosm underwent in the philosophy of the Renaissance. For Bovillus, as for Pico and Cusanus, the motif no longer implied the unity of man and the world; rather, they stressed the moment of *opposition*, the polarity of 'subject' and 'object' implied by the correlation in the motif. With that, we are on the threshold of Leibniz's theory of the monad. For the *monad*, by its very nature and essence, must be detached from the world of *phenomena*, so that it can completely express, and be a 'living mirror' of, that world.

[34] Cf. Burdach, *Reformation, Renaissance, Humanismus*, pp. 171ff.

to the plaintiff, the peasant, go the honours of battle. 'The battle is not without reason. You have both fought well. Suffering forces the one to accuse; the other is forced by the accuser's attack to tell the truth. Therefore, accuser, Honour is yours; to you, Death, belongs victory.'[35] And yet, this victory of death is also a defeat. For now, although his physical power is confirmed and sealed, his spiritual power is broken. The destruction of life, the fact that God makes it subject to death, no longer signifies the nullity of life. For though it be destroyed in its being, life nevertheless retains an indestructible value: the value that the free man gives to himself and to the world. The faith of humanity in itself guarantees the re-birth of humanity.

The allegorical form of the poem acts as a thin veil through which we can clearly and sharply see the great line of artistic creativity and the direction of thought. And in it we recognize clearly the basic view of the coming Renaissance. In the accusing speech of the peasant against death, in which he lauds man as the most free and, therefore, most perfect and magnificent of God's creatures, Burdach sees the same spirit that will express itself more than two generations later in Pico's *Oration on the Dignity of Man*. 'Angel, devil, hobgoblin, witch—those are all spirits restrained by God's nature; of all God's creations, man is the most precious, the most adroit, and the most free.'[36] Another characteristic feature of this accusing speech is its decisive rejection of the pessimistic features of Christian dogma. Its unshakable faith in the personal powers of man and in his God-given good nature contains an element of Pelagianism within it.[37] Thus, it also anticipates a view that soon received its conceptual expression and its conceptual justification in German philosophy. The poet of the *Peasant from Bohemia* ignores the corruption of man that came about through Adam's fall, was proclaimed by God's curse, and passed on to the whole human race with each new generation. Soon, Nicholas of Cusa will inveigh against this doctrine almost in the same words. *Omnis vis illa quae se esse cognoscit ab optimo, optime se esse cognoscit. Omne id, quod est, quiescit in specifica natura sua, ut in optima ab optimo. Datum igitur naturale qualecumque in omni eo quod est, est optimum . . . de sursum igitur est ab omnipotentia infinita.*[38]

---

[35] *Der Ackermann aus Böhmen*, eds. Alois Bernt and Konrad Burdach (Berlin, 1917), in *Vom Mittelalter zur Reformation. Forschungen zur Geschichte der deutschen Bildung*, vol. 3, chap. xxxiii, p. 85.

[36] *Ackermann aus Böhmen*, chap. xxv, p. 58. Cf. Burdach's comments, p. 323.

[37] Burdach, loc. cit., p. 315.

[38] Cusanus *De dato patris luminum* 1. *Opera* fol. 284f.; cf. above, chap. i, n. 52.

With these words, we have reached the point at which the Adam motif undergoes the inner transformation that enables it to merge with the Prometheus motif. No change in the content of the thought is necessary to complete this transition; a slight shift of *accent* suffices. Man is a creature; but what distinguishes him above all other creatures is that his maker gave him the gift of creation. Man arrives at his determination, he fulfils his being, only by using this basic and primary power. The myth of Prometheus, the man-making artist, was not unknown to medieval thinkers; we find it in Tertullian, in Lactantius, and in Augustine. But the medieval view seizes primarily upon the negative feature in this myth. It sees in the myth only the pagan travesty of the biblical story of creation, and it tries to re-establish the orthodox story in the place of this perversion. The true Prometheus, the one whom the Christian faith may recognize and allow, is not man, but the one God: *Deus unicus qui universa conditit, qui hominem de humo struxit, hic est verus Prometheus.*[39] If we compare Boccaccio's euhemeristic interpretation of the Prometheus legend with the medieval interpretation, we shall see that a change in basic attitude has taken place. In his *Genealogia deorum*, he distinguishes between two creations; the one called man into existence, and the other conferred upon this existence an intellectual content. The rough and ignorant man that came forth from the hands of nature could only be perfected by another act of creation. The first gave him his physical reality; the second gave his specific form. Here, Prometheus is a human hero of culture, the bringer of wisdom and of political and moral order. Through these gifts, he 'reformed' man in the true sense, i.e., he impressed upon him a new form and a new essential character.[40]

Renaissance philosophy moves farther and farther away even from this version of the motif, for it transfers the power of giving form ever more definitely to the individual subject. The activity of the individual

[39] For the development of the Prometheus motif in the Middle Ages, especially by Lactantius (*Divin. Institut.* ii. 2.), and by Tertullian (*Apolog.* 18; *Adv. Marc.* i. 1.) cf. the detailed evidence in J. Toutain, 'Prometheus', in Daremberg-Saglio, *Dictionnaire des antiquités*, IV, 684. For the re-adoption of the motif in the plastic arts of the Renaissance, cf. Georg Habich, 'Uber zwei Prometheus-Bilder angeblich von Piero di Cosimo', *Sitzungsberichte der bayrischen Akademie der Wissenschaften, Philosophisch-philologische Klasse* (1920).

[40] Boccaccio *De genealogia Deorum* iv. 4: 'Verum qui natura producti sunt rudes et ignari veniunt, immo ni instruantur, lutei agrestes et beluae. Circa quos secundus Prometheus insurgit, id est doctus homo et eos tanquam lapideos suscipiens quasi de novo creat, docet et instruit et demonstrationibus suis ex naturalibus hominibus civiles facit moribus, scientia et virtute insignes, adeo ut liquide pateat alios produxisse naturam et alios reformasse doctrinam.'

is juxtaposed to the activity of the Creator and to that of the Saviour. This basic view enters even into the thought of the Christian Platonists; even in Ficino's thought, this heroic individualism sometimes breaks through. Man is not a slave of creative nature, according to Ficino: rather, he is its rival, completing, improving, and refining its works. *Humanae artes fabricant per se ipsas quaecumque fabricat ipsa natura, quasi non servi simus naturae, sed aemuli.*[41] We have already seen that this thought was subsequently sharpened and strengthened by Bovillus. And in his *De sapiente*, Bovillus also refers to the Prometheus legend, interpreting and transforming the legend in a manner consistent with his natural philosophy and with his metaphysics. This metaphisics postulates four levels, i.e, it divides all being into the four basic orders of *Esse*, *Vivere*, *Sentire*, and *Intelligere*. In the play of analogies that dominates his entire doctrine, earth corresponds to the first of the cosmic elements, water to the second, and air to the third; whereas fire, taking the highest position, becomes the analogue and the image of 'reason'. This represents a fusion of Stoic thoughts with a kind of 'metaphysics of light' derived from Neoplatonic sources, and later systematically revived by the natural philosophy of the Renaissance, especially by Patrizzi.[42] Bovillus uses the Prometheus motif as the connecting link joining his philosophy of nature with his philosophy of mind. When he makes the heavenly out of the earthly man, the actual out of the potential man, intellect out of nature, the wise man is imitating Prometheus, who arose to the heavens to take from the gods the all-animating fire. The wise man becomes his own creator and master; he acquires and possesses himself, whereas the merely 'natural' man always belongs to a foreign

[41] Ficino *Theologia Platonica* xiii. fol. 295. The lack of unity in Ficino's concept of 'humanitas' expresses, itself among other ways, in his explanation of the word itself. Sometimes he plays with etymology, as did the medieval thinkers, and lets the word derive from *humus* (*homo dicitur ab humo, Epistolae* i. fol. 641). But at other times, he emphatically rejects this derivation. '(humanitatem) cave ne quando contemnas forte existimans humanitatem humi natam. Est enim humanitas ipsa praestanti corpore nympha, coelesti origine nata Aetherea ante alias dilecta Deo.' (*Epistolae* v. fol. 805.) Here again, we perceive the opposition that had received artistic expression at the beginning of the century in the dialogues between the peasant and death. (Cf. especially chaps. xxiv and xxv of *Der Ackermann aus Böhmen.*) Burdach's commentary (op. cit., pp. 310, 317) accepts the 'De contemptu mundi sive de miseria conditionis humanae' by Innocent III as the direct or indirect source of inspiration for death's discourses. If this is true, it is another example of the close interplay between religion, philosophy, and humanism in the Renaissance. For it was precisely Innocent's work that Giannozzo Manetti attacked with his *De dignitate et excellentia hominis* (1452); and this work, in turn, seems to have been the direct literary model for Ficino's defence of 'humanity'. (For further details, cf. Gentile, op. cit., pp. 153ff.; also see above, pp. 83f.)

[42] Cf. Patrizzi *Pancosmia* iv (*Nova de universis Philosophia*, Ferrariae 1591, P. IV. fol. 73ff.).

power and remains its eternal debtor.[43] As soon as we proceed to the order of *value*, we find a reversal of the temporal succession of the man of 'nature' and the man of 'art'—a reversal, that is, of the *primus homo* and the *secundus homo*: the second in time becomes the first in value. For man attains his purpose as a man only when he gives it to himself; only when, as Pico says in his Oration, he becomes his own, free maker (*sui ipsius quasi arbitrarius honorariusque plastes et fictor*).

Later, in Giordano Bruno, we encounter this thought again, completely dislodged from its original religious grounding and, in fact, in conscious departure from it. The only passion that reigns in Bruno is the passion of the self-affirmation of the Ego, heightened to titanic and heroic proportions. Although the Ego recognizes that there is something transcendent, something that lies beyond human powers of conception, it nevertheless does not want to receive this super-sensible something as a simple gift of grace. The man who passively receives such a gift may perhaps possess a greater good than the man who tries to attain a knowledge of the divine through his own power; but this objective-good does not counterbalance the specific value of independent striving and action. For man must grasp the divine not as a vessel or as an instrument, but as an artist and as an active cause. Thus, Bruno distinguishes the merely faithful receivers from those who feel in themselves the drive to ascend and the power of upward movement— the *impeto razionale* towards the divine. *Gli primi hanno più dignità, potestà ed efficacia in sè, perchè hanno la divinità; gli secondi sono essi più degni, più potenti ed efficaci, et son divini. Gli primi son degni come l'asino che porta li sacramenti; gli secondi come una cosa sacra. Nelli primi si considera et vede in effetto la divinità et quella s'admira, adora et obedisce; negli secondi si considera et vede l'eccellenza della propria humanitade.*[44] By bringing

---

[43] Bovillus *De sapiente* 8: 'Sapiens . . . celestum hominem inde profert, e tenebris emendicat elicitque splendorem: ex potentia actum, ex principio finem, ex insita vi opus, ex natura intellectum, ex inchoatione perfectum, ex parte totum et ex denique semine fructum. Hac enim in parte celebrem illum Prometheum imitatur, qui (ut poetarum fabulae canunt) aut divum permissione aut mentis et ingenii acumine admissus nonnunquam in ethereos thalamos, posteaquam universa celi palatia attentiore mentis speculatione lustravit, nichil in eis igne sanctius, preciosius ac vegetius reperit. Hunc ergo quem dii tantopere mortalibus invidebant illico suffuratus mortalium indidit orbi eoque luteum ac figulinum hominem (quem fixerat prius) animavit. Ita et sapiens vi contemplationis sensibilem mundum linquens penetransque in regiam celi conceptum ibidem lucidissimum sapientie ignem immortali mentis gremio in inferiora reportat eaque sincera ac vegetissima flamma naturalis ipsius tellureusve homo viret, fovetur, animatur. Sapiens nature munera studioso homine compensat, seipsum insuper acquisivit seque possidet ac suus manet. Insipiens vero . . . manet perpes nature debitor, substantiali homine oberatus et nunquam suus.'

[44] Bruno, *De gli heroici furori*, Dial. III, *Opere ital.* (ed. Lagarde), 641.

these sentences from Bruno's dialogue *Degli eroici furori* together with the sentences of the *De docta ignorantia*, in which Nicholas Cusanus defined the concept and the ideal of *humanitas*, we can encompass the whole movement of thought of the fifteenth and sixteenth centuries. Cusanus does not merely try to fit this ideal into a religious framework of thought; for him, the ideal signifies the completion and the fulfilment of the basic doctrines of Christianity. The idea of humanity merges and becomes one with the idea of Christ. But as philosophy develops further, the bond becomes weaker, and finally dissolves completely. With characteristic precision, Giordano Bruno reveals the forces that press towards such a dissolution. The ideal of humanity includes the ideal of *autonomy*; but as the ideal of autonomy becomes stronger, it dissociates itself more and more from the realm of religion—the realm into which Cusanus and the Florentine Academy had tried to force the concept of humanity.

2

Up to now we have observed the gradual transformation of the problem of freedom, and the ever stronger advance of the principle of freedom within the religious thought of the Renaissance. In the face of this advance, dogmatic theology had gradually but necessarily to retreat. This retreat was, indeed, difficult, for the founder of dogmatic theology was esteemed even by the philosophers of the Renaissance as a classical author and as a philosophical and religious authority. *Petrarch* had led the way in this veneration of *Augustine*. He had picked him out of the array of the great models of antiquity and prized him as the one who was to him 'dearest among thousands'.[45] In much the same vein, the Florentine Academy always saw in Augustine the most exemplary 'Christian Platonist'. Only by keeping in mind these historical facts can we measure the magnitude of the obstacles that now had to be overcome. And yet, the removal of the obstacles would of itself not have sufficed to assure the victory of the idea of freedom. Before this could be realized, the battle had to be taken up against another power, one tied to the intellectual life of the Renaissance by a thousand threads.

In his *Theodicy*, Leibniz distinguished three forms of fate: the *Fatum Christianum*, to which was opposed the *Fatum Mahumetanum* and the

---

[45] Petrarca *De secreto conflictu curarum suarum, Prefatio.*

Fatum Stoicum. The three basic directions of thought expressed in these concepts were still thoroughly vital forces in the Renaissance. *Astrological* thought, nourished from pagan and Arabic sources, was no less influential than Christian thought. And although *antiquity* could be utilized against the Christian-medieval tradition and against Christian-medieval dogmatic theology, it was powerless, at first, against the new opponent. Indeed, antiquity seemed to support astrology, because—in the beginning, at least—the path to the 'classical' epoch of Greek philosophy was closed to the Renaissance. It could only see this philosophy disguised by its Hellenistic garb; it could only see Plato's doctrine through the medium of Neo-Platonism. Thus, with the revival of ancient thought, the ancient world of myth also moved closer to the Renaissance. Even in Giordano Bruno, one still senses that this world has by no means disappeared; it invades philosophical thought itself and becomes one of its determining factors. And whenever one sought to explain the relationship between the Ego and the world, between the individual and the cosmos not through conceptual thought but through artistic feeling and emotion, the influence of the ancient world of myth became stronger and deeper. As these forces emerge more independently and express themselves more uninhibitedly in the Renaissance, the barriers set up by the Middle Ages against the system of astrology begin to fall more easily. The Christian Middle Ages were able neither to dispense with astrology nor to completely overcome it. They adopted the astrological system, just as they tolerated and continued ancient pagan conceptions. The old gods lived on; but they were demoted to demons, to spirits of inferior rank. No matter how strongly the primitive fear of demons might assert itself, it was allayed and held in bounds by faith in the omnipotence of the one God to whose will all opposing forces must bow. Thus, although medieval 'knowledge', especially medicine and natural science, was saturated with astrological elements, medieval *faith* represented a constant corrective against them. Faith neither denied nor removed them; it simply subjected them to the power of Divine Providence. By virtue of this subjugation, astrology could remain undisturbed as a principle of worldly wisdom. Even Dante accepted it in this sense; indeed, in the *Convivio*, he gives a complete system of knowledge that corresponds in every detail to the system of astrology. The seven sciences of the Trivium and the Quadrivium are assigned to the seven spheres of the planets: grammar corresponds to the sphere of the moon, dialectics to that of Mercury, rhetoric to Venus, arithmetic to the sun, music to Mars, geometry to Jupiter, and astronomy to Saturn.[46]

Early *Humanism* brings no change in attitude towards astrology. Petrarch adapts himself completely to the basic Christian view; his position towards astrology is no different from that of Augustine, to whose arguments he expressly refers.[47] In his youth, *Salutati* had a tendency to believe in astrological fate; but he completely overcame this temptation and expressly fought against this belief in his later work, *De fato et fortuna*. The stars possess no independent power; they may only be considered instruments in the hand of God.[48] And yet, as we move further into the Renaissance, we feel more and more that the advance of the worldly spirit and of worldly culture strengthens the tendency towards the basic doctrines of astrology. In Ficino's life, generally so orderly and balanced, there is a moment of unrest and of constant inner tension as a result of his ambiguous intellectual and moral position towards astrology. He, too, bows to the Christian-ecclesiastical point of view; he, too, stresses that the heavenly bodies may indeed exercise power over the bodies of men but that they can exert no pressure on the mind or on the will.[49] From this position he also fights against any attempt to predict the future by means of astrology. *Si diligentius rem ipsam consideramus, non tam fatis ipsis, quam fatuis fatorum assertoribus agimur.*[50] And yet, it is clear that this theoretical conviction, which he struggled to reach, cannot change the essence of his feeling about life. That feeling is still dominated by the belief in the power of the stars, above all by the belief in the evil power of Saturn, the planet ascendant in Ficino's own horoscope.[51] The wise man ought not to attempt to escape from the power of his star. Only one thing remains for him to do: to channel this power towards the good by strengthening in himself the beneficent influences that come from his star, and, whenever possible, rejecting the harmful ones. The possibility of giving

---

[46] Dante *Convivio*, trattato secondo, chap. xiv.

[47] Petrarca *Epist. rerum familiarium* iii. 8 (details in Voigt, op. cit., I, 73ff.).

[48] A. v. Martin, *Coluccio Salutati und das humanistische Lebensideal* (Leipzig and Berlin, 1916), pp. 69ff., 283ff., gives details about Salutati's essay 'De fato et fortuna' (1396).

[49] Ficino to Cavalcanti *Epistolae* i. *Opera* fol. 633: 'Corpus . . . nostrum a corpore mundi fati viribus tanquam particula quaedam a tota sui mole violento quodam impetu trahitur, nec in mentem nostram fati vis penetrat, nisi ipsa se sua sponte prius in corpus fato subjectum immiserit. . . . Recipiat a corporis peste seipsum animus quisque et in mentem suam se colligat, tunc enim vim suam fortuna explebit in corpore, in animum non transibit.'

[50] Ficino *Epistolae* iv. fol. 781.

[51] Cf. Ficino's letters to Cavalcanti; *Epistolae* iii. fol. 731 and 732.

a form to life is based upon this ability to shape it to unity and perfection *within* the prescribed circle. Our striving neither can nor should reach beyond this boundary. In the third book of his work *De triplici vita*, which he entitled *De vita coelitus comparanda*, Ficino developed a complete and detailed system for shaping one's life according to the determination and the power of the stars.[52]

With an example like this before us, we can see with particular clarity that the new Renaissance sense of life and the Renaissance concept and ideal of humanity had to fight against two different forces. A necessity of a double kind and character stands opposed to every attempt to liberate the Ego: both the *regnum gratiae* and the *regnum naturae* demand the recognition and submission of the Ego. The more vigorously the claim of the *regnum gratiae* was rejected, the more vigorously did the *regnum naturae* arise and declare itself to have the only valid claim. A transcendent bond is replaced by an immanent bond; a religious and theological bond is replaced by a naturalistic bond. And the latter was a harder one to surmount and surpass. For ultimately the Renaissance concept of *nature* was nourished by the same intellectual forces that gave birth to its concept of mind and its concept of man. What was required here was nothing less than that these forces turn, so to speak, against themselves, and that they put their own limits around themselves. The battle against Scholasticism and against medieval doctrinal theology had been directed towards the outside; now it was to turn inwards. Clearly, it would have to be a bitter and stubborn battle.

The basic magical-astrological view of causality is strongly interwoven in the whole Renaissance philosophy of nature, from its inception in the fifteenth, throughout its life in the sixteenth, and even through the beginnings of the seventeenth century. To understand nature according to its own principles (*juxta propria principia*) seemed to mean nothing but to explain it by the *forces* innate in nature. But where did these forces appear more clearly, where were they more graspable and more general than in the movements of the heavenly bodies? If the immanent law of the cosmos, the all-embracing universal rule even for particular occurrences was readable at all, it must be here. During the Renaissance, therefore, astrology and magic do not conflict with the 'modern' concept of nature; on the contrary, they become its

[52] For details about Ficino's essay 'De vita triplici', and about his attitude towards astrology cf. especially Erwin Panofsky, Fritz Saxl, 'Dürers Melancolia I', *Studien der Bibliothek Warburg*, No. 11 (Leipzig and Berlin, 1923), pp. 32ff.

most powerful vehicle. Astrology and the new empirical 'science' of
nature enter into a personal as well as an objective union. We must recall
the effect this union had on the lives of individual thinkers; we must
observe the form it took in the autobiography of such a man as Cardano.
Only then can we measure completely the power it exercised over the
theoretical conception and the practical shaping of life itself. This union
was dissolved only by *Copernicus* and *Galileo*. And yet, the dissolution
does not represent a simple victory of 'experience' over 'thought', nor
of calculation and measurement over speculation. Before it could be
successful, a transformation had first to be completed in the mode of
thought itself; a new logic of the conception of nature had to be formed.
To know the great *systematic* complexes in Renaissance philosophy,
nothing is more important than to trace the course of this logic. For
what is decisive and essential here is not the end as such but the path by
which it was attained. This path seems to lead us through a hodge-podge
of fantastic superstition; even in the work of such thinkers as *Bruno*
and *Campanella* the line between myth and science, between 'magic'
and 'philosophy' cannot be drawn with certainty. Nevertheless, we
must look ever deeper to find the dynamic of that slow and continuous
intellectual process by which the 'differentiation' between these two
fields was first accomplished.

The continuity of this process does not imply that the *systematic* succession of thoughts is represented and reflected by a *temporal* succession.
We are not dealing with a continuous temporal 'progress' that leads in
a straight line to some specific goal. Not only do the old and new proceed
together for long periods of time, but both continually merge with
each other. One can, therefore, speak of 'development' only in the
sense that the individual thoughts, precisely through this process of
merging and separating, gradually distinguish themselves from each
other more sharply and emerge in definite, *typical* configurations. These
typical configurations make clear to us the immanent forward movement of thought, which by no means necessarily corresponds to its
temporal and empirical course. Two different steps can be distinguished
in the conquest of the astrological view of the world: the one consists in
negating the *content* of this view; the other, in the attempt to clothe the
content in a new *form* and to give it a new methodological foundation.
The latter attempt is characteristic of that view of nature which is not
based on the study of the phenomena themselves, but which tries
instead to look at the phenomena through the medium of Aristotelian-

Scholastic concepts of nature and to adapt them to the system of these concepts. From this comes forth a peculiar mixture—a kind of Scholastic astrology and astrological Scholasticism, whose prototype may be found in certain medieval systems, particularly Averroism.

In the Italian Renaissance, this type of thought once again found a characteristic embodiment in Pomponazzi's work *De naturalium effectuum admirandorum causis sive de incantationibus* (1520).[53] At first glance, the content of this work appears to be nothing more than a compendium of ancient and medieval superstitions. The various kinds of omens and of miraculous phenomena, the different forms of divination and magic are gathered together and ordered according to groups. Although Pomponazzi is critical and sceptical about some of the miracles reported, he never attacks the truth and credibility of the genus itself. This truth seems to him to be guaranteed by 'experience'; and experience the philosophical critic must simply accept without changing its content. No matter how strange and improbable certain kinds of effects may seem, theory may not dispute the 'that-ness', i.e., the reality of these effects, but must rather seek the 'why' of the 'that', the reason for the phenomenon. Theory may not regulate observations; rather, it must 'save' them. But reasons can only be found if we do away with the 'isolation' in which the phenomena at first appear to us, i.e., if we trace every particular effect, no matter how puzzling it appears as such, to a general form of *regularity*. And for Pomponazzi, precisely this form is present in the influence of the heavenly bodies, in astrological causality. Thus, astrological causality becomes for him nothing more nor less than the basic postulate upon which any explanation of natural phenomena must be founded. No event can be considered fully understood if it is not brought into this sort of connection with the ultimate knowable causes of all being and of all becoming. And, on the other hand, there is no fact of nature which cannot be explained, at least in principle and in possibility, by the influence of the stars upon the lower world. Therefore, in Pomponazzi's view, each particular 'miracle' is traceable to *one* of these influences. He constantly seeks to prove that this power suffices to explain the effects of sorcery, the phenomena of magic, the interpretation of dreams, chiromancy and

---

[53] Pomponazzi *De naturalium effectuum admirandorum causis seu de incantationibus* (Basel, 1567) 10. 122f.: 'Et certe (cognosces) superos in haec inferiora non operari nisi mediantibus corporibus coelestibus. . . . Ex quibus concluditur omnem effectum hic inferius aut per se aut per accidens reduci ad coelum et experitia corporum coelestium miranda et stupenda posse cognosci et pronuntiari.'

necromancy, etc. Popular belief can only make these phenomena understandable by seeing in them the *tours de force* of personal powers and personal acts of the will; but the theoretician must reject this assumption, for it makes natural events subject to arbitrariness. So far as he is concerned, the law governing these events will not suffer any interference, be it demonic or divine. Even the influence of God upon the world is carried out only through the medium of the heavenly bodies. They are not only signs of the divine will, they are its genuine and indispensable intermediaries. Whether we can show these intermediary causes for every particular happening, whether we can trace them in an uninterrupted series, is of little consequence; it suffices to know that the series exists, that it is absolutely *necessary*.[54] The philosophical understanding may not waive this requirement in any individual case, nor may it be satisfied by any explanation that evades the medium of astrological causality or prematurely breaks off its investigation. For if even one exception were admitted to this basic rule, the natural order would lose all its inner consistency. If angels or demons could exercise a direct influence upon the objects of nature or the world of man without the heavenly bodies, the significance and the necessity of these cosmic bodies, the function they fulfil in the totality of the world, would no longer be understandable.[55]

Obviously, we have here before us a peculiar form and a peculiar foundation of astrology. It is dominated neither by the longing to reach into the future to wrest its secret, nor by empirical observation or mathematical theory. Here, a *logic* is operative seeking to deduce *a priori* the form of astrology as the only one adequate to our knowledge of nature. Astrological causality becomes, to use a modern phrase, the 'condition of the conceivability of nature'. For Pomponazzi, it does not signify a surrender to the world of miracles but actually the only salvation from that world, the only sure guarantee for the unconditional validity of the laws of nature. Though it may seem paradoxical at first glance, we are dealing with a thoroughly 'rational' astrology. The unconditional dominance of the stars over everything on earth is

---

[54] Ibid., 131, 134: 'Ultimo supponitur, quod in rebus difficilibus et occultis responsiones magis ab inconvenientibus remotae ac magis sensatis et rationibus consonae sunt magis recipiendae quam oppositae rationes. . . . His modo sic suppositis tentandum est sine daemonibus et angelis ad objecta respondere. . . . Effectus inferior immediate non fit a Deo super nos, sed tantum mediantibus ejus ministris. Omnia enim Deus ordinat et disponit ordinate et suaviter legemque aeternam rebus indidit quam praeterire impossibile est.' Cf. 12. 223, *et passim*.

[55] Cf. ibid., 10. 142; and 13. 299, *et passim*.

asserted only in order that the unconditional primacy of scientific reason may be guaranteed. In this case, Pomponazzi's object is the same as it is in all his other philosophical works. He wants to put 'knowledge' in the place of 'belief'; he is striving for a purely 'immanent' rather than a transcendent explanation. His *ethic* is also oriented in this direction. He tries to determine it from its own bases and to derive it from an original, autonomous certainty of reason, independent of any assumption about immortality and a future life. And this also true of his *psychology*, in which he combats the dualistic opposition of 'soul' and 'intellect', trying to show that even the highest intellectual functions are not to be understood except in organic connection with the senses and thus with the functions of the body.

What Pomponazzi sought to do for ethics and for psychology in *De immortalitate animi*, he sought to achieve for the philosophy of nature in *De incantationibus*. Here, he tries to show that 'magical' activities, the reality or possibility of which cannot be doubted, are incapable of breaking through the framework of the one, immanent causality of nature. For nature, nothing is common or uncommon; it is only our power of conception that establishes these differences. Thus, things that seem at first to lead beyond the sphere of nature, upon deeper investigation lead us back into it again. The accidental and individual dissolves in the necessary and general. At first, this result seems to be a triumph for the astrological view of the world. But upon closer investigation it becomes clear that this view of the world has disintegrated in a peculiar fashion. Warburg has shown from its history that astrology, from its very inception, presents a double intellectual front. As a theory, it seeks to place before us the eternal laws of the universe in clear outline; whereas its practice stands under the sign of the fear of demons, the 'most primitive form of religious causation'.[56] Although Pomponazzi's *De incantationibus* is still within the ambit of the astrological view, it nevertheless executes a sharp and conscious *separation* between these two basic moments of theory and practice, which hitherto had been inextricably intertwined. Therein lies the intellectual and historical significance of the work. In this sense, the work, which at first seems to be an arsenal of superstition, contains genuinely *critical* thought. The purely 'primitive', the demonic element in astrology is removed, and

[56] See Aby Warburg, 'Heidnisch-antike Weissagung in Wort und Bild zu Luthers Zeiten', *Sitzungsberichte der Heidelberger Akademie der Wissenschaften, Philosophisch-historische Klasse* (1919), pp. 24, 70.

in its place remains only the thought of the one, inviolable regularity of occurrences, recognizing no exceptions and no accidents: the 'demonic' causality of faith gives way to the causality of science.[57] This remains, to be sure, thoroughly bound to the traditional world of astrological representations, since there was as yet no *mathematical science of nature* for Pomponazzi. But it can be easily foreseen that once this framework is broken, and once the astrological concept of causality is replaced by that of mathematics and physics, the development of the new concept will find no inner obstacles to resist it. In this completely mediate sense, even Pomponazzi's strange and abstruse work helped pave the methodological way for the new, exact scientific conception of natural occurrences.

This accomplishment brought with it another consequence. Pomponazzi's strict naturalism was rendered possible only by conferring upon the naturalistic view exclusive power and dominion over the whole of *intellectual life*. There can be no barriers and no lines of separation, just as there can be no doubt that the connection between causes and effects is to be thought of as unique and clear. Because of this uniqueness of the causal nexus, no region can possibly exist beyond the realm of complete determination which we call nature. Even all of intellectual life, which we are accustomed to considering the field of free becoming and creative productivity, can only be truly understood when we have reduced it to the same all-encompassing laws upon which the entire order and the interrelationships of the world of appearances are based. In Pomponazzi's language, this simply means that astrological causality is not only the principle that explains all natural occurrences, but the constitutive principle of history as well. Like all natural being and becoming, all historical development, too, is subject to the power of the stars. The stars give history its initial impulse and decisively determine all its further progress. The radicalism of this thought is especially revealed in its application to the *history of religion*. Pomponazzi is not the only one to apply this thought to religion; indeed, he is only expressing a consequence towards which astrology had tended for a long time. That each of the forms of faith, like the forms of nature, has its own 'epoch', its periods of blossom and decay, and that these may be read in the heavens, is a view well known to astrology. Thus,

---

[57] Cf. especially the opposition of the 'philosophical' (Peripatetic) and the 'religious' concepts of causality: *De incantationibus* 10. 198, and 13. 306f. *et passim*. Cf. also Andrew H. Douglas, *The Philosophy and Psychology of Pietro Pomponazzi* (Cambridge, 1910), pp. 270ff.

the Jewish faith had been traced to the conjunction of Jupiter with Saturn, the Chaldean to that of Jupiter with Mars, the Egyptian to that of Jupiter with the sun, and the Mohammedan to that of Jupiter with Venus. Nor does this astrological construction of history stop short of Christianity. In 1327, Cecco d'Ascoli died at the stake for his attempt to determine the nativity of Christ in this way. *Burckhardt* says of these attempts that they necessarily brought with them as an ultimate consequence a 'complete eclipse of everything supersensible'.[58] Perhaps nowhere does this consequence appear with such conscious intention as in Pomponazzi's work. He *needs* precisely this eclipse so that the autarchy and the autonomy of the laws of nature may stand out the more clearly and brightly against it. He goes to the farthest limits, drawing consequences which had perhaps never before been so sharply and openly formulated. The changes in the heavens necessarily bring with them a 'change in the form of the gods'.

We now seem to be in a completely 'irrational' sphere, one inaccessible to the causality of nature. Does the ultimate foundation of religion not lie in *revelation*, in the immediate inspiration which its proclaimers and prophets receive? Just at this point, Pomponazzi's peculiar method begins to operate. He certainly does not deny revelation; but he does require that even revelation fit itself into the general course and law of nature. Even at this point, there is no exception possible to the basic rule that the divine does not influence the lower world immediately, but only through definite intermediary causes. The entire development of the various religions is bound to such intermediary causes, for it is an empirical and temporal development. Even the awakening of the founder of a religion presupposes a natural 'disposition' in him; furthermore, to become effective, it requires certain conditions. If we survey these natural conditions and try to penetrate to their ultimate unified cause, we shall again be led to the power of the stars. All intellectual being and happening is dependent upon the constellation; it produces not only the artist and the poet, but the religious seer, the *vates*, as well.

Here again, the idea of an external, divine or demonic 'possession' is to be avoided. Although God as the source of all being is ultimately also the source of the seer's illumination, it nevertheless takes place according to the cosmic situation of the world which, in turn, is indicated by the disposition of the heavenly bodies. Through this disposition

[58] Cf. Burckhardt, *The Civilization of the Renaissance*, p. 490.

the power of the prophet is awakened and its success or failure determined.[59] No form of faith may claim to stand, so to speak, as eternal truth *above* time; rather, each shows itself to be determined by time and bound to time. Faith, like all natural existence, has a period of blossoming and a period of decay, of rise and fall. Even paganism had its day in the world, during which its gods were dominant, its prayers and invocations completely effective. And the same is true of Judaism and Islam: for it cannot be denied that the mission of Moses and that of Mohammed were announced and attested by certain 'miracles'. But such signs and omens are never miracles in the absolute sense; they are never phenomena that are simply *against* nature and outside her order. What we call miracles are simply those infrequent and uncommon phenomena that repeat themselves only at great intervals of time, and that are concomitants of every great intellectual revolution in the world. They are richest and most effective when a new faith rises, only to become dissipated and weak as soon as it begins to grow old and is about to be conquered by another, stronger faith. It is as true of the gods as it is of their expressions, their annunciations and oracles, that they have their definite hour, written in the stars. *Neque enim signum vel scriptura, vel vox hoc ex se facere possunt, sed virtute corporum coelestium hoc fit faventium tali legislatoribus et ejus stigmatibus. . . . Nam veluti nunc orationes factae valent ad multa, sic tempore illorum deorum hymni dicti in eorum laudem proficiebant tunc: proficiebant autem quia tunc sidera illis favebant, nunc vero non favent, quoniam propitia sunt istis qui nunc sunt.*[60] Christianity itself, according to Pomponazzi, stands in the midst of this realm of becoming and transpiring, not above it. In Christianity we are not confronted with something that will exist eternally, but rather with simply another instance of the ever valid rule of rise and fall. And Pomponazzi does not hesitate to interpret the signs of the times in such a way that they point to the approaching end of the Christian faith. Even the sign of the cross, which once conquered pagan gods and pagan cults, does not possess unlimited power and validity; for there is nothing in this

[59] Pomponazzi *De incantationibus* 12. 230f.: 'Illa oracula non semper reperiuntur vera: quoniam stellae non sunt semper secundum eundem et unum motum: et vulgares attribuebant hoc numinibus iratis, cum veram causam ignorarent. Sed haec est consuetudo vulgi, ascribere daemonibus vel angelisquorum causas non cognoscunt. . . . Deus autem non tantum unius est causa, verum omnium; quare et omnium vaticiniorium causa est, secundum tamen alteram et alteram dispositionem coelorum . . . dat unum vaticinium et secundum alteram alterum. . . . Modo quis est tam philosophiae expers, qui nesciat secundum dispositionem varietatem et effectus variari.'
[60] Ibid., 12. 287f.

earthly life, neither in the spiritual nor in the natural realm, whose end is not prescribed together with its beginning.[61]

Pomponazzi's work opens before us a view that includes the most general problems with which the philosophy of the Renaissance had to wrestle, as well as the contradictions it had to overcome in itself. A new concept of nature and a new concept of humanity want to arise. But they cannot immediately unite, for they seem to embody not only different but diametrically opposed intellectual tendencies. The more clearly and sharply they are defined, the more unrelenting the conflict between them becomes. Seen from the point of view of 'nature', the world of freedom always remains a mystery, a kind of miracle. This miracle cannot be recognized without losing the specific *sense* of the concept of nature, as the Renaissance conceived of it. For this sense consists in nothing other than in the idea of the unity and the uniqueness of the explanation of nature. Above all, this monism of *method* seems to exclude any dualism in the contents of being. The intellectual and historical world cannot exist aside from the natural world as a 'state within a state', but must be taken back into it and reduced to its basic laws. But the *sense of life* of the Renaissance constantly rebels against this reduction that seems so inevitable from the point of view of the Renaissance *concept of knowledge*. In Pomponazzi's *De incantationibus* we have, in a sense, one pole of this movement; in Pico's polemic against astrology the other. But aside from these, there is no dearth of attempts to create a balance and to mediate between the two polar opposites. Such a balance seemed to offer itself as soon as one referred back to one of the basic motifs of the Renaissance, the motif of 'microcosm'. It seemed to be a middle ground where the Renaissance concept of nature and its concept of *humanitas* met and reciprocally determined each other. As a symbol, as an image of nature, man is as much related to nature as he is *distinct* from it. He embraces nature within himself, without being completely absorbed by it; he contains all its powers, and also adds a specifically new one, the power of 'consciousness'.

With this, a new motif penetrates into astrology and gradually

[61] Ibid., 12. 286: 'Ita est in talibus legibus veluti in generabilibus et corruptibilibus. Videmus enim ista et sua miracula in principio esse debiliora, postea augeri, deinde esse in culmine, deinde labefactari, donec in nihil revertantur. Quare et nunc in fide nostra omnia frigescunt, miracula desinunt, nisi conflicta et simulata; nam propinquus videtur esse finis. . . . Non enim influit aliqua virtus de coelo nisi in quodam tempore, et non ultra: ita est etiam de virtutibus imaginum.'

transforms it from within. The astrological vision of the world had always been bound to the idea of the microcosm. Indeed, astrology seemed to be nothing other than the simple consequence and carrying out of that idea. Ficino's presentation of the system of astrology in his work *De vita triplici* begins with the thought that inasmuch as the world is not an aggregate of dead elements but rather an animate being, there can be in it no mere 'parts' that possess an independent existence next to and outside the whole. What appears externally to be a part of the universe is, when more deeply grasped, to be understood as an *organ* possessing its definite place and its necessary function in the whole complex of life of the cosmos. The unity of this universal complex of activities must necessarily be articulated through a multiplicity of organs. But this differentiation does not signify an isolation of the part from the whole; rather, it signifies an ever new *expression* of the whole, a particular aspect of its self-presentation. On the other hand, the integrity of the cosmos, this *concordia mundi*, would not be possible if a hierarchical *order* of the particular forces did not exist in addition to their mutual *interpenetration*. The activity of the universe not only maintains a definite form but shows throughout a definite *direction*, too. The path leads from above to below, from the intelligible to the sensible realm. From the heavenly spheres above, currents continuously flow down, and these sustain earthly being and always fructify it anew.

This *emanatistic* sort of physics presented by Ficino is still completely in accord with the old presentations, especially with the *Picatrix*, the classical handbook of late Hellenistic magic and astrology.[62] But it cannot be sustained much longer, for its most solid foundation was destroyed when the philosophical thought of the Quattrocento completed its decisive criticism of the concept of the graduated cosmos. In the new cosmology, which begins with Nicholas Cusanus, there is no absolute 'above' or 'below', and, therefore, there can no longer be just one direction of influence. The idea of the world organism is here expanded in such a way that every element in the world may with equal right be considered the central point of the universe (see above, pp. 22ff.) The hitherto one-sided relationship of dependence between the lower and higher world now takes on more and more the form of a relationship of pure *correlation*. And therewith, the type and the foundation of astrological thought must gradually be transformed even where the

---

[62] For details on the Picatrix, see Hellmut Ritter, 'Picatrix, ein arabisches Handbuch hellenistischer Magie', *Vorträge der Bibliothek Warburg*, I (1921/22), pp. 94ff.

general presuppositions of astrology remain in force. In Germany, this transformation takes place most clearly in the philosophy of nature of *Paracelsus*.

Paracelsus rigidly maintains the relationship and the general correspondence between the 'great' and the 'little' worlds. In his view, this constitutes the basis of all medical knowledge. Philosophy is the 'first foundation of medicine', and astronomy is its 'other foundation'. 'First of all, the physician must know that he has to understand man in that other half which concerns the *astronomicam philosophiam*, and that he must transfer man into it and transfer the heavens into man. Otherwise he will be no healer of men, for the heavens contain in their sphere half the body and also half the number of diseases. Who can be a doctor and not be acquainted with the diseases of this other half? . . . What is a doctor who is not expert in cosmography? It is a subject in which he ought to be especially well versed . . . for all knowledge originates in cosmography, and without it nothing happens.' Knowledge of the *harmony* between man and the world constitutes the object of all theoretical medical science. But this harmony is no longer understood in the sense of simple dependence. 'Of two twins who look alike, which has taken after the other, so that he may look like him? Neither. Why then do we call ourselves children of Jupiter and the moon, when actually we are to them as the twins to each other?' To interpret this relationship of similarity as a causal relationship, it would be necessary to move its centre of gravity from 'external' being to 'internal', from the being of things to the being of the 'mind'. In fact, then, it would be more proper to say that Mars takes after man than that man takes after Mars, 'for man is more than Mars and the other planets'.[63]

Here again, we recognize that the tight circle of naturalistic astrological thought is being penetrated by a new and fundamentally foreign idea. The purely causal mode of observation becomes teleological. And through this transformation, all definitions of the relationship between the macrocosm and the microcosm receive, in a sense, a new accent, even though their content may remain the same. The ethical self-consciousness of man opposes the astrological motif of destiny. This curious juxtaposition reveals itself even in the external structure of Paracelsus' medical doctrine and natural philosophy. The *Buch*

---

[63] Karl Sudhoff (ed.), *Theophrast von Hohenheim, gen. Paracelsus, Medizinische natur-wissenschaftliche und philosophische Schriften*, (Munich, 1924), VIII, 68ff., 91ff., 103f., *et passim*.

Paragranum seeks to determine the 'four columns' of medical knowledge. Besides the three columns of *Philosophia*, *Astronomia*, and *Alchimia*, it places *Virtus*: 'let the fourth column be virtue, and let it remain with the doctor unto death, for it integrates and sustains the other three columns'.[64] The Renaissance version of the idea of the microcosm not only permits but even calls for such a μετάβασις εἰς ἄλλο γένος, such a transition from physics to ethics. In this transition, cosmology immediately joined not only with physiology and psychology, but with ethics as well. If this idea requires that the Ego of man be understood by means of the world, it also requires, conversely, that genuine and true knowledge of the world must pass through the medium of self-knowledge. In the work of Paracelsus, both requirements are still immediately juxtaposed. On the one hand, he sees man as nothing but an 'image in a mirror, put together out of the four elements'; and 'just as the image in the mirror can never make his being understandable to anyone, can never let anyone know what he is, because he only stands there as a dead image, so, too, is man in himself; and nothing comes from him, but only from external knowledge, for whose configuration he is the mirror'.[65] And yet this 'dead image' includes in itself all the powers of pure subjectivity, all power of knowing and of willing; and for precisely that reason it becomes, in a new sense, the nucleus and the central point of the world. 'For man's mind is such a great thing that no one can express it. And just as God himself, and prime matter, and the heavens are all three eternal and immutable, so, too, is the mind of man. For that reason, man finds bliss through and with his mind. And if we men rightly knew our minds, nothing would be impossible for us upon this earth.'[66]

Thus, even where the general astrological view of the world remains unquestioned, we can observe the clear attempt to conquer a new place for subjectivity *within* this view of the world itself. Here, Paracelsus is only taking up the thoughts of a man whom he—generally so chary with praise of his predecessors—called 'the best Italian doctor'.[67] Ficino evidently owes the compliment to his three books *De vita*, in which he attempts to present a complete structure of medicine on an astrological basis. Yet in this work Ficino modifies in a peculiar way the doctrine of the stellar radiations that through their influence govern man's entire

---

[64] Paracelsus *Das Buch Paragranum*, loc. cit., p. 56.
[65] Ibid., p. 72.
[66] Paracelsus *Liber de imaginibus* 12. *Opera* ed. Joh. Huser (Basel, 1589ff.), ix. 389f.
[67] Ibid., vii. Paracelsus' letter to Christoph Clauser.

physical and moral state. To be sure, there is a bond, says Ficino, that joins every man to 'his' planet from the moment of his birth; and that bond is indestructible. He constantly complains of the influence exercised upon him and upon the entire course of his life by the evil star ascendant in his horoscope. That ease and certainty in the conduct of life which Jupiter so liberally bestows upon others, is denied to him, the 'child of Saturn'. And yet, this recognition of astrological fate does not imply that he must for ever renounce his independence in the shaping of his own life. The tired and painful resignation with which Ficino surrenders to the will of destiny gradually gives way to a new and freer tone. To be sure, man cannot choose his star, and thus he does not choose his physical and moral nature and his temperament. But he is free to exercise his choice within the limits prescribed by his star. For every constellation contains within its circle a multiplicity of different, even of contradictory possibilities of life, and it leaves the final choice among them open to the will. Saturn is not only the demon of inertia and of unfruitful, self-indulgent melancholy; he is also the genius of intellectual observation and meditation, of intelligence and contemplation. This polarity, which is in the stars themselves, found its recognition and its most clear and visible expression precisely in the system of astrology. Now, it clears the way for the free will of man.

Although the sphere of man's volition and action is rigidly circumscribed, the *direction* of his will is not. This direction may be towards the higher or the lower, towards the intellectual or the sensible powers, all of which are contained as indifferent possibilities within the planet. Depending on whether the direction is towards the one or the other, the resulting forms of life can be not only different but opposed. And, like the form of life, happiness and unhappiness, too, are dependent upon this impulse of the will. The *same* planet can become the friend or foe of man; it can unfold those powers that bring bliss or those that bring evil, according to the inner attitude that man assumes towards the planet. Thus, Saturn becomes the foe of all those who lead vulgar lives; but the friend and protector of those who try to develop the deepest virtues that lie within him—those who surrender themselves with their whole souls to divine contemplation. Ficino retains the idea of 'being children of the planets'; but in addition to this natural descendance from the planets he also recognizes an intellectual descendance —he recognizes the possibility, as has been said, of being a 'planet's child by choice'. A man is born under a certain star and has to conduct

his life under its dominion; but it is nevertheless up to him to decide
which of the powers and possibilities contained by this star he will
develop and bring to full maturity in himself. Indeed, according to the
intellectual tendencies and aspirations that he allows to flourish and
nourishes within him, he can place himself now under the influence of
one star, now under the influence of another.[68]

In this manner, Ficino attempts to build the basic doctrines of astrology into his *theological* system. For him, there is a threefold order of
things, which he calls *providentia, fatum, natura*. Providence is the realm
of the mind, fate the realm of the soul, and nature the realm of the body.
Bodies, in their movements, are subject to the laws of nature; the
'rational' soul, so long as it is bound to the body and dwells within it
as its moving force, is affected by the influences of the world of bodies
and is, therefore, bound by the necessity of this world; the purely
intellectual principle in man, on the other hand, is able to free itself
from all such connections. Thus, although man is subject to this threefold order, he can, nevertheless, transfer himself from the one to the
other. Therein consists what we call the 'freedom' of man. Through
our mind we are subject to providence; through our imagination and
sensibility, to fate; through our particular natures, to the general laws
of the universe. And yet, by virtue of our reason, we are the unfettered
masters of ourselves (*nostri juris*), for we can submit now to the one,
now to the other.[69] With this, even Ficino's astrological system flows
into that realm of thought of the Florentine Academy, the realm in
which resides Pico's oration 'On the Dignity of Man'. In any order of
being, man only possesses the place he *gives* himself in it. Ultimately,
the individual definition of man depends upon his determination, and

---

[68] I shall not discuss in detail here Ficino's *De vita triplici*. Instead, I refer the reader to
Erwin Panofsky and Fritz Saxl, op. cit., p. 32. Appendix IV contains many examples taken
from Ficino's works.

[69] See Ficino *Theologia Platonica* xiii. fol. 289f.: 'Iis quasi tribus rudentibus toti machinae
colligamur, mente mentibus, idolo idolis, natura naturis. . . . Anima per mentem est
supra fatum, in solo providentiae ordine tanquam superna imitans et inferiora una cum
illis gubernans. Ipsa enim tanquam providentiae particeps ad divinae gubernationis
exemplar regit se, domum, civitatem, artes et animalia. Per idolum est in ordine fati
similiter, non sub fato . . . Per naturam quidem corpus est sub fato, anima in fato naturam
movet. Itaque mens super fatum in providentia est, idolum in fato super naturam, natura
sub fato, supra corpus. Sic anima in providentiae, fati, naturae legibus non ut patiens modo
ponitur, sed ut agens. . . . Denique facultas illa rationalis quae proprie est animae verae
natura, non est ad aliquid unum determinata. Nam libero motu sursum deorsumque
vagatur . . . Quamobrem licet per mentem, idolum, naturam quodammodo communi
rerum ordini subnectamur, per mentem providentiae, per idolum fato, per naturam
singularem universae naturae, tamen per rationem nostri juris sumus omnino et tanquam
soluti, modo has partes, modo illas sectamur.'

this is not so much a consequence of his nature as a consequence of his free *action*.

Despite Ficino's constant wrestling with the problem, he leaves us with only an apparent solution, with a compromise; but with Pico's polemic against astrology, we are on completely new ground. With one blow, he destroys the sphere of influence of astrology. That Pico could succeed in such a feat must at first seem a strange historical anomaly, for his entire doctrine, his philosophy of nature as well as his philosophy of religion, is strongly influenced by magical and cabbalistic thought. To this realm belong no fewer than seventy-one of those nine hundred theses, the defence of which marks the beginings of his philsophical career. Pico himself expressly calls them cabbalistic conclusions.[70] It is understandable, therefore, that Franz Boll, one of the leading experts on the history of astrology, should express his amazement at Pico's unconditional rejection of astrology. In Pico's divided nature, Neo-Platonic and Neo-Pythagorean mysticism was even stronger than his acute critical sense. Indeed, he was a representative of nearly *all* the basic philosophical tendencies that had traditionally nourished and strengthened faith in astrology.[71] If we examine the peculiar intellectual nature of Pico's work, we shall find that the success of his solution cannot be ascribed, as Boll ascribes it, to an external cause, i.e., to the staggering impression made by Savonarola's preaching. Rather, there are independent inner forces at work in his thought. Ultimately, these forces are based not on Pico's view of nature, but on his total *ethical* view. In his metaphysics, in his theology, and in his philosophy of nature, Pico is indissolubly bound to the past; but in his ethics he becomes one of the first proclaimers and pioneers of the true spirit of the Renaissance. And his treatise attacking astrology builds upon this foundation of ethical humanity.

The dominant idea of Pico's oration 'On the Dignity of Man' finds its full and pure expression in this treatise. *Nihil magnum in terra praeter hominem, nihil magnum in homine praeter mentem et animum, huc si ascendis, coelum transcendis, si ad corpus inclinas et coelum suspicis, muscam te vides et musca aliquid minus.*[72] These sentences resuscitate and give vigour to a genuinely Platonic motif, for they require a kind of 'transcendence' that recognizes no *spatial* standard because it goes beyond the form of

[70] Joh. Pici Mirandulae Conclusiones DCCCC; see *Opera* fol. 63ff., 107ff.
[71] Fr. Boll, *Sternglaube und Sterndeutung* (2nd ed., Leipzig, 1919), p. 50.
[72] Pico della Mirandola *In astrologiam libri XII* iii. 27. fol. 519.

space. Simple and unassuming as this thought appears, it nevertheless attacks one of the basic presuppositions of the Hellenistic-Neo-Platonic and Christian-medieval view of the world. This view is characterized by its acceptance of the Beyond-motif, the Platonic ἐπέκεινα, in *both* a spatial and an intellectual sense; and by the fact that it inextricably intertwines both meanings. Although Pico is generally unable to free himself from Neo-Platonism and its syncretistic confusion of intellectual motifs, he does succeed here in becoming master of the confusion and in sharply drawing the lines between the motifs. And therewith he succeeds in enriching and in deepening the entire conception of ancient thought. This was the first step on the long and difficult road that was to lead from Plotinus back to Plato, from Hellenistic to classical Greek thought. The first sentences of Pico's work affirm that astrology is completely foreign to genuinely Hellenic, classical Greek thought. Plato and Aristotle never even mention it; and through this contemptuous silence they condemned it more than they would have done with a detailed refutation.[73] To this historical argument are then added the really decisive systematic arguments.

To demonstrate his thesis, Pico must become a critic of *knowledge*; he must distinguish the form of mathematical-physical causality from astrological causality. The latter is based upon the acceptance of occult qualities; the former is satisfied with what we learn from experience, from the empirical view of things. It does not consider the bond that connects the heavens and the earth to be in some mysterious stellar 'effluvia' that seize hold of things related to individual stars through sympathy. Instead of such chimerical inventions, mathematical-physical causality posits only the phenomenon that offers itself to observation and can be empirically attested and demonstrated. In Ficino's astrological physics, all earthly and natural effects are conditioned by stellar radiations, by means of which the all-animating pneuma passes from the higher to the lower world. Pico rejects not only the details but the whole of this explanation; he rejects not only the details but the whole of this explanation; he rejects not only the content, but the method. Phenomena are to be understood by their *own* principles (*ex propriis principiis*), by their proximate and particular causes. However, we need not look far for the proximate cause of whatever the heavens contain of *real* influences; for it consists simply of the powers of *light* and *heat*, that is, of well-known, sensibly demonstrable phenomena. These

[73] Ibid., i. fol. 415.

powers alone constitute the vehicle for all heavenly influences. They are the medium through which things ever so widely separated in space are dynamically conjoined.[74] What Pico is giving here seems to be nothing more than a philosophical theory of nature, such as we shall later encounter in *Telesio* and *Patrizzi*. But if we look at the context of this theory, we recognize that it contains a great deal more. For what he has discovered and definitely established is nothing less than the concept of *vera causa*, which Kepler and Newton will later embrace, and upon which they will base their fundamental conception of induction. Even the direct historical connection seems certain. Even in his first methodological work, his defence of Tycho, Kepler based himself on Pico and on his refutation of astrology. The reasons we think up, in a purely conceptual manner, for the explanation of any phenomenon are not always 'true'; they first become true if they prove to be verifiable, i.e., if they prove to be determinable through observation and measurement. Although Pico does not enunciate this principle with the same clarity as do the founders of the mathematical science of nature, he nevertheless makes constant use of it as an immanent criterion.

With the help of this principle, Pico becomes one of the first to fight against the acceptance of forces localized in mere place. Place is a geometrically ideal, not a physically real determination. Therefore, no concrete, physical effects can derive from place.[75] Astrology misconstrues as real, and adorns with real powers, not only what is ideal, but also what is purely fictitious. The lines the astrologer draws in the heavens for the purpose of orentiation; the individual houses into which he divides the heavens; the whole apparatus of this calculative thought; all this, in astrology, is subject to a curious hypostasis: it becomes a being *sui generis*, endowed with demonic power. But all these constructions disappear as soon as one becomes aware that they have no ontological but merely significative meaning. Like astrology, the genuine science of nature also cannot do without the significative, the operation with pure signs. But in science, these signs are not something final, let alone something independently existent; rather they merely form a medium of thought—they are a stage on the road that leads from the

---

[74] Ibid., iii. 5. fol. 461: 'Praeter communem motus et luminis influentiam nullam vim caelestibus peculiarem inesse.' Cf. especially Lib. iii. 19. fol. 503: 'Pastores, agricolae et ipsum saepe vulgus ineruditum statum aeris praecognoscunt non a stellis, sed ab aeris ipsius dispositione. . . . Quare raro fallunt, aerem scilicet ex aere, sicut medici aegrum ex aegro praejudicantes, hoc est ex propriis principiis, non quod faciunt astrologi, ex remotis et communibus in universalibus, immo, quod pejus est, fictis imaginariis fabulosis.'

[75] Ibid., vi. 3. fol. 584f.

sensible perception of phenomena to the intellectual conception of their causes. But this presupposes more than a vague correspondence, more than a mere analogical relationship between spatially and temporally separated elements of being. To be able to speak of a really causal connection, we must be able to follow step by step and member by member the continuous series of changes which originate at a certain point in the universe; we must be able to set up a unitary law which all these changes obey. If we cannot empirically demonstrate such a form of heavenly influence, it is idle to consider the heavens as a sign of future happenings, and to try to decipher the signs. For the heavens can truly only indicate those things which they can cause: *Non potest coelum ejus rei signum esse, cujus causa non sit*.[76] With these fundamental propositions, Pico goes beyond a mere criticism of astrology; he draws a sharp line separating the magical signs of astrology from the intellectual signs of mathematics and mathematical physics. Now the way is clear for an interpretation of the 'cipher writing' of nature through mathematical-physical symbols which are, at the same time, conceived of *as symbols*. They no longer confront the mind as strange powers but as its own creations.

The ultimate roots of Pico's criticism of astrology do not, however, lie in such logical or epistemological considerations. The pathos that inspires his work against astrology is not so much an intellectual as an ethical pathos. Time after time, he opposes the basic vision of his ethical spiritualism to astrology. To accept astrology means to invert not so much the order of being as the order of *value*—it means making of 'matter' the master of spirit. To be sure, this objection seems to be invalid if we consider astrology in its basic form and in its historical origin. This basic form considers the heavenly bodies not as something merely material, as cosmic masses but rather as masses animated by spiritual principles, i.e., by intelligences that give them life and determine their course. If human destiny is made subject to the heavens, the being of man is not tied and bound to material principle; rather, a definite place is assigned to man's being in the hierarchy of *intelligible* forces that pervade the universe. Just at this point we feel the force of Pico's interpretation and definition of the concept of freedom, given in his oration *De dignitate hominis*. This concept of freedom becomes

---

[76] Ibid., iv. 12. fol. 543: 'Non potest igitur coelum significare inferiora, nisi quatenus causa effectum indicat suum, quare qui causam quidem non esse victi ratione fatentur, signum tamen esse contendunt, hi vocem suam ignorant.'

invalid if the mind of man is subjected not only to the causality of nature, but to any kind of determination not established by the mind. Man asserts his pre-eminence over all other natural beings, and even in the 'realm of spirits' and of intelligences; and this pre-eminence is based on the fact that man does not receive his being as something finished but that he *forms* it by virtue of his free will. This formation excludes the possibility of any determination from without, be it 'material' or 'spiritual'. Through this faith in the pure, creative power of man and in the autonomy of his creative power, through this purely humanistic faith, Pico conquers astrology.

The most telling proofs for his thesis are to be found in his opposition of the world of human culture to the world of astrology. The world of human culture is not a product of cosmic forces but a work of genius. In genius we seem to encounter, to be sure, an 'irrational' force, one not reducible to its elements and its causal origins. And the recognition of genius brings us again to a limit of understanding. But *this* limit is of a human, not of a mystical sort. We may rest at it, for when we have penetrated to it, we have traversed the whole sphere of human being and human determination. We stand before those ultimate reasons which are only conceivable by us because they express our own being. Any attempt to connect these reasons to something anterior to them, any attempt to 'explain' them through cosmic forces and influences ends in self-deception. In the work of the great thinkers, statesmen, and artists, we must recognize and venerate not the power of the stars but the power of humanity. Not their better star, but their better *Ingenium* raised Aristotle and Alexander above their contemporaries and gave them their significance and their power. And the *Ingenium* is traceable not to the star, not to some bodily cause, but immediately to God as the source and origin of all spiritual being. The wonders of the mind are greater than those of the heavens; to try to derive the former from the latter means not to understand them but to deny and to debase them.[77]

[77] Ibid., iii. 27. fol. 517ff.: 'Admiraris in Aristotele consummatam scientiam rerum naturalium, ego tecum pariter admiror. Causa coelum est, inquis, et constellatio, sub qua natus est; non accedo, non tam vulgata ratione, quod nati eodem astro multi non fuerunt Aristoteles, quam quod praeter coelum, sub quo tanquam causa universali et Boetiae sues et philosophi . . . pariter germinant, causae proximae sunt Aristoteli propriae et peculiares, ad quas singularem ejus profectum referamus. Primum utique . . . sortitus est animam bonam, et hanc utique non a coelo, siquidem immortalis et incorporeus animus, quod ipse demonstravit nec astrologi negant. Tum sortitus est corpus idoneum, ut tali animae famularetur, nec hoc etiam a coelo, nisi tanquam a communi causa, sed a parentibus. Elegit philosophari. Hoc et principiorum opus quae diximus, hoc est animi et corporis, et

Thus, the astrological vision of the world was overcome, essentially, neither by empirical and scientific reasons, nor by new methods of observation and of mathematical calculation. The decisive blow had fallen before these methods were completely perfected. The agent of liberation was not the new view of nature but the new view of the value of humanity. The power of *Fortuna* is confronted with the power of *Virtus*; destiny is confronted with the self-confident and self-trusting will. What may be really and truly called the destiny of man does not flow to him from above, from the stars, but rather arises from the ultimate depths of his innermost self. We ourselves make of Fortune a goddess and raise her to the heavens; whereas, in truth, destiny is the daughter of the soul: *sors animae filia.*[78]

Kepler himself took up Pico's idea and developed it further. And that is characteristic for the manner in which the individual motifs derived from various spheres of thought interpenetrate and mutually fructify each other in the philosophy of the Renaissance. As an investigator of nature, as a mathematician, and as an astronomer, Kepler was by no means completely outside the ambit of astrology; only gradually did he liberate himself from it. And in this process of liberation, we can again see all those mediations and transitions that we observed within the development of the philosophy of the Renaissance. The process was impeded and held back—and not exclusively by those reasons of a social and economic nature which even in Kepler's times required a personal union between astronomy and astrology. Kepler spoke of the 'foolish daughter' astrology, who had to support that most wise but poor mother astronomy.[79] But his pronouncements on astrology do not always show the same ironical and serene superiority. In a work of the year 1623 he still attributed to the conjunctions of the planets, if not

sui arbitrii fuit; profecit in philosophia, hic arrepti propositi et suae industriae fructus. . . . At profecit plus longe quam coaetanei et quam discipuli. Sortitus erat non astrum melius, sed ingenium melius: nec ingenium ab astro, siquidem incorporale, sed a Deo, sicut corpus a patre, non a coelo . . . Quod vero ad id attinet, quod principaliter hic tractatur, nego quicquam in terris adeo magnum fieri vel videri, ut autorem coelum mereatur. Nam miracula quidem animi (ut diximus) coelo majora sunt, fortunae vero et corporis, utcumque maxima sint, coelo collata minima deprehenduntur.'

[78] Ibid., iv. 4. fol. 531.
[79] Johannes Kepler *De stella nova in pede Serpentarii* (1606), *Opera*, ii. 656f.: 'Quod astrologica attinet, e quidem fateor, virum illum (Fabricium) auctoritati veterum et cupiditati praedictionum, ubi haec duo conspirant, alicubi succumbere et quodam quasi enthusiasmo praeter rationem abripi: verum ista cum ingenti doctorum virorum turba communia habet. Quo nomine vel solo veniam meretur. Quid ringeris, delicatule philosophe, si matrem sapientissimam sed pauperem stulta filia, qualis tibi videtur, naeniis suis sustentat et alit.'

a direct influence upon the lower world, at least a 'spur and a stimulus'. And from this idea of *causality* which, to be sure, is only mediate, he then returns to the idea of simple 'correspondence'; the relationship between 'cause' and 'effect' is replaced by a relationship of correlation. The heavens do not originate any new action; but they do 'beat the drum' for those which occur for natural reasons, from physical causes, human emotions and passions.[80] But Kepler takes the really decisive argument against astrology from the world of intellectual creation, not from natural phenomena. His awareness of the aboriginal power of the mind and the power of genius brings him to the final decision. Neither Mercury nor Mars, he says in the *Harmonia mundi*, but Copernicus and Tycho Brahe were his stars. It would be futile for an astrologer to seek in his horoscope the reasons for his discovery, in the year 1596, of the proportions between the distances of the planets or the reasons for his discovery of the laws of planetary motion in 1604 and in 1618. *Non influxerunt ista cum charactere coeli in flammulam illam facultatis vitalis nuper incensae inque actum productae, sed partim intus in penitissima animae essentia latebant secundum Platonicam doctrinam . . . partim alia via per oculos nimirum, introrsum recepta sunt; sola et unica thematis genethliaci opera fuit ista, quod et emunxit illos ingenii judiciique igniculos et instigavit animum ad laborem indefessum auxitque desiderium sciendi; breviter: non inspiravit animum, non ullam dictarum hic facultatum, sed excivit.*[81] The idea of mutual determination, which had already been established in Pico's work against astrology, received its confirmation here. The problem of freedom is closely allied to the problem of knowledge; the conception of freedom determines that of knowledge, just as, conversely, the latter determines the former. The spontaneity and productivity of knowledge finally become the seal of the conviction of human freedom and human creativity.

Earlier, we pointed to the progressive unfolding of the Prometheus myth in Renaissance thought, and to its significance in the gradual transformation of the medieval-theological view of the world. Now it becomes clear that the very same motif supplies the vital force in the battle against astrology and against the Weltanschauung of late antiquity, and finally decides the victory over them. In his *Spaccio della bestia trionfante*, Giordano Bruno created the characteristic symbol for

---

[80] Cf. Johannes Kepler, 'Discurs von der grossen Conjunction und allerlei Vaticiniis über das 1623 Jahr', *Opera* vii. 697ff., especially 706f.
[81] Johannes Kepler, 'Harmonice mundi' iv. 7, *Opera* v. 262f.

this whole intellectual movement. To man, who is subject to illusions and superstition, the constellations of the zodiac appear to be the highest masters of his fate. These constellations must be toppled and replaced by other powers. A new moral philosophy must be established—one which presents the object purely according to the 'inner light' that resides in the watchtower, or at the helm of our soul. This principle of conscience and of consciousness, the principle of 'sinderesis', as Bruno calls it,[82] replaces the unconsciously active, cosmic-demonic forces. 'Let us put in order the heaven that intellectually lies within us (*che intellettualmente è dentro di noi*)—and then that visible heaven that presents itself bodily to your eyes. Let us remove from the heaven of our mind the bear of roughness, the arrow of envy, the foal of levity, the dog of evil calumny, the bitch of flattery; let us ban the Hercules of violence, the lyre of conspiracy . . . the Cepheus of hard-heartedness. When we have thus cleansed our house and created our heaven anew, then, too, shall reign new constellations, new influences and powers and new destinies. Everything depends upon this higher world, and out of contradictory causes must necessarily flow contradictory effects. Oh we happy ones, we truly blissful ones, if we only rightly cultivate our minds and our thoughts. If we want to change our condition ,we change our habits; if we want the former to become good and better, the latter should not become worse. If we purify the drive within us, then it will not be hard to pass from this transformation in the inner world to the reformation of the sensible and outer world.' (purghiamo l'interiore affetto: atteso che dall' informatione di questo mondo interno non sarà difficile di far progresso alla riformatione di questo sensibile et esterno.)[83] There is a decidedly ethical stand even in the natural philosophy and cosmology of Bruno, a thinker whom we are accustomed to considering the typical representative of the 'naturalistic' tendencies of the Renaissance. Through the heroic passion that ignites within him, man becomes equal to nature and able to comprehend its infinity and its incommensurability.

[82] Giordano Bruno, *Lo spaccio della bestia trionfante, Opere ital.* 412.
[83] Ibid., 439f.

CHAPTER FOUR

THE SUBJECT-OBJECT PROBLEM IN THE
PHILOSOPHY OF THE RENAISSANCE

I

THE relationship of the Renaissance to the Middle Ages and to antiquity has two sides and two meanings; and nowhere does this duality show itself more clearly than in the Renaissance position on the problem of self-consciousness. All the intellectual currents that nourish the Renaissance flow into this central problem. But now, new systematic questions suddenly emerge from the manifold and contradictory historical conditions. The conscious formulation of these questions is, of course, one of the latest products of Renaissance philosophy, first attained by Descartes—indeed, in a certain sense, first by Leibniz. Descartes discovered and defined the new 'Archimedian' point from which the conceptual world of scholastic philosophy could be raised out of its hinges. And thus we date the beginning of modern philosophy from Descartes' principle of the *Cogito*. This beginning appears not to have been historically mediated; it rests, as Descartes himself felt and said, upon a free act of the mind. With one blow, with an independent, unique decision, the mind rejects the whole of the past and must now go along the new path towards thoughtful reflection upon itself. This is not a question of a gradual evolution but of a genuine 'revolution in the mode of thought'. And the significance of this revolution is by no means lessened if we trace the development and the steady growth of the intellectual and the general forces which finally gave it birth.

At first, these forces do not constitute a unity, nor do they show any rigid organization. They rather work against than with one another; they seem to have completely different points of departure and to be pursuing different objectives. Nevertheless, they all have one negative result in common: they loosen up, so to speak, the earth out of which will come forth the new, specifically modern view of the relationship of 'subject' and 'object'. There is scarcely a single branch of Renaissance philosophy that did not participate in this work—not only metaphysics but natural philosophy and empirical knowledge of nature; not only psychology but ethics and aesthetics. In this work, even the differences between the various schools are harmonized. The movement that emerged from Platonism converges at this point with the movement that started with a renewed and reformed Aristotelianism. Both the historical and the systematic consciousness of the epoch are placed before the same basic questions and forced to make certain definite decisions.

One of the fundamental accomplishments of Greek philosophy was that it was the first to succeed in removing the concept of self-consciousness and the concept of the world from the sphere of mythical thought. Both tasks reciprocally condition each other, for it is precisely the new image of the cosmos moulded by Greek thought that paves the way for a new view of the Ego. The view of the Ego seemed to be even more deeply and more tightly interlaced with mythical constitutive elements and presuppositions than the view of the world of things. In Plato himself, the problem of the Ego is indissolubly bound to the problem of the soul. So much so that even Plato's philosophical language knows no other terms for this problem than those that in some way go back to the basic meaning of ψυχή. In Plato's thought, this relationship expresses itself in a constant tension, dominating his whole doctrine from beginning to end. Even the new insights which Plato has gained as a *dialectician* by means of ever further analysis and of ever deeper foundation of knowledge must dress themselves in the language of his metaphysical psychology. The conceptual determination of the *a priori* and the demonstration of the reasons for its necessity takes place in the form of the Platonic *anamnesis* doctrine. The distinction of degrees and kinds of certainty seeks its support in the separation of different parts of the soul. The high point of Platonic speculation, marked by Plato's late dialogues, certainly seems to have attained the sure and sharp delineation of the individual problems. In the *Theaetetus* he still defines the unity of consciousness as the unity of the soul, as ἕν τι ψυχῆς; but it is a concept of the soul that has rejected all primitive and mythical constitutive elements, and all recollections of the Orphic concept of the soul and faith in the soul. Now it stands, so to speak, only as a symbol for the continuous process and function of unification that pure thought exercises upon the contents of perception. Nevertheless, the polarity of motifs and of representational means continue to exist.

Plato's philosophy recognizes two contrary forms of representation, one of which is valid for the realm of being and the other for the realm of becoming. Strict knowledge is only possihle of the always-being, i.e., of that which remains identical with itself and always behaves in the same way. That which is becoming, that which is temporally conditioned and changeable from moment to moment, is not susceptible of apprehension through such knowledge. It can only be described, if at all, in the language of myth. One might well ask which means of knowledge, according to this fundamental distinction in the Platonic theory of knowledge, are proper and adequate for the conception and representation of the soul; but the question has no clear answer. For the soul breaks through the original Platonic separation; it belongs to the realm of being as well as the realm of becoming; and in a certain sense it belongs to neither. It is an in-between, a hybrid nature, incapable of renouncing either the pure being of the idea or the world of appearances and of becoming. In keeping with its nature, every human soul has contemplated being, and is capable of apprehending pure relationships of being; but at the same time each soul also bears within it the direction, the tendency, the striving towards sensible multiplicity and toward sensible becoming. Precisely this double *movement* expresses the constitution and the true substance of the soul. Thus it remains an 'intermediary' between becoming and being, between appearance and idea. It is *related* to both poles, to being and becoming, to the identical and the different, without ever being completely absorbed by, or even bound to, the one or the other. Whether it be in relation to the pure idea or in relation to phenomena, i.e., to the contents of sensual perception, the soul remains something independent unto itself. As the 'subject' of thought and of perception, it does not coincide with the *content* of what is thought or perceived. To be sure, the mythical language of the Platonic *Timaeus* blurs this distinction. Since this mythical language knows only the one dimension of temporal occurrence, it must convert all qualitative differences to differences of temporal origin and of temporal creation. Thus the soul becomes a mixed being in whom the creator, the demiurge, has impressed and, so to speak, fused the contrary natures of the same and of the different, of the ταὐτὸν and the θάτερον. In keeping with the nature and peculiarity of mythical expression, ideal differences of significance become converted into ontological differences of being and of origin. And it was essentially in this form that the Platonic doctrine of the soul influenced posterity. Throughout the

whole Middle Ages, the *Timaeus* was considered one of the fundamental works of philosophy. In the translation of Chalcidius, it was
practically the only Platonic dialogue known and read. Thus, in the
Middle Ages, the Platonic-Socratic concept of the soul, which conceives of the soul as the *principle* of subjectivity, could only be thought
of in a mythical guise and in a mythical objectification.

This process of objectification had already begun in ancient thought
itself. Aristotle considers the soul the *form* of the body; and as such, it is
also the active force and the power of movement immanent in the
body. The soul is the final cause that expresses the ideal 'determination'
of the body; and it is the moving force by means of which the body is
led to this determination. In this conception of it as the 'entelechy' of
the body, the soul again becomes a pure potency of nature, a force of
organic life and of organic structure. Indeed, at a decisive point in his
doctrine, Aristotle sees himself forced to modify and amplify his original
concept of the soul. For although this concept may encompass and explain the phenomena of *life*, it does not suffice to encompass all the
determinations of *knowledge*. In its highest and purest form, knowledge
is no longer related to the individual, but to the general; it is not related
to a 'material', but to a purely intelligible content. Therefore, the power
of the soul, which realizes this knowledge in itself, must be of the same
nature as the object; it must be thought of as free and as unmixed with
any corporeality (χωριστός καί ἀμιγής). But this distinction is again
translated immediately into metaphysical-ontological terms. The
Aristotelian νοῦς, which is the subject of pure thought and of thought
about 'eternal truths', is also an objective 'intellectual being'; just as the
soul, as the form of the organic body, is a natural being. This latter is
a moving force, whereas the other is a thinking force that enters into
men from without (θύραθεν).

Neo-Platonism accepts this definition. But at the same time it
divests the thinking force of that specific and special character it had in
Aristotle. It accomplishes this by again placing the thinking force in
the general hierarchy of powers leading down from the one to the
many, from the intelligible to the sensible, and by fixing its definite
position within that hierarchy. As Neo-Platonism develops this position
further, a host of half-divine, half-demonic intermediate beings press
themselves between the thinking power as such and the form in which
it appears in man as a concrete individual. This development terminated
and found its consequential systematic formulation in the Arabic

philosophy of the Middle Ages, especially in the Averroistic doctrines. By letting the soul re-enter completely into the sphere of objective-metaphysical forces, Averroism abandons not only the principle of subjectivity but the principle of individuality as well. The basic force of thought is placed above every form of individuation; for the intellect as such is considered to be not something manifoldly divided but an absolute unity. As a mere living entity, the Ego is relegated to a state of isolation. The act of thought consists in abandoning and overcoming this isolation and fusing with the One Absolute Intellect, the *intellectus agens*. The possibility of this fusion is necessary not only to *mysticism*, but to *logic* as well; for this fusion alone seems capable of really explaining the process of thought and of establishing its necessary validity. The true subject of thought is not the individual, the 'self'. Rather, it is a non-personal, substantial being common to all thinking beings; one whose connection with the individual Ego is external and accidental.

At this point, the logical-metaphysical system developed out of the interpenetration of Aristotelianism and Neo-Platonism comes into open conflict with the system of *faith*, to which it had hitherto seemed to give staunch support. The *Christian* faith, at least, cannot abandon the principle of 'subjectivism', the principle of the independence and *personal value* of the individual soul, without, at the same time, being unfaithful to its own basic religious assumptions. The great Christian thinkers of the thirteenth century perceived this conflict and, to escape it, continually fought against the systematic conclusions drawn by Averroism. Thomas Aquinas dedicated a whole work to its refutation (*De unitate intellectus contra Averroistas*). The basic thought of this work consists in the affirmation that the Averroistic thesis, while claiming to *explain* thought, actually *destroys* it. One cannot ask what the intellect is in itself, what it is according to its general nature without exercising the *function* of thought. But this function itself we can know empirically only in individual form, in relation to a thinking *self*. To exclude this self means to annihilate the *fact* upon which any theory of knowledge must base itself. Moreover, Averroism threatens not only the theory of knowledge, it threatens even more the religious consciousness of self in its peculiarity and in its innermost core. For this consciousness requires that both members of the basic religious relationship. God and the self, retain their independence. We can grasp and adopt the universal, absolute content of faith only if we place ourselves at the centre of religious *life*. In this connection, personality is no merely accidental barrier or limitation but rather functions within that life as its indispensable constitutive principle.

This conclusion had already been drawn in all its sharpness by *Augustine*, the first great systematizer of Christianity. It is well known that his *religious* subjectivism led him directly to those basic conclusions that Descartes later formulated as a *logician* and as a critic of knowledge. His religious idealism and Descartes' logical idealism rest upon one and the same principle of interiorization, of reflection upon oneself. *Noli foras ire, in te ipsum redi: in interiore homine habitat veritas.* Actual being, knowing, willing, the actual *esse, nosse, velle* constitute the unshakable point of departure for all theory; for the mind knows nothing better than what is present in it, and nothing is more present in it than itself.[1] These sentences establish the primacy of the religious experience above all the dogmatic conclusions of a metaphysical doctrine of the soul and of God. The Ego is no longer placed in a constructed schema of objective knowledge, because such mediate determination cannot arrive at the specific nature and the specific value of the Ego, which is a value completely *sui generis*.

To understand the transformation that takes place with the beginning of the philosophy of the Renaissance, we must keep in mind this opposition, this tension, which already existed in the medieval system of life and learning. Despite all the attacks it had suffered in the classical systems of Scholasticism, the theoretical foundation of Averroism seemed to be completely unshaken in the 14th and 15th centuries. For a long time, it was the reigning doctrine in the Italian universities. In the actual academic citadel of Scholastic studies, in Padua, Averroistic doctrine maintained itself from the first half of the fourteenth century on into the sixteenth and seventeenth centuries.[2] But gradually, a counter movement emerges ever more clearly. Characteristically, this counter movement is by no means restricted to the environs of the school, but rather receives its strongest impulses from other quarters. The men of the new humanistic ideal of culture and of personality are the first to sound the call to battle against Averroism. Here, too, Petrarch leads the way. His passionate, lifelong feud against Averroism is not free of theoretical misunderstandings; but that detracts little from its value, for the entire question concerns something more than mere

[1] Augustinus *De trinitate* xiv. 7, *De vera religione* 29. *et passim*.
[2] For details cf. Ernest Renan, *Averroes et l'Averroisme* (3rd ed.: Paris, 1866).

speculative, theoretical discussion. Here, we have a highly gifted personality; by right of its original feeling for life, it rebels against conclusions that threaten to limit or to weaken this right. The artist and virtuoso who rediscovered the inexhaustible wealth and value of 'individuality' now sets up his defences against a philosophy that considers individuality to be something merely casual, something purely 'accidental'. And Augustine becomes his guide in this battle.

Petrarch was one of the first of those who did not concern themselves with the merely objective content of historical creations. Instead he looked behind these creations to the lives of the creators, to feel them and re-live them. By virtue of this gift, he leaps over the centuries and comes into direct contact with Augustine. The lyrical genius of individuality takes fire at the religious genius of individuality; in the characteristic form of Petrarch's mysticism, religion and poetry merge and flow together. Unlike Averroistic mysticism, his is not cosmologically but purely psychologically oriented. And though it does seek and pine for the union of the soul with God, this union is nevertheless not the only and essential goal at which to rest. Rather, his mysticism immerses itself time and again in contemplation of the inner mobility of the Ego, to admire it in its multiplicity, and to enjoy it precisely in its contradictions. Thus we can understand why Petrarch, in his fight against Averroism, always stresses his faith. We can also understand that in this battle, he considers himself to be a completely orthodox Christian defending the simplicity of faith against the pretensions of human reason. And yet, Petrarch's Christianity bears a completely personal stamp, more aesthetic than religious. If Averroism was to be mastered through *philosophical* thought, it would be necessary to take a different tack. Instead of immersing itself in the feeling and enjoyment of individuality, philosophical thought would have to try to set up a new and deeper *principle* for it. We saw such a principle attained for the first time in Cusanus' doctrine.

The Averroism of the Paduan School was at the high point of its development just at the time Cusanus was studying there. But there is nothing to show that he was intellectually influenced by it in any important way. In his later systematic works, he expressly fought against its basic doctrines, using arguments derived not so much from his metaphysics as from his theory of knowledge. His theory of knowledge recognizes no absolute separation between the realm of sense and that of intellect. Although the sensible and the intellectual are opposed to each other, the intellect *needs* precisely this opposition and this resistance of sensual perception, for they are the necessary means through which the intellect attains its own fulfilment and its full actuality (see above, pp. 42f.). Thus no intellectual function can conceivably exist dissociated from the realm of sensible material. To become effective, the mind requires a body corresponding and 'adequate' to it. For this reason, furthermore, the differentiation and the individualization of the act of thought must be in harmony with the organization of the body. 'The vision of *your* eye cannot be the vision of any other eye, even if it could be detached from your eye and connected to the eye of another, for it would not find in the other eye the measure it had in yours.— And the power of distinction in *your* vision cannot be the power of distinction in someone else's vision. So, too, *one* intellect cannot think in all men.'

Here a thought emerges that will only find its complete systematic development and articulation in Leibniz. The sensible and corporeal is not a merely indifferent, undifferentiated *sub-stratum* for the pure act of thought. Neither is it a mere *organ* that simply exists like a dead tool outside the pure act of thought. Rather, the power and the achievement of this act consist in its ability to grasp as such the differences that lie in the sensible world and to completely represent them within itself. Thus, the *principium individuationis* cannot be sought in the mere 'matter' of thought but must be based in its pure *form*. As the active power of thought, the soul is not just enclosed in the body, as in some external lodging place; rather, it expresses with more or less clarity all the differences that are in the body, and all the changes that are taking place within it. Thus, between the soul and the body there exists not only a relationship of connection but also of complete 'concinnity', of continuous proportion, as Cusanus calls it.[3] A completely opposite conception is offered in the doctrines of Averroes and of certain Neo-Platonists. But the *Renaissance* Neo-Platonism of the Florentine Academy quite characteristically sides completely with Cusanus in this decisive problem. In the *Theologia Platonica* as well as in his letters *Ficino* constantly combats the doctrine of the unicity of the

---

[3] Cusanus *Idiota* iii, 'De mente', 12. fol. 167f.: 'Sicut enim visus oculi tui non posset esse visus cujuscuncque alterius, etiam si a tuo oculo separaretur et alterius oculo jungeretur, quia proportionem suam, quam in oculo tuo reperit, in alterius oculo reperire nequiret: sic nec discretio, quae est in visu tuo, posset esse discretio in visu alterius. Ita nec intellectus discretionis illius posset esse intellectus discretionis alterius. Unde hoc nequaquam possibile arbitror unum esse intellectum in omnibus hominibus.'

'active intellect'. In this battle, he, too, bases himself upon immediate experience which always shows us our Ego and our thought in individual form. No essential difference can exist, however, between the *nature* of the self and that as which it is *given* to us in our immediate consciousness, *quid enim menti naturalius, quam sui ipsius cognitio?*[4]

This process seeks to work out the *theoretical* foundations and conditions of 'subjectivity'. But beside it, there is another process, one that makes clear to us for the first time the actual forces that, in the final analysis, determine and dominate this whole intellectual movement. Ficino builds his doctrine of the soul and his doctrine of individual immortality not so much upon his view of human knowledge as upon his view of human *will*. The actual pivot of Ficino's psychology is the doctrine of *Eros*. It becomes the central point of all the philosophical efforts of the Florentine Academy. As Cristoforo Landino's *Disputationes Camaldulenses* reveal, the doctrine of Eros constituted the eternal, inexhaustible topic of academic conversation.[5] This central theme is the source of the entire influence exercised by the Academy on the intellectual life, on the literature, and on the visual plastic arts of the Quattrocento. At the same time, a constant reciprocal action is taking place here. On the one hand, Girolamo Benivieni, in his *Canzone dell'amor celeste e divino*, gives poetic form to the basic thoughts in Ficino's theory of love; on the other hand, Pico della Mirandola reconducts these thoughts back into the purely philosophical sphere through his commentary on Benivieni's poem.[6] Ficino and Pico seem to want only to reproduce, as faithfully as possible, the *Platonic* theory of Eros. Both thinkers base themselves directly upon Plato's *Symposium*, to which Ficino wrote a very detailed commentary. And yet, perhaps nowhere does the particularity and the special character of the 'Christian' Platonism of the Florentine Academy emerge as clearly as it does in this question.

In a letter to Luca Controni, accompanying his *De Christiana Religione* and the commentary on the Symposium, Ficino writes: *Mitto ad te amorem, quem promiseram. Mitto etiam religionem ut agnoscas et amorem meum religiosum esse et religionem amatoriam.*[7] Ficino's doctrine of Eros is the point at which his psychology and his theology meet, and at

---

[4] Ficino *Epistolae* i. fol. 628.
[5] For the value of Landino's *Disputationes Camaldulenses* as a documentary source for the history of the Florentine Academy, cf. especially Arnaldo della Torre, *Storia dell'Accademia platonica di Firenze* (Florence, 1902), pp. 579ff.
[6] Pico della Mirandola *Opera* fol. 734ff.   [7] Ficino *Epistolae* i. fol. 632.

which they indissolubly fuse with each other. In Plato, too, Eros belongs to a middle realm of being. He stands between the divine and the human, between the intelligible and the sensible worlds, and he must relate and join them to each other. He can only effectuate this union insofar as he himself does not belong exclusively to either world. Eros is neither fullness nor want, neither knowing nor ignorant, neither immortal nor mortal; rather, his 'demonic' nature is a mixture of all these opposites. This contradictory nature of Eros constitutes the truly active moment of the Platonic cosmos. A dynamic motif penetrates the static complex of the universe. The world of appearance and the world of love no longer stand simply opposed to each other; rather, the appearance itself 'strives' for the idea (ὀρέγεται τοῦ ὄντος). This striving is the basic force from which all becoming emerges; this inner insufficiency represents the eternally animating 'unrest' that prescribes a certain direction to all occurrences—the direction towards the immutable being of the idea. But in the Platonic system, this direction is not reversible. There is, indeed, a 'becoming towards being', a γένεσις εἰς οὐσίαν: but there is no opposite action of being towards becoming, i.e., from the idea to the appearance. The idea of χωρισμός is retained in all its rigour. The idea of the good is a 'cause' of becoming only in the sense that it represents its aim and its end; not in the sense that it interferes as a motive force in the workings of empirical-sensible reality. Later, in the Neo-Platonic system, this methodological relationship will be metaphysically interpreted and hypostatized. In Neo-Platonism, too, the drive to return to the first cause is a property of all conditioned and derivative being. But this striving of the conditioned for the unconditioned has no corresponding counterpart in the latter. The super-being and the super-one of Neo-Platonism also stands 'above life' (ὑπὲρ τὸ ζῆν). The pure *objectivity* of the absolute stands, as such, above the sphere of subjective consciousness, no matter whether this be conceived of as practical or as theoretical consciousness. For knowledge, like striving, is a property foreign to the absolute. All knowledge presupposes a relationship to something else; but the pure autarchy of the absolute, its being closed within itself, would exclude the possibility of such a relationship.[8]

Ficino's theory of love goes beyond this doctrine in that it conceives of the process of love as a completely *reciprocal* process. Man's striving towards God, represented in Eros, would not be possible without a

---

[8] Cf. especially, Plotinus *Ennead* vi. 7. 35; vi. 7. 41. *et passim.*

counter-striving of God towards man. Thus, Ficino resuscitates the basic notion of *Christian mysticism* and thereby gives his Neo-Platonism a new stamp. God, the absolute objective being, is tied to subjectivity, and bound to it as a correlate and necessary counterpart; just as all subjectivity is related and directed towards him. Love itself cannot be realized in any but this double form. It is as much the drive of the higher for the lower, of the intelligible for the sensual, as it is the yearning of the lower for the higher. In a free act of love, God turns towards the world; in a free act of his grace, He redeems man and the world; and the same double direction of striving is essential to all intelligences. 'It is the peculiarity of all divine spirits that, while they contemplate the higher, they do not cease to look at the lower and to care for it. It is also characteristic of our soul that it is concerned not only for its own body but for the bodies of all earthly things and for the earth itself, to cultivate them and further them.' This cultivation, this 'culture' of the sensible world constitutes a basic moment and a basic task of the spirit.

This conception of the Eros doctrine sheds new light upon the problem of *theodicy* with which Neo-Platonism constantly wrestled. Only now does a theodicy in the strict sense become possible. For matter is no longer conceived of as the mere opposite of form and, therefore, as 'evil' pure and simple; instead, matter is that with which all activity of the form must begin and through which the form must realize itself. Eros has become in a true sense the 'bond of the world'. He overcomes all the diversity of the world's various elements and realms by taking every one of them into his domain. He reconciles and resolves the *substantial* diversity of the elements of being by letting them be recognized as subjects and as central points of one and the same *dynamic function*. The spirit descends to the sensible and corporeal through love, and love raises it again out of this realm. But in both movements the spirit is not following some strange impulse or some fatalistic compulsion; rather, it is following its own free decision. *Animus nunquam cogitur aliunde, sed amore se mergit in corpus, amore se mergit e corpore.*[9] Here, we

[9] Ficino *Theologia Platonica* xvi. 7. fol. 382. Giuseppe Saitta, *La filosofia di Marsilio Ficino* (Messina, 1923), has very rightly emphasized this important moment in Ficino's theory of love (pp. 217ff.). But on this point, as on many others, Saitta has considerably exaggerated Ficino's originality when compared to Cusanus. 'Ciò che differenzia il Ficino dai filosofi precedenti, compreso il Cusano, è l'intuizione travolgente dell'amore come spiegamento assoluto, infinito di libertà. . . . Il vero mistico s'appunta nella assoluta indistinzione o indifferenza, laddove il pensiero di Ficino respira nell'atmosfera sana della libertà come continua differenziazione.' Ibid., p. 256.) But Cusanus' concept of creation and his concept of divine love moved precisely in this 'atmosphere of freedom'. Cf. e.g., *De beryllo*, chap. xxiii, fol. 275: 'Ad omnem essendi modum sufficit abunde primum principium

have a spiritual circle, a *circuitus spiritualis*, that needs no external purpose, because it has its aim and its limit within itself, and because it
contains within itself both the principle of movement and the principle
of rest.[10]

The philosophy of the Renaissance took up these ideas in Ficino's
doctrine of love and sought to develop them in natural philosophy and
ethics, and in the theory of art and the theory of knowledge. So far as
the doctrine of knowledge is concerned, the Neo-Platonic, mystical
literature of the Middle Ages had already bound knowledge and love
indissolubly to each other. The mind cannot turn to consider any object
in a purely theoretical fashion unless it be driven to it by an act of love.
In Renaissance philosophy, this doctrine is again taken up and systematically developed by *Patrizzi*. The act of knowledge and the act of love
have one and the same goal, for both strive to overcome the separation
in the elements of being and return to the point of their original unity.
Knowledge is nothing but a specific stage on this road back. It is a form
of striving, for the 'intention' towards its object is essential to all knowledge (*intensio cognoscentis in cognoscibile*). The highest intellect became an
intellect, a thinking consciousness, only when it was moved by love to
divide itself in two, and to confront itself with a world of objects of
knowledge as objects of contemplation. But the act of knowledge that
initiates this division, this sacrifice of the original unity for multiplicity,
is also capable of *overcoming* it. For to know an object means to negate
the distance between it and consciousness; it means, in a certain sense,
to become *one* with the object: *cognitio nihil est aliud, quam Coitio quaedam
cum suo cognobili*.[11]

Ficino's version of the doctrine of Eros had an even stronger and
deeper influence on the Renaissance view of the essence and meaning of
art than it did on the theory of *knowledge*. Many of the great artists of
the Renaissance embraced the basic speculative doctrines of the Floren-

---

unitrinum: licet sit absolutum et superexaltatum, cum non sit principium contractum, ut
natura, quae ex necessitate operatur, sed sit principium ipsius naturae. Et ita supernaturale,
liberum, quod voluntate creat omnia. . . . Istud ignorabant tam Plato quam Aristoteles:
aperte enim uterque credidit conditorem intellectum ex necessitate naturae omnia facere,
et ex hoc omnis eorum error secutus est. Nam licet non operetur per accidens, sicut ignis
per calorem . . . (nullum enim accidens cadere potest in ejus simplicitatem) et per hoc
agere videatur per essentiam: non tamen propterea agit quasi natura, seu instrumentum
necessitatum per superiorum imperium, sed per liberam voluntatem, quae est essentia
ejus.'

[10] Ficino *Theologia Platonica* ix. 4. fol. 211.

[11] Francesco Patrizzi *Panarchia* xv: 'De intellectu' (*Nova de universis philosophia*; Ferrara,
1591), fol. 31.

tine Academy with great fervour. That they should have done so is explainable if we remember that, for them, the doctrines signified a great deal more than mere speculation. They saw in them not only a theory of the cosmos very compatible with their own basic view; but, even more important, they found the secret of their own artistic creation interpreted and expressed in these doctrines. The enigmatic double nature of the artist, his dedication to the world of sensible appearance and his constant reaching and striving beyond it, now seemed to be comprehended, and through this comprehension really justified for the first time. The theodicy of the world given by Ficino in his doctrine of Eros had, at the same time, become the true theodicy of art. For the task of the artist, precisely like that of Eros, is always to join things that are separate and opposed. He seeks the 'invisible' in the 'visible', the 'intelligible' in the 'sensible'. Although his intuition and his art are determined by his vision of the pure form, he only truly *possesses* this pure form if he succeeds in realizing it in matter. The artist feels this tension, this polar opposition of the elements of being more deeply than anyone else. But, at the same time, he knows and feels himself to be the mediator. Here lies the essence of all aesthetic harmony; but here, too, lies the eternal insufficiency inherent in all harmony and beauty, viz., that it cannot reveal itself except through matter.

We encounter Ficino's doctrine of love in this form and in this depth in *Michelangelo's* sonnets. And if we compare this general influence of the doctrine with its further development by Patrizzi in epistemology, and by Giordano Bruno in ethics, we can begin to see fully the basis for its extraordinary fertility. Florentine Platonism, to be sure, still conceived of ideas completely as forces, as objective and cosmic potencies; but in addition to this it discovered a new concept of intellectual *consciousness* in its doctrine of Eros. This consciousness now emerges in its unity and in its multiplicity, in its division into the basic activities of knowledge, volition, and aesthetic creation, as well as in its immanent autonomy and identity. The self, the 'subjective spirit', is separated into the various directions of activity, and from these is derived the manifoldness of culture, the realm of the 'objective spirit'. In a reference to Plotinus, Giordano Bruno also calls Eros the one who truly opens the realm of subjectivity to man. As long as our eye is given to the mere contemplation of the perceived object, the phenomenon of beauty, like that of love, cannot be born. Beauty and love can both emerge only when the mind retreats from the external forms of the image and conceives of itself in its own, indivisible form, removed from all visibility.[12]

The *spiritualism* of the Renaissance determines its conception of the problem of the soul and of the problem of consciousness. But the development of both problems seems to take a completely new direction when one looks at it within the framework of the *concept of nature* and naturalistic psychology. The basic tendency in the critical renewal of Aristotelian psychology, brought about at the turn of the sixteenth century in the School of Padua, consists in a turn towards naturalism, i.e., in an attempt to fit the principle of the 'soul' into the general complex of nature, and to explain it purely immanently through nature. Pomponazzi's *De immortalitate animi* represents the first systematic result of this development. In this work too, the central concern is the battle against Averroism. Averroistic doctrine believes it can save the *unity* of the intellect only by letting it coincide with the intellect's *universality* and by viewing individuality not as an essential, but as an accidental characteristic of the thinking principle. Now if, instead of describing the given *phenomena* of psychical life, we inquire about their *cause*; and if, furthermore, we define this cause in such a manner as to lose the distinguishing empirical character of all the soul's activities, then we no longer have psychology, but metaphysics. Before we try to explain the character of the soul's activities, we must recognize what it is. But Averroism sins precisely against this basic methodological principle; it explains thinking consciousness in such a way that it makes it disappear *qua* consciousness. At best, its unitary 'active intellect' can be considered a cosmic being and a cosmic force; but this force lacks precisely that moment which could transform it into self-consciousness, transform it, that is, from a mere 'being-in-itself' to a 'being-for-itself'. Since consciousness is only possible in this form of 'for itself', it is only conceivable in its concrete particularization; for the one characteristic implies the other. And from here, Pomponazzi's demonstration goes one step farther. The particularization of the subject of consciousness is unthinkable unless we juxtapose to it a corresponding *objective* particularization. An individual soul can only be conceived of as such if it is thought of as the form of an individual *body*. In fact, one can say that what we call the animation of a body consists in nothing other than in

[12] Cf. Giordano Bruno *De umbris idearum, Opera latina*, ed. Imbriani, ii. 48: 'Notavit Platonicorum princeps Plotinus. Quamdiu circa figuram oculis dumtaxat manifestam quis intuendo versatur, nondum amore corripitur: sed ubi primum animus se ab illa revocans figuram in se ipso concipit non dividuam, ultraque visibilem, protinus amor oritur.'

this its complete individualization. Through this, the body is distinguished from mere 'matter'; through this, it becomes an *organic* body which, in its individual determination, becomes the vehicle of a definite, concrete and individual *life*. The 'soul', therefore, is not added to the 'body' as an external principle of movement or animation; rather, it is the very thing that forms the body in the first place; it is that which makes it a whole, differentiated within itself and articulated within this differentiation. This strict, correlative relationship may be reversely expressed. If the soul is not a mere *forma assistens*, but the genuine *forma informans*, it follows that its *function* of giving form can only be accomplished through a definite physical *substratum*, without which the function would not only lose its support but its entire meaning as well.

At this point, Pomponazzi parts company not only with Averroism but with every kind of spiritualistic psychology as well. Just as the soul cannot be disjoined as a separate entity from the body, whose form it is, so, too, there is no absolute separation in the soul to distinguish its 'higher' from its 'lower' functions. The soul is only 'intellect' or 'spirit' insofar as it is also 'life'; and as life, it can only reveal itself through a definite organic body. Consequently, if we follow the pure principles of reason rather than revelation, all proofs for the immortality of the soul, for its continued existence apart from the body, must fail. Studied closely, all these proofs can be shown to be based on a simple *petitio principii*. They argue from the universality of the thought-function and from the independent *accomplishments* of 'pure' thought as compared to sensual perception, to the independent *existence* and to the possible separation of the thinking substance. Because there are general ideal *significations*, because there are logical and ethical *values* independent of sense experience, an independent power of thought is postulated as the vehicle of these values. In fact, however, a sharper analysis of the act of thought itself shows that such a supposition is unwarranted. For the mind grasps the meaning of a general concept or of a general rule only by contemplating this meaning in something particular, i.e., in the content of perception or of the sensible fantasy. Without this concrete fulfilment, without this relation to something particular, the universal thought would remain empty. Thus, logic and psychology point to the same conclusion—a conclusion that stands unalterably opposed to the content of Christian doctrine.

Pomponazzi never tries to reconcile this opposition. He sets it up with the greatest precision, only to retreat then to the doctrine of the 'double truth'. But this purely formal limitation only throws the radicality of his thesis into even sharper relief. In his fight against Averroism, he constantly makes use of the proofs used by Thomas Aquinas to combat the doctrine of one intellect in all men. But now his argumentation turns against Thomas himself, and thus against the foundation of all Scholastic psychology. With true mastery, he reveals first of all the conflict that exists between the Platonic and the Aristotelian elements in the Thomistic concept of the soul. Platonism, for which soul and body are originally separate and fundamentally different substances, at least remains, according to Pomponazzi, true to itself in this strict metaphysical dualism. It conceives of the 'connection' between body and soul neither as a correlation nor as an inner and essential relationship; rather, it sees the soul as something that acts from without. To be sure, the unity of 'body' and 'spirit', of 'sense' and 'intellect', which we believe we immediately experience in human consciousness, is herewith explained as essentially an illusion, no different, say, from the unity that exists between the ox and the plough. But how could an Aristotelian be satisfied with that kind of unity if, according to Aristotle's definition, the soul is nothing other than the reality, the 'entelechy' of the body itself? This explanation contradicts the assertion that the soul is capable of a double kind of existence, i.e., its existence during earthly life and the existence it has as a discrete substance after its separation from the body. Since substance is never given in its absolute being, in its pure 'in itself', but is instead recognizable only in its operations, in its mode of functioning, it follows that we cannot ascribe to one and the same substance two completely different and disparate forms of functioning. If, in addition to the empirically conditioned and empirically known mode of functioning that the soul possesses as 'form of the body', we attribute to it still another function which it may exercise independently of the body, we are left not with the alleged *real* identity, but in fact with only a *verbal* identity. We are supposing two substances, two conceptually different essences, upon which we arbitrarily place the same *name*. And this is the basic fault of the Thomistic doctrine.

Thomas cannot avoid recognizing the epistemological foundations of the Aristotelian doctrine. Like Aristotle, he starts with the principle that no thought, no exercise of any purely intellectual function is possible if the thought is not in some way related to sensible representation. The mediate, the 'representative' act of thought always needs support in something immediately given and directly present in consciousness. Now, *this* kind of presence is proper only to the 'fantasms', i.e., to the images of perception and to the sensible power of imagination. But this epistemologically necessary consequence is denied and annulled by the metaphysics of Thomas Aquinas. To separate the soul from the body means to remove it from the only substratum upon which it could exercise its function. And yet, this change in the presuppositions of the soul's ability to think is not supposed to destroy thought itself but rather only to give it a new form, radically different from the earlier. But such a form is derived from thought, not from experience. Nor is it even capable of being experienced in any sense. All empirical help fails; here, we are no longer moving in the field of psychological or logical analysis, but in the empty field of speculation. Neither as a scientist nor as a psychologist does Aristotle ever recognize such a transition of *one* mode of the soul's functioning into another that is its direct opposite.[13] Since the concept of being must be defined according to the concept of function, such a transition would in fact mean nothing less than a kind of mythical transformation, a metamorphosis such as takes place in Ovid's wondrous tales.[14]

The break with Scholastic psychology could hardly be sharper. The whole Scholastic metaphysic of the soul now becomes a mere fable, a fiction that cannot be substantiated by any facts or by any 'natural' criterium or sign. To affirm a double being of the soul—one in the body and one outside it—would require showing two specifically different kinds of knowledge about the soul: in one it would be related to the sensible and in the other completely free of it. But the observation of psychical *phenomena* themselves offers no proof whatsoever of such freedom. And rational explanation is concerned with the interpretation and the 'salvation' of these phenomena, not with the arbitrary acceptance of another 'world', nor with the soul's condition there. From our point of view, these things are simply transcendent and inconceivable. 'Reason' must necessarily arrive at the same conclusion as

---

[13] Pomponazzi *De immortalitate animi* (1516), chaps. iv, ix *et passim*. 'Ridiculum videtur dicere animam intellectivam . . . duos habere modos intelligendi, scilicet et dependentem et independentem a corpore, sic enim duo esse videtur habere.' 'Neque plures modi cognoscendi ab Aristotele in aliquo loco sunt reperti, neque consonat rationi.'

[14] Ibid., 9: 'Dicere enim . . . ipsum intellectum duos habere modos cognoscendi, scilicet sine phantasmate omnino, et alium cum phantasmate, est transmutare naturam humanam in divinam. . . . Sic anima humana simpliciter efficeretur divina, cum modum operandi divinorum assumeret, et sic poneremus fabulas Ovidii, scilicet naturam in alteram naturam transmutari.'

the one arrived at by the true and rightly understood Aristotle. For both reason and Aristotle, the human soul is and remains the form of the organic body and as such, 'mortal by its very nature' (*simpliciter mortalis*)—even though the soul can, in a certain sense, be called 'conditionally-immortal' (*secundum quid immortalis*), since it can direct itself through the individual to the universal, through the sensible and transitory to the timeless and eternal.[15]

These propositions would seem to constitute the direct antithesis to the doctrine of the soul of the Florentine Academy. Indeed, Pomponazzi's treatise *De immortalitate animi* seems to be the negative pole to Ficino's work bearing the same title. And yet, above and beyond this contradiction, there exists a common systematic interest. Both Ficino and Pomponazzi wrestle with the problem of individuality. Both want to make the 'Ego' the centre of psychology, but they pursue this aim in completely different ways. For Ficino, only the purely spiritual nature of man makes of him an 'independent being' in the strict sense and raises him above the sphere of mere things. The freedom of man, in which his true Ego emerges, presupposes the possibility of the soul's liberation from the body. For Pomponazzi, on the other hand, individuality must be asserted not *against* nature but must be deduced and demonstrated *from* it. For him, individuality is not a prerogative of the spirit but rather represents the basic character of all *life*. 'Life' means nothing but existence in an individual form and in a completely individual configuration. In championing the rights and the particular character of the individual Ego, Ficino calls supernaturalism and transcendence to his aid; in the same cause, Pomponazzi calls for help from naturalism and immanence. He considers the ultimate foundation of individuality and its true justification to lie not beyond but within nature. Pomponazzi considers the organic body to be the best example, the prototype of 'individuation'. With this, he pays homage to Aristotle the *biologist* rather than to Aristotle the *metaphysician*. Pomponazzi is looking for a theory of the soul which, in principle, is not distinct from, but a direct continuation and completion of, the theory of the body. The image of the 'outer world' seems to model the image of the 'inner world' after itself; but conversely, the basic experience of individual psychical life has also become the key to the whole of nature.

[15] On this whole question, cf., besides *De immortalitate animi*, Pomponazzi's commentary on Aristotle's *De anima*, ed. Ferri (Rome 1876). For further evidence, cf. my *Erkenntnisproblem*, I, 105ff. Also see A. H. Douglas, *The Philosophy and Psychology of Pietro Pomponazzi*, chaps. iv and v.

Nevertheless, neither Ficino's nor Pomponazzi's path led to the modern view of nature and to the modern view of consciousness. The true sources of these views are to be found in an intellectual movement that wants to *subordinate* neither the 'subject' to the 'object' nor the 'object' to the 'subject'. Instead, it seeks, so to speak, a new ideal equilibrium between them. To effect this balance, to win and secure a new concept of intellect and of mind within a new concept of nature, it was necessary to abandon the path of metaphysics as well as of that of mere psychology. The goal was attained neither by supernaturalistic metaphysics nor by naturalistic psychology, but by the scientific and artistic observation of nature. Such observation gave birth to a concept of the necessity and the order of nature. Far from conflicting with the freedom and autonomy of the mind, this concept became instead its surest support and confirmation.

2

In its philosophical and scientific form, the *psychology* of the Renaissance shows us only the beginnings of that great intellectual movement from which was to emerge the newer, deeper concept of 'subjectivity'. Renaissance psychology could not yet encompass and formulate the *whole* of the new problem because it was unable to view in true unity the two opposite moments that constituted the problem. The old fight between 'spiritualism' and 'naturalism' could not be decided on this battlefield. Essentially, the psychological systems of the early Renaissance possess only one virtue: that of having brought the basic conflict into the sharpest possible focus. In this period, the concept of 'nature' and the concept of 'spirit' fight once again for the possession of man's 'soul'. The theoretical doctrine of the soul is torn between two basically divergent views. When it follows the path of spiritualism, as in the Florentine Academy, it must conclude by deeply disparaging the value of nature; when it conceives of 'soul' and 'life' as a unity, as in Pomponazzi's psychology, it sacrifices the pre-eminence of the spirit and of the 'higher' intellectual and ethical functions. The view that sees the spirit as eternal and indestructible must necessarily negate nature; whereas the view that sees the complex of nature as a singular and all-embracing continuity must necessarily deny immortality. And the ultimate reason for this reciprocal exclusion lies in the fact that the opposition is still conceived of in a purely substantival manner. So long as 'nature' and 'spirit' are thought of as two 'parts' of being, the question of which encompasses, and which is encompassed by, the other can never be settled. In this incessant competition, they are contending, so to speak, for the whole world of reality. For *Telesio*, the spirit becomes a special *region* of nature, dominated and moved by the general forces of nature, the forces of warmth and coldness. For *Ficino*, instead, nature is the lowest *level* of being—below the realm of grace, below the levels of *providentia* and *fatum*. For naturalism, the spiritual domain constitutes a single 'province' of being, to be viewed not as a 'state within a state', but as subject to the all-encompassing laws of being. For spiritualism, nature is the last link in the chain that connects the world of 'form' with that of 'matter'.[16] And so the investigation goes on, always with images of this sort. Indeed, these are more than images; they are the typical casts of a common basic form of observation. A real change in the solutions to this problem will take place only with the gradual abandonment of the presupposition common to both the spiritualistic and the naturalistic psychology of the Renaissance; i.e., when 'body' and 'soul', 'nature' and 'spirit' are no longer related substantively, as one thing to another, but rather *functionally*.

By itself, the metaphysics of the period would have been unable to establish and to give form to this new relationship. Had it not received decisive help from other quarters, it would not have been able to burst out of the basic Scholastic forms which lived on in both the spiritualism and the naturalism of the Renaissance. On the one hand, metaphysics was aided by exact and empirical *research*; on the other, by the *theory of art*. The union of these two constitutes one of the most remarkable and one of the most fruitful moments in the whole intellectual development of the Renaissance. The theory of science (i.e., knowledge of nature) and the theory of artistic creation not only point out a new path to philosophy; they even precede it on this path by creating a new sense for the orderliness of nature. And with this, the basic question of 'freedom'

---

[16] Generally speaking, Humanism did not change the medieval classification and hierarchy of knowledge, according to which the science of nature occupied the lowest rung on the ladder. Thus, Salutati considers jurisprudence to be higher than medicine because the former is a direct testimony of divine wisdom both through its concept of *aequitas* and in the form of laws; whereas the latter, based as it is on change and transitoriness, is to be considered more an art than a science. Medicine does not strive for the Good but for subordinate truths. Inasmuch as it makes use of 'experientia et instrumenta' in a purely empirical manner, it is concerned with temporal existence, not with trying to attain eternal rational principles through speculation. For a detailed discussion, cf. Paul Joachimsen, 'Aus der Entwicklung des italienischen Humanismus', *Historische Zeitschrift* (CXXI, 1920), 196f.; and Ernst Walser, *Poggius Florentinus* (Leipzig, 1914), pp. 250ff.

and 'necessity' reaches a new stage. Neither the theory of science nor the theory of art in the Renaissance could avoid this question, for it was the intellectually pivotal problem of the epoch. But they find a new solution to it, a solution that lies outside the sphere of the metaphysical oppositions of the schools. The antinomy freedom-necessity is transformed into a correlation. For the common characteristic joining the world of pure knowledge to that of artistic creation is that both are dominated, in different ways, by a moment of genuine intellectual generation. In Kantian language, they both go beyond any 'copy' view of the given; they must become an 'architectonic' construction of the cosmos. As science and art become more and more *conscious* that their primary function is to give form, they conceive of the law to which they are subject more and more as the expression of their essential freedom. And with that, the concept of nature and, indeed, the whole world of objects, takes on a new significance. The 'object' is now something other than the mere opposite, the—so to speak—*ob-jectum* of the Ego. It is that towards which all the productive, all the genuinely creative forces of the Ego are directed and wherein they first find their genuine and concrete realization. The Ego recognizes itself in the necessity of the object; it recognizes the force and the direction of its spontaneity. Nicholas Cusanus understood this basic notion of philosophical idealism in all its sharpness and depth. Nevertheless, this notion exercised its true influence and achieved its full maturity not in abstract speculation but in the new form of scientific knowledge and artistic vision.

The first testimony to this decisive change in the concept of nature is certainly not to be sought in mere theory, be it philosophical, scientific, or aesthetic; we find it rather in that transformation in the *feeling for nature* that began in the thirteenth century. The spell with which dogmatic medieval ideas had bound nature was first broken by *Petrarch's lyric poetry*. Nature is now divested of everything strange, everything disquieting and demonic. The lyrical mood does not see in nature the opposite of psychical reality; rather it feels everywhere in nature the traces and the echo of the soul. For Petrarch, landscape becomes the living mirror of the Ego. To be sure, we have here not only a liberation but, at the same time, a limitation to the feeling for nature; for precisely in this function of reflecting the soul, nature itself possesses only a mediate and, as it were, reflected reality. Nature is not sought and represented for its own sake; rather, its value lies in its service to modern man as a new *means of expression* for himself, for the liveliness and the infinite polymorphism of his inner life. In Petrarch's letters, this peculiar polarity of his feeling for nature sometimes emerges with startling clarity and consciousness. Sometimes, this feeling leads him away from self-expression and towards the representation of nature; but then, precisely in this observation of nature, he feels brought back to himself, to his own Ego. For him, landscape loses its independent value and its own *content*. The feeling for nature again degenerates and becomes the mere foil for self-awareness: *quid enim habet locus ille gloriosius habitatore Francisco?*[17] Petrarch's depictions of nature are full of this duality and this curious oscillation. It emerges unmistakably even in the most famous of these depictions, the narration of his ascent of Mont Ventoux. The scene is well known. Having reached the peak of the mountain after great hardships, Petrarch does not spend time viewing the panorama that offers itself to him; instead, his glance falls upon the book he always has with him. He opens it and happens upon the passage in Augustine's *Confessions* that speaks of how men go forth to admire high mountains, and wide seas, and the course of the stars, but therewith forget themselves.[18] Here, the contradiction between the mode of thought and the general mood is completely pressed into one sentence. The drive towards nature, the desire to immediately contemplate nature is obstructed by the Augustinian admonition that sees in this attitude nothing but a danger to the one truly immediate relationship, the relationship of the soul to God. *Noli foras ire, in te ipsum redi, in interiore homine habitat veritas.*[19] This Augustinian motto seems to bar any direct access to nature, the world of 'external' contemplation. Petrarch's feeling for nature is characterized by the same tension that is typical of his whole vision of the world. He sees nature and man, the world and history in a new splendour; but time and again this splendour itself seems to him blinding and seductive. The book that discusses this inner conflict, and that contains the confession of this 'secret battle of his heart's woes', might well be called the first presentation of the modern soul and modern man; and yet he gave it also the thoroughly medieval title *De contemptu mundi*. Petrarch feels about nature the same way he feels about worldly life and fame, which for him is the essence of all worldly life; although he feels himself pas-

[17] Petrarca *Append. litt. epist.* vi, ed. Fracassetti; cf. Voigt, *Wiederbelebung*, I, 113.
[18] Petrarca *Epistolae famil.* iv; cf. Burckhardt's presentation in *The Civilization of the Renaissance*, pp. 296f.
[19] Augustinus *De vera religione* 39.

sionately and irresistibly drawn to them, he is unable to devote himself
to them easily and with good conscience. This is not a 'naive', but a
completely 'sentimental' relationship to nature. Nature cannot be
understood, felt, and enjoyed *per se*, but only as a dark or light back-
ground for the Ego.

The following periods, the Quattrocento and the Cinquecento, had
to steer a different course. Theirs was the task of making the concept of
nature independent and of securing for it a strong, strictly 'objective'
character. When this had been accomplished, one could—indeed, one
had to—again raise the question of the relationship of this new realm of
nature to the world of 'consciousness' and 'spirit'. Once again, the
'correspondence', the 'harmony' of these two worlds is sought; but
now it presupposes the autonomy and the independent determination
of each member of the relationship. It seems manifest that the Renaissance discovered and championed this independence of nature by means
of immediate, *sensible-empircal observation*. Certainly, this is the opinion
that even today reigns almost unopposed in the history of philosophy,
and in cultural and intellectual history. *Burckhardt* depicted this steadily
progressing 'discovery of the world' in one of the most brilliant chap-
ters of his book. It seemed sufficient to receive the forms of this world
purely and objectively, instead of relating them to man; it seemed
sufficient to accept them in their simple and sensible determination and
to describe and to order them as such, thereby gaining a new image of
reality as pure reality of experience. The beginnings of such a mode of
observation may be seen emerging everywhere in Italy in the fourteenth
and fifteenth centuries, steadily gaining strength and scope. There is a
steady increase in the wealth of directly observed *material* from which
the new image of the world will emerge; and the main features of this
image, as well as the fine and finest contours of the details become ever
clearer. The urge towards systematic description and order derives
from and corresponds to the urge towards direct observation. Soon,
the strong urge to collect things leads to the establishment of botanical
and zoological gardens and also lays the first foundation for a new,
exact form of nature description. Cesalpino's work *De plantis* (1538),
attempting to set up for the first time a 'natural system' of the plant
world, opens the way to scientific botany.

At first, the Renaissance philosophy of nature also seems to start out
of this purely empirical path. *Telesio* demands, as *Bacon* did after him,
that nature no longer be observed through the medium of abstract

Aristotelian categories; instead, it must be understood through itself and investigated according to its own principles (*juxta propria principia*). These principles do not lie in the logical concepts of 'form' and 'matter', of 'actuality' and 'potentiality', of 'reality' and 'privation', but rather are to be sought in the constant, concrete, and universally uniform phenomena of nature. According to Telesio, the primary phenomena are the basic forces of warm and cold, and they must be grasped in direct, sensible observation. These forces mutually balance each other; they successively impress different forms on matter. And matter is no longer to be thought of as a merely logical *subject* of the change, but as its real, physical *substratum*. From this successive impression of different forms derives all the multiplicity of events. On the other hand, the multiplicity is recognized as a strict, law-bound unity, precisely because it is traceable to this triad of principles. Telesio proclaims sensory perception to be the principal means for attaining knowledge of nature. It must precede all the work of the intellect; it must precede the intellectual ordering and comparing of single facts, for sensory perception alone is able to produce the contact between 'subject' and 'object', between 'knowledge' and 'reality'. Telesio's system of nature and his system of knowledge interpret this contact in a thoroughly literal sense. Every abstract conception of an object presupposes a sensible contact with it. We only have consciousness of an object when it acts upon us; in fact, only when, by virtue of this action, it penetrates us. What we call 'spirit' is a mobile substance whose state of movement is determined and modified by external actions; and each sensory perception represents a special variety of this modification. What is different is the manner in which the original stimulus is transported. And this manner is partly determined by the nature of the medium that serves as the vehicle of transmission. In visual sensation, the forces of warmth and cold are transported by means of light; in aural sensation, by means of air, which also serves as the vehicle for olfactory sensation. But since all these mediate transportations must finally end in a direct contact, the sense of touch becomes for Telesio the sense of all senses. In the final analysis, even all 'higher' intellectual functions are reducible to it; even all our thought and reasoning represents a kind of 'touching at a distance'. The act of deductive reasoning consists simply in the mind's reception of impressions from without, which are the modifications of cold and warm and its preservation of them within itself. Under certain conditions, the mind is capable of renewing within itself a state of movement that was originally due to an external influence. Thus, it can repeat earlier impressions and therewith achieve a connection of the present with past states, making it capable furthermore, of reaching into the future and anticipating coming impressions. This ability to look back to the past and forward into the future we generally call the reflexive power of thought, the power of 'rational conclusion'. But this is not an expression of the independent, detached power of an autonomous 'active intellect'; instead, it is, so to speak, the mechanical continuation of the movements within us that were originally caused from without. When Aristotle lets memory derive from the senses, experience from memory, and knowledge from experience, he implicitly recognizes this fundamental relationship of the individual psychical functions and their collaboration in the construction of knowledge—although he later explicitly denied this relationship in his doctrine of the νοῦς. In fact, there can only be fleeting differences between sense and representation, between representation and memory, and between memory and knowledge. The intellect itself is only a mediate and derivative sense. Precisely because of this mediateness, it remains necessarily imperfect and preserves only a kind of outline, an analogue, a simile of the true constitution of the impression.[20]

Thus, in its very first appearance as a closed system, the *naturalism* of the Renaissance seems to take on a strictly empirical and sensualistic character. Its entire foundation seems to consist only in empirical observation, excluding from the picture of nature everything that cannot be supported by the direct testimony of sensory perception. And yet, if we trace the subsequent influence of Telesio's ideas on the natural philosophy of the Renaissance, we soon notice a curious reversal. Even the direct successors of Telesio, the men who considered themselves his immediate disciples, abandoned the path of exact observation of nature and the methodology of strictly descriptive knowledge. Telesio's basic tendency is opposed not only to the Aristotelian-Scholastic explanation of nature but also, and just as relentlessly, to the 'occult' sciences. By demanding the explanation of nature from its 'own principles', he is also condemning the occult sciences of astrology and magic. But no sooner does this autonomy of empirical science seem attained, than it is lost again. The Renaissance philosophy of nature never succeeds in removing magic from its path. In the writings of *Giordano Bruno*, the

[20] Telesio *De rerum natura juxta propria principia*; cf. especially viii. 3, 11 (Neapoli, 1587), fol. 314f., 326f.

problems of 'natural magic' take up so much room that they threaten to stifle the speculative-philosophical problems. And *Campanella*, who in the whole tendency of his doctrines of nature and of knowledge seems to come closest to Telesio, gives his main work on natural philosophy the title *De sensu rerum et magia*. Clearly, the 'empiricism' announced and formulated here does not, of itself, possess enough power to become a system of 'pure experience', and to keep itself free of fantastic admixtures. At every turn, it reverses itself immediately into its very opposite, i.e., into theosophy and mysticism. No direct path leads from Telesio's concept of nature to modern science. Campanella was deceiving himself when he believed that he could be both a representative of Telesian principles and, at the same time, an apologist for Galileo.[21] The sharp dividing line in the *method* of knowing nature reveals itself right here. The path of Leonardo and Galileo seeks the 'reason' in experience, the *ragioni* of the real; and it is sharply and clearly divergent from the path of the sensualistic theories of nature. The former leads ever more clearly and definitely to mathematical idealism, the latter always leads back to primitive forms of animism.

This relapse is no mere accident, no simple historical regress. It is founded not only in those dark passions and emotions through which man strives for dominion over nature, but even more in the general theoretical presuppositions of the Italian philosophy of nature. The common principle that serves as its point of departure is that to 'know' a thing means to become one with it. But this unity is only possible if the subject and object, the knower and the known, are of the same nature; they must be members and parts of one and the same vital complex. Every sensory perception is an act of fusion and reunification. We perceive the object, we grasp it in its proper, genuine being only when we feel in it the same life, the same kind of movement and animation that is immediately given and present to us in the experiencing of our own Ego. From this, Panpsychism emerges as a simple corollary to the theory of knowledge, just as, conversely, this theory is coloured by Panpsychism from the very beginning. The connection is so close that *Patrizzi* can append the presentation of his theory of knowledge to a work entitled *Panpsychia*. In it, he reproves Aristotle for having developed only half way the basic idea of Panpsychism and for having made the world into a monster by considering only the heavenly spheres to be animated and everything else to be unanimated. In

[21] Cf. Campanella *Apologia pro Galileo mathematico florentino* (Frankfurt, 1622).

reality, the unity of life knows no such divisions and barriers. It is contained, complete and undivided, even in things that seem to be just material; it functions in the greatest as in the smallest, in the highest as in the lowest, in the stars as well as in the simple elements. True being and genuine value can only be attributed to animated things; and the elements would be deprived of both if we were to deny them any life of their own.[22] Even *Telesio's* theory of knowledge seeks to demonstrate the unity of intellect and senses by letting all the functions of thought and of 'rational' deduction be rooted in the *single* function of drawing analogies: *intellectionis cujusvis principium similitudo est sensu percepta.*[23] Now the attempt is made to define this process of drawing analogies more sharply by giving it a metaphysical sub-structure. The theoretical conclusion of the 'analogy' is rooted in the fundamentally common nature of all being and would be invalid without it. All conception, every mediating ratiocination goes back to an original act of *empathy* by which we assure ourselves of the community that binds us with all being. Even Cardano's theory of nature is completely dominated by such analogical thought-games. Indeed, they want to be more than mere games; they want to be an immediate, intuitive grasping of the complex of nature. For Cardano, metals are only 'buried plants' leading an underground existence; stones have their development, their growth, and their maturity.[24] Such a view not only tolerates but even requires magic, for it sees in it the true fulfilment of the science of nature.

In the nine hundred theses and in the *Apologia*, composed to defend the theses against the charge of heresy, Pico defines magic as the sum of all natural wisdom and as the practical part of natural science. With this, he is only repressing a conviction common in the natural philosophy of the Renaissance. In this view, magic is nothing but the active side of the knowledge of nature; what this knowledge theoretically recognizes as related, as belonging together, magic actively connects and leads to a common goal. Thus, magic itself does not work miracles, but simply supports, like an industrious servant, the operative forces in nature. 'It investigates that bond in the universe which the Greeks call

---

[22] Francesco Patrizzi, *Panpsychia* (*Nova de universis Philosophiae tomus III*; Ferrariae, 1591) iv. fol. 54ff.

[23] Telesio *De rerum natura* viii. 3; further details about Telesio's epistemology in my *Erkenntnisproblem*, I, 232ff.

[24] Cardanus *De subtilitate libri xxi* (Basel, 1554), v. fol. 152: 'Metallica vivere etiam hoc argumento deprehenditur, quod in montibus non secus ac plantae nascuntur, patulis siquidem ramis, radicibus, truncis ac veluti floribus ac fructibus, ut non aliud sit metallum aut metallica substantia quam planta sepulta.'

'sympathy'; it penetrates into the understanding of the nature of all things; it draws from the lap of the earth and from its secret storerooms the hidden wonders and brings them to light as though it had created them itself. Just as the peasant weds the vine to the elm, so the magician weds heaven and earth and brings the lower world into contact with the forces of the higher world.'[25] Magic can be accepted in its full scope —under the *one* condition that the foundation of its effectiveness no longer be sought outside or above nature but in the midst of it. Not the interference of demonic powers, but the observation of the course of events and of the rules within them sets the direction and fixes the aim of all magical activity.

In his work on 'natural magic', *Giambattista della Porta* established the concept of magic in this sense. Nature is not so much the object as it is the subject of magic. The source and the seed of all magical power is the attraction of like things and the repulsion of unlike things that takes place within nature.[26] In his *De sensu rerum et natura*, *Campanella* elaborates upon these basic propositions of Porta. But whereas the latter takes as his point of departure the simple fact of σύμπνοια πάντα, i.e., the 'fact' of universal sympathy, Campanella seeks to derive this fact from its speculative 'foundations'. Thus, in keeping with that paradoxical mixture of motifs so characteristic of Renaissance philosophy, Campanella becomes the rational methodologist of magic. He explicitly defines it as his task to trace natural magic back to its final causes. In his work Porta had treated natural magic as a historically and factually determined set of facts; now Campanella wants to give it, for the first time, a truly rational form.[27] Porta's work is steeped in the myriad of analogies that exist between the macrocosm and the microcosm, between the world of man and the world of elements, between the plants and the animals; Campanella wants to trace this multiplicity back to a single principle. Not satisfied with the fact of their harmony, he asks for the 'why'—and he believes he has found it when he points to the capacity for sensory perception as the foundation for all connection, for similarity and dissimilarity, for sympathy and antipathy. In varying degrees, the capacity for sensory perception is proper to all

[25] Pico della Mirandola *Apologia*, *Opera* fol. 170f.; cf. especially his oration, *De hominis dignitate*, ibid., fol. 327f.
[26] Giambattista Porta *Magiae naturalis Libri viginti* i. 2.
[27] Campanella *De sensu rerum et magia* ed. Tob. Adami (Frankfurt, 1620), iv. 1. 260: 'Conatus est bis . . . studiosissimus Porta hanc scientiam revocare, sed historice tantum, nullas reddendo dictorum suorum causas. (Ex quo autem hunc librum meum vidit, audio ipsum rationalem magiam struere.)'

parts of being, no matter what their individual constitution may be. And this capacity connects all of them not only mediately but immediately, not only empirically but, in a sense, also *a priori*. Sense becomes the original, ontological, essential determination of *all* being. It lies beyond all individual differences and, therefore, bridges the separation of the elements of being from one another, as well as their apparent disparity. Sense is neither born nor dies, it is to be found not only in the individual, organic entities of nature, but rather is common to all its forms. For, just as it is true that nothing can be in the effect which was not pre-formed in the cause, so it is equally true that out of things not endowed with life, with sense, nothing with sensation, with life, can come forth.[28]

We are concerned here not with the metaphysical consequences brought about by this doctrine in Campanella's system but with the methodological characteristics it contains. In this respect, it becomes quite clear that Campanella's concern with the sensible plethora of the world of phenomena and the attempt to grasp it immediately and 'drain' it completely, not only failed to create the new, specifically modern concept of 'nature' but actually even obstructed and arrested it. So long as definite *criteria* of experience were not created through the medium of mathematics and through the other new intellectual means furnished by it, the empiricism of the Renaissance lacked objective standards of value and any principle of selection among the teeming phenomena. The single 'facts' cluster around each other in colourful abundance but in completely chaotic disorder. The appeal to experience could offer no firm foundation so long as the concept of experience still contained such completely heterogeneous constitutive elements.

The theory of nature of the fifteenth and sixteenth centuries laid the first foundation for exact description and exact experimentation; but closely connected with this, we find also the attempts at the foundation of an 'empirical magic'. The difference between 'natural' and 'demonic' magic[29] lies in that the latter is based on the acceptance of supernatural

---

[28] Campanella *Universalis philosophiae seu metaphysicarum rerum juxta propria dogmata partes tres* (Paris, 1638), P. II, vi. 7; for Campanella's relationship to Giambattista Porta cf. Fiorentino, *Bernardino Telesio* (Florence, 1872ff.), II, 123ff.

[29] This distinction between 'natural' and 'demonic' magic was made throughout Renaissance philosophy. We find it in Pico's nine hundred theses and in his *Apologia*, as well as in Ficino's *De vita triplici*, and in Pomponazzi's *De admirandorum effectuum causis sive de incantationibus* i. 5. 74: 'Nemini dubium est ipsam (magiam naturalem) in se esse veram scientiam factivam et subalternatam philosophiae naturali et Astrologiae, sicut est medicina et multae aliae scientiae; et in se est bona et intellectus perfectio . . . et, ut sic, non facit hominem habentem ipsam malum esse hominem.'

forces whereas the former wants to remain completely within the framework of nature and of its empirical uniformity, claiming for itself no method other than inductive observation and the comparison of phenomena. But, this form of 'induction' does not yet recognize any kind of analytical-critical limitations, such as are presupposed and lie at the base of every genuine 'experiment'. Thus, the world of experience here borders on the world of miracles, and both constantly overlap and merge with each other. The whole atmosphere of this 'science' of nature is filled to the brim with miracles.

Kepler hails *Giambattista della Porta* as the discoverer of the telescope. Whether this attribution be correct or not, Porta certainly did make decisive contributions to the foundation of the science of optics. But it was Porta, too, who, in the *Accademia dei Secreti* founded by him in Naples, established the first great centre for the 'occult' sciences. His indefatigable zeal as a collector and investigator and his long trips through all of Italy and through France and Spain enabled him to make a compilation of everything that had any relation at all to the investigation of the secret forces of nature. He worked steadfastly to extend and enrich the compendium of natural magic he had already composed at the age of fifteen. With Porta, as later with Campanella, empiricism leads not to the refutation but to codification of magic. To conceive of experience itself as a mere aggregate, to define it, with Campanella, as *experimentorum multorum coacervatio*, means that there can be no analysis of its elements and no evaluation of the role played by each individual element in the systematic construction of 'nature'. Such an analysis and evaluation could only be made after a separation of the basic elements of experience had been achieved elsewhere—after an inner 'crisis' had taken place in experience itself. This separation of the 'necessary' from the 'accidental', this distinction between that which obeys laws and that which is fantastic and arbitrary, was brought about not by the empiricism and sensualism of the philosophy of nature but by the intellectualism of mathematics. And yet, the issue was not decided by purely intellectual motifs alone. In a manner that is characteristic and determinative of the total intellectual picture of the Renaissance, the logic of mathematics goes hand in hand with the *theory of art*. Only out of this union, out of this alliance, does the new concept of the 'necessity' of nature emerge. Mathematics and art now agree upon the same fundamental requirement: the requirement of 'form'. In this common pursuit, the line of demarcation between the theory of art and the theory of science disappears. Thus, Leonardo can immediately take up Cusanus. And in a famous passage of his dialogue on the two chief systems, Galileo uses Michaelangelo, Raphael, and Titian to demonstrate his conception of the human intellect and the role it plays in the construction of empirical knowledge.[30] Here, we have a new synthesis within the world of mind, and together with it a new correlation of 'subject' and 'object'. Reflection on human freedom, on man's original, creative force, requires as its complement and its confirmation the concept of the immanent 'necessity' of the natural object.

This double process emerges with complete clarity in the manuscripts of *Leonardo*. His notes are laden with references to his constant battle against those 'deceitful' sciences that flatter man with false hopes and that give man the illusion of direct dominance over nature and her secret forces. He reproaches these sciences for disdaining mathematics, which is the only true medium for knowing nature. 'The man who blames the supreme certainty of mathematics feeds on confusion and can never silence the contradictions of sophistical sciences which lead to an eternal quackery.'[31] With these words Leonardo parts company once and for all with the 'enthusiasts' of natural philosophy, those *vagabundi ingegni*, as he calls them. True, they do seem to reach for the highest goals and to penetrate to the ultimate reasons of nature; nevertheless, the greatness of the *object* of their science ought never delude us as to the uncertainty of the *foundations* of this wisdom. 'But you, who live in dreams, are better pleased by the sophistical reasons and frauds of wits in great and uncertain things than by those reasons which are certain and natural and not so far above us.'[32] This single blow changes the standard of value which the medieval system had used to determine the rank of the individual sciences. We will recall that Salutati still ranked jurisprudence higher than medicine because the former is concerned with law, which is to say with the spiritual and the divine, whereas medicine, like natural science generally, is only concerned with lower, material things. In Salutati's *De nobilitate legum et medicinae*, medicine says: *Nos curamus temporalia sed leges aeterna, ego de terra creata sum, lex vero de mente divina*. Laws are 'more necessary than medicine', inasmuch as they derive immediately from God.[33] But now another

---

[30] Galilei, *Dialogo sopra i due massimi sistemi del mondo* (Ed. nazionale, VII), 129f.
[31] Jean Paul Richter (ed.), *The literary works of Leonardo da Vinci* (2 vols.; London, 1883), No. 1157.
[32] Ibid., No. 1168.
[33] See above, n. 16; cf. especially Walser, *Poggius Florentinus*, pp. 250f.

concept and another norm of necessity is created, according to which necessity no longer depends upon the excellence and dignity of the *object* of the knowledge but upon the *form* of the knowledge, upon the specific quality of its certainty. This *certezza* becomes the true, the only *fundamentum divisionis*. And with this, mathematics moves into the focal point of knowledge. For certainty is only present wherever one of the mathematical sciences can be applied, or wherever the object in question can be discussed in connection with mathematical principles.[34] Passage through the forms of mathematical demonstration becomes the *conditio sine qua non* for all true science: *nessuna investigazione si può dimandare vera scienza, s'essa non passa per le mathematiche dimostrazioni.*[35]

Although Leonardo emphatically enunciates this principle, a look at all of his notebooks might nevertheless give us the impression that he oscillated between two opposite definitions of the methodological foundations of the knowledge of nature. Sometimes mathematics, sometimes experience is considered the basic principle. Wisdom is the daughter of experience; the experiment is the only true interpreter between artful nature and the human species.[36] Error is never rooted in the experience, in the sense data, but in reflection, in the wrong judgment we make about them. Therefore men complain unjustly about experience when they call it guilty of being deceptive. 'But leave experience alone and turn such lamentations against your own ignorance which makes you hasten, in your vain and foolish desires, to promise yourself things which are not within its power.'[37] Nevertheless, these propositions do not recognize a second principle of certainty beside or above mathematics.

The decisive point in Leonardo's thought is precisely that a dualism between the abstract and the concrete, between 'reason' and 'experience', can no longer exist. Both moments are related and bound to one another; experience completes itself only in mathematics, just as mathematics first 'comes to its fruition' in experience. There is no competition, let alone a conflict; there is only a purely complementary relationship. For there is no true experience without an analysis of phenomena, i.e., without breaking down into its basic elements that which is given and complex. And the only way to conduct this analysis is through

---

[34] Charles Ravaisson-Mollien (ed.), *Les manuscrits de Léonard de Vinci*, G fol. 96ᵛ.
[35] Leonardo da Vinci, *Trattato della pittura*, ed. Ludwig (Leipzig, 1882), I, 33.
[36] *Il codice Atlantico di Leonardo da Vinci* (Milano, 1894), fol. 86ʳ.
[37] Ibid., fol. 154ʳ.

mathematical demonstration and mathematical calculation. What we call the world of facts is nothing but a tissue of 'rational principles', i.e., of determining elements. In concrete being and events, they are infinitely and multifariously interconnected and superimposed upon each other. Only the power of thought can separate them and show their individual significance and validity. The true value of the experiment consists in its accomplishment of this analysis. It takes the single factors that constitute a complex phenomenon, makes them visible in themselves, and traces their separate activities. Thus, experience, to speak in Aristotelian language, is the πρότερον πρὸς ἡμᾶς, whereas the mathematical rational principle upon which it is based remain the πρότερον τῇ φύδει. And there is no doubt that what experience and the world of phenomena actually show us is only a fragment, only a limited segment of the infinitely multifarious realm of rational principles. Nature conceals within it countless principles which have never come forth as sensible phenomena.[38] The true path of investigation, then, is to bring a definite measure and a fixed rule to the indistinct mass of phenomena by constantly relating experience to mathematics; and that is done by transforming empirical accidentality into orderly necessity. Now, we have found the criterion vainly sought by the Renaissance philosophy of nature; we have a clearly drawn line of demarcation between the methodological orientation based on experience and mere 'speculation.'[39] Rules are established for distinguishing the true from the false and for separating the scientifically feasible from the impossible and the fantastic. Now, man understands the purpose of his knowledge as well as its limits. He is no longer immersed in that fruitless uncertainty which causes him to despair and leads him to scepticism.[40]

When anyone asks about Leonardo's part in the foundation of exact science, it is customary to begin by pointing to individual results of modern statics and dynamics that he anticipated in his notes. And in these notes we do, indeed, find scattered everywhere hints that clearly anticipate the basic principles of Galileo's theory of motion. These hints deal with the law of inertia and with the principle of the equality of action and reaction; with the problem of the parallelogram of forces and the parallelogram of velocity; with the principle of the lever and with the 'principle of virtual velocity' later formulated by *Lagrange*.

[38] Richter, op. cit., No. 1151.
[39] Ravaison-Mollien, op. cit., B fol. 14ᵛ. 'Fuggi i precetti di speculatori che le loro ragioni non son confermate dalla sperienzia.'
[40] *Il codice Atlantico*, fol. 119ʳ.

But all this, important and fundamental as it is,[41] by no means exhausts the whole of Leonardo's theoretical accomplishment. This accomplishment lies not so much in the results as in the new formulation of problems. It lies in the new concept of the 'necessity of nature' which he establishes and applies everywhere. From the point of view of methodology, his definition of 'necessity' is truly fundamental: *La neciessità è maestra e tutrice della natura; la neciessità è tema e inventrice della natura e freno e regola eterna*.[42] Leonardo's true intellectual greatness lies in this formulation of the *problem*, of the 'theme' of exact science. Reason is the immanent, unbreakable law governing nature.[43] Sense, sensation, or the immediate feeling for life can no longer serve as the means by which we assimilate nature and discover her secret. Only thought proves to be truly equal to nature; only 'the principle of sufficient reason', which Leonardo considers a principle of mathematical explanation.

Now, we can begin to grasp and appreciate the significance of Leonardo's influence on Galileo. Leonardo's formulation of *individual* laws of nature may sometimes be vague and ambiguous; but he is always certain about the idea and the definition of the law of nature itself. On this point, Galilelo bases himself directly on Leonardo, simply continuing and explicating what the latter had begun. For Galileo too, nature does not so much 'have' necessity, but rather *is* necessity. This is the decisive characteristic that distinguishes what we call nature from the realm of fiction and poetic invention. If Galileo fights as hard against the speculative natural philosophy of his time as he does against Aristotle and Scholasticism, it is because both schools completely blur this distinction in their explanations. Both schools, says Galileo in his *Saggiatore*, look upon philosophy as a book, a product of fantasy, like the *Iliad* or the *Orlando Furioso*, in which the matter of least concern is whether the things written in it are true. 'But that is not the case. Rather, philosophy is written in the great book of nature, which lies constantly before our eyes, but which no one can read unless he has first learned to understand the ciphers in which it is composed, i.e., the mathematical figures and their necessary relationships.'[44] The logical and mathematical connections of being and of events are re-

[41] For a discussion of Leonardo's mechanical investigations, cf.—in addition to Duhem's exhaustive studies—the newest work by Ivor B. Hart, *The mechanical Investigations of Leonardo da Vinci* (London, 1925).

[42] Richter, op. cit., No. 1133.

[43] Ravaisson-Mollien, op. cit., C fol. 23ᵛ. 'Lan ature è costretta dalla ragione della sua legge che in lei infusamente vive.'

[44] Galileo, *Il saggiatore* (Edizione nazionale VI), p. 232.

vealed to us only in these relationships, i.e., in the strictly univocal relationship of the 'cause' to the 'effect' and of the 'effect' to the 'cause'.

Although Leonardo and Galileo are very close in their view of nature, they did not reach this result in the same way. For when Galileo draws the dividing line between the objective truth of nature and the world of fable and fiction, both poetry *and art* are relegated to the latter world. But for Leonardo, art never signifies a mere outpouring of the subjective fantasy; rather, it is and remains a genuine and indispensable organ for the understanding of reality itself. Its immanent truth value is not inferior to that of science. Neither in art nor in science does Leonardo admit even the slightest subjective arbitrariness. In both, he honours all-pervading necessity as the theme and discoverer, the rein and eternal rule of nature. Leonardo, like Goethe after him, sharply distinguished artistic 'style' from mere individual manner. And, again like Goethe, he considered style to be based on the 'deepest foundations of knowledge, on the essence of things, inasmuch as it is allowed us to recognize this essence in visible and graspable forms'. Even as a *scientist*, Leonardo insists upon this visibility, this graspability of the form. He considers it the limit that bounds all human knowledge and conception. To traverse the realm of visible forms completely; to grasp each of these forms in its clear and certain contours; and to keep them in their full definiteness before both the internal and the external eye: these are the highest aims recognized by Leonardo's science. Thus, the limit of vision is also, of necessity, the limit of conception. Both as artist and as scientist, he is always concerned with the 'world of the eye'; and this world must present itself to him not in bits and pieces but completely and systematically.[45]

If we fail to recognize this essential form of Leonardo's question, if we try to foist upon him problems that were—and could only be—posed by the later mathematical science of nature, we run the risk of measuring his concept of knowledge and his scientific achievement by a false standard. From two different quarters the attempt has been made recently to cast doubt upon this concept and to limit its significance for the history of knowledge. In an essay on 'Leonardo as a Philosopher', *Croce* ranks him very close to the great modern investigators of nature, Galileo and Newton; but he denies him any vision of the

---

[45] On the relationship between 'seeing' and 'knowing' in Leonardo's thought, cf., e.g., Arturo Farinelli, 'La natura nel pensiero e nell'arte di Leonardo da Vinci', *Michelangelo e Dante* (Torino, 1918), pp. 315ff.

inner world, which is the true sphere of mind and of speculative knowledge.[46] In his *History of Scientific Literature in the Modern Languages*,
Olschki raised the opposite objection. 'It is,' he writes, 'as though he
[Leonardo] were afraid of making a scientifically usable generalization
that could be reached either deductively or inductively. It is as though
he felt incapable of indulging in even the most obvious abstraction and
satisfied himself instead with the intuitive proofs acquired through his
sketches.' One of these judgments measures Leonardo by the norm of
speculative idealism and the other measures him by the norm of modern
positivism. But both forget that there is, to use Goethe's words, such a
thing as an 'exact sensible fantasy', with its own rules and its own
immanent standards. And Leonardo has shown, better than anyone,
just what this form of exact fantasy can do for empirical research.
Nothing is more wrong than to see in his scientific writings a *mixture*
of sharply observed facts and of fantastic 'visions'.[47] Fantasy here is
not an addition to perception; it is its living vehicle. Fantasy guides
perception and gives it its significance, its sharpness, and its definiteness.
It is certainly true that Leonardo's ideal of science aims at nothing but
the perfection of seeing, the *saper vedere*. It is also true that representational, pictorial material preponderates even in his notes on mechanics,
optics, and geometry. For Leonardo, 'abstraction' and 'vision' collabor-
ate intimately.[48] The highest results of his investigations are due precisely to this collaboration. He himself has stated that he first noticed,
as a *painter*, how the pupils dilate and contract according to the amount
of light that falls upon them, and that he discussed the phenomenon
theoretically later on.[49]

Leonardo's vision of nature proved to be a methodologically necessary transition point, for it was artistic 'vision' that first championed
the rights of scientific abstraction and paved the way for it. The 'exact
fantasy' of Leonardo the artist has nothing to do with that chaotic
surging and billowing of subjective feeling which threatens to coalesce
all forms into an undifferentiated whole. His 'exact fantasy' knows how
to insist firmly upon visually real, as opposed to merely conceptual and
abstract distinctions. True and objective necessity is found *in* vision,

---

[46] Benedetto Croce, 'Leonardo filosofo' in *Saggi filosofici* (Paris, 1913), III.
[47] Olschki, *Geschichte der neusprachlichen wissenschaftlichen Literatur* I, 261, 300f., *et passim*.
[48] Ibid., I, 342, 379.
[49] Ravaisson-Mollien, op. cit., D fol. 13ʳ; cf. Solmi, *Nuovi studi sulla filosofia naturale di Leonardo da Vinci*, p. 39: 'Analizzare un fatto col discorso o analizzarlo col disegno non sono (per Leonardo) che due modi di un medesimo processo.'

not above or below it. And with this, necessity receives a new meaning and a new accent. Hitherto, as the *regnum naturae*, necessity had been the opposite of the realm of freedom and of mind; but now it becomes the seal of mind itself. 'Oh wonderful necessity,' writes Leonardo, 'with the highest reason you force all effects to participate in their causes. With the greatest despatch, every natural activity is obedient to you, as to a highest and irrevocable law . . . Who can explain this miracle that raises human reason up to divine vision? . . . Oh mighty instrument of artful nature, it is yours to obey the law that God and time have given to creative nature.'[50] This dominion of necessity and this, its profound content, were first truly revealed by artistic vision. Goethe has said that the beautiful is a manifestation of secret laws of nature which, without such a manifestation, would be eternally hidden from us. This is completely in harmony with Leonardo's ideas—indeed, it expresses the kernel of his thought. For Leonardo, the innermost order of proportion is the true middle term, the connecting link between nature and freedom. The mind rests in proportion, as in something solid and objective. In proportion, the mind re-discovers itself and its own rule.

It is worth dwelling upon this complete parallel between the *theory of art* and the *theory of science*, for it reveals to us one of the most profound motifs in the entire intellectual movement of the Renaissance. One might say that nearly all the great achievements of the Renaissance are gathered here as in a focal point. One might say, furthermore, that these achievements are nearly all rooted in a new attitude towards the *problem of form*, and in a new sensitivity to form. In this respect, poetry and the visual arts point to the same basic relationship. Borinski has demonstrated the significance of *poetics* for the whole human and intellectual ideal of life in the Renaissance. 'This change in the intellectual way of understanding the world . . . can also make clear for the first time the significance of classical antiquity in the . . . new intellectual era. Certainly the Middle Ages . . . had enough ties to antiquity. A complete rupture with antiquity had never come about, thanks to the church, the cultural power that replaced it. Indeed, in the Carolingian, Ottonian, and Hohenstaufen ages, we find anticipatory hints of the great intellectual movement [i.e., the Renaissance revival of antiquity]. On the whole, the influence of antiquity on the Middle Ages was, as has been generally and accurately pointed out, an influence of *content*. And

[50] *Il codice Atlantico*, fol. 345^r.

this 'antiquity of content' continued to exercise its influence on into the actual Renaissance period for a considerable time. A change in the attitude of the personality towards antiquity expressed itself in form—starting with the form of the individual in his feeling, thinking, and living, and going on to the renewal of ancient and classical forms in poetry and art, state and society.'[51]

This primacy of form in Renaissance life and thought is demonstrable in practically every intellectual field. Lyrical poetry leads the way by becoming the first and the most potent vehicle of the new will to form. In Dante's *Vita nuova* and in Petrarch's sonnets, the feeling for form is, as it were, advanced beyond the feeling for life; whereas the latter still seemed bound to medieval views and sentiments, the former became a truly liberating and redeeming force. The lyrical expression does not merely describe a complete inner reality that already has its own form; rather, it discovers and creates this reality itself. The new lyrical style becomes a source of the new life. The *philosophical* sources of this style lead back to medieval philosophy, especially to Averroism. We can understand the entire allegorical and conceptual language of this lyrical poetry and the content of its problems only if we derive them from their historical presuppositions—from the poetic tradition of the troubadors and from the scientific tradition of the Scholastics.[52] But the new form into which this traditional content was poured was destined gradually to change the content. And the same relationship of content and expression that we have seen in lyric poetry also shows itself in logic. In logic, too, the new Renaissance feeling for language, cultivated in humanistic circles, acted as a constant and direct incentive to thought. The striving for purity of language, for freedom from the 'barbaric' deformities of Scholastic Latin, leads to a reform of dialectics. Valla's *Elegantiarum linguae latinae libri* have the same aim as his dialectical disputations: both strive for clarity, simplicity, and purification of the language, which, in turn, will immediately lead to neatness and purity of thought. The theory concerning the structure of an oration is further developed and transformed into a theory of the general structure of thought; stylistics becomes the model and the guide for the theory of categories. Whatever genuine content philosophy, logic, and dialectics may possess, they borrowed from 'queen eloquence': *omnia*

---

[51] Borinski, *Streit um die Renaissance*, pp. 20f. (Cf. above, introduction, n. 8.)

[52] For further details see Karl Vossler, *Die philosophischen Grundlagen zum 'süssen neuen Stil' des Guido Guinicelli, Guido Cavalcanti und Dante Alighieri* (Heidelberg, 1904).

quae philosophia sibi vendicat nostra sunt, says the humanist and orator Antonio Panormita in Valla's dialogue *De voluptate.*[53] And thus it has been said of humanism that its deepest root, and the common bond that joined all humanists, was neither individualism nor politics, neither philosophy nor common religious ideas, but simply artistic sensibility.[54]

Clearly it was artistic sensibility that gave concrete determination to the *concept* of nature formulated by Renaissance science. Leonardo's artistic work and his scientific achievement are joined not only in a kind of personal union, as is generally thought, but, rather, in a really essential union by virtue of which he attains a new vision of 'freedom' and 'necessity', of 'subject' and 'object', of 'genius' and 'nature'. It seemed as though the terms in each of these pairs were separated by an abyss, created apparently by the older art theory of Renaissance thinkers whose ideas Leonardo took up and developed further. In his *Trattato della Pittura*, Leon Battista Alberti warned artists not to trust the power of their own genius (*ingegno*), but rather to contemplate the great model of 'nature'. The artist must avoid the error of those fools who, proud of their talent, believe they can earn laurels in painting, without ever having taken from nature any examples that they can follow with their eye or with their understanding.[55] Leonardo, on the other hand, resolves this opposition. For him, the creative power of the artist is as certain as that of theoretical and scientific thought. Science is a second creation made with the understanding; painting is a second creation made with the imagination (*la scienza è una seconda creazione fatta col discorso; la pittura è seconda creazione fatta colla fantasia*). But the value of both these creations consists not in their departure from nature and from the empirical truth of things, but precisely in their grasp and revelation of this truth.

Such a peculiar reciprocal relationship between 'nature' and 'freedom' was impossible so long as the opposition between them was thought of in ethical and religious categories. In the realm of the will, the ethical-religious Ego saw itself placed before an alternative. It could choose

[53] Valla *De voluptate* i. 10, *Opera* fol. 907.

[54] Ernst Walser, *Studien zur Weltanschauung der Renaissance*, p. 12.

[55] Leon Battista Alberti *Trattato della pittura* iii, ed. Janitschek (Vienna, 1877), 151: 'Ma per non perdere studio et faticha, si vuole fuggire quella consuetudine d'alcuni sciocchi, i quali presuntuosi di suo ingegnio, senza avere essemplo alcuno dalla natura quale con occhi o mente seguano, studiano da sè ad sè acquistare lode di dipigniere. Questi non imparano dipigniere bene, ma assuefanno sè a' suoi errori. Fuggie l'ingegni non periti quella idea della bellezza, quale i beni exercitatissimi appena discernono.'

one or the other; it could decide against freedom and grace and for nature; or for the *regnum gratiae*, for freedom and providence, against nature. But Leonardo, from the very beginning, stands above this conflict that constitutes the basic theme of Pico's 'Oration on the Dignity of Man'. For Leonardo, nature no longer signifies the realm of the formless—the mere matter that opposes itself to the principle of form and its dominion. Viewing it only through the medium of art, Leonardo does not see nature devoid of form but rather as the very realm of perfect and complete form itself. Necessity does, indeed, reign as the bond and the eternal rule of nature—but this is not the necessity of mere matter; it is the necessity of pure proportion, intimately related to the mind. Proportion may be found not only in numbers and measurements but also in tones, weights, times and places, and in whatever power it happens to be.[56] Through inner measure and harmony, nature is, so to speak, redeemed and ennobled. It no longer stands opposed to man as an inimical or strange power. For, although nature is simply inexhaustible and infinite, we are nevertheless certain that it is the infinity of the *infinite ragioni* of mathematics. And although we can never encompass their entire extension, we nevertheless can grasp their ultimate foundations, their *principles*. The ideality of mathematics lifts the mind to its greatest heights and brings it to its true perfection. It thrusts aside the medieval barrier between nature and mind, and between the human and the divine intellect. Later, *Galileo*, too, explicitly draws this bold conclusion. In his dialogue on the two chief systems of the world he tells us that the standard of knowledge may be understood in either of two senses, depending on whether one takes knowledge in its intensive or in its extensive signification. If one chooses the latter, if one takes as the point of departure the multiplicity of the *knowable*, then, compared to that, human understanding may be considered a nullity. But if, instead of looking at the objects of knowledge, one goes back to its *foundation* and to its principle, i.e., to that which makes it knowledge, then it is quite different. 'For here I say that the human mind understands some things as perfectly and possesses as absolute a certainty of them as does nature itself. And the pure mathematical sciences are of this kind. To be sure, the divine intellect knows the mathematical truths in infinitely greater fullness than does ours, for it knows them all; but of the few which the human intellect grasps, I believe that the knowledge of them is equal to divine knowledge in

---

[56] Ravaisson-Mollien, op. cit., fol. 49ʳ.

objective certainty, since man can see their *necessity*, and there can be no higher degree of certainty than that.'[57]

This establishes the basic relationship between artistic imagination and reality, and between 'genius' and 'nature': there is no conflict between them. True artistic imagination does not soar above nature into the realm of mere fictions and fantasies but, rather, seizes upon nature's own eternal and immanent laws. On this point, too, Leonardo and Goethe are in agreement. 'The law, manifesting itself in complete freedom and under its own conditions, brings forth the objectively beautiful, which then, of course, must find subjects worthy of comprehending it.'[58] The creative power of the artist, the imagination that creates a 'second nature', does not consist in his inventing the law, in his creating it *ex nihilo*; it consists in his discovery and demonstration of the law. The act of artistic seeing and of artistic representing separates the accidental from the necessary; in this act the essence of things appears and is visibly expressed in its form. The scientific theory of *experience*, in the version to be given it by Galileo and Kepler, will base itself on the basic concept and on the basic requirement of 'exactness' as formulated and established by the theory of art. And both the theory of art and the theory of exact scientific knowledge run through exactly the same phases of thought.

Throughout the entire Middle Ages, the 'bond between the *pulchrum* and the *bonum*' had firmly relegated art to the realms of theology and metaphysics. The loosening of that bond has rightly been called one of the most significant moments in the Renaissance theory of art, for it paved the way for the autonomy of aesthetics, which then received its theoretical foundation more than three centuries later.[59] And yet, this loosening is counterbalanced by a strengthening: as the *pulchrum* moves farther and farther from the *bonum*, it comes always closer to the *verum*. Leonardo warns artists not to 'imitate the manner of another'. He considers those who study authors instead of the works of nature to be not the children but the grandchildren of nature,[60] So, too, Galileo wages a constant battle against that Scholastic method which, instead of analysing and interpreting phenomena, indulges in the analysis of authors. But, like Leonardo, Galileo also constantly emphasizes that the

[57] Galilei, *Dialogo sopra i due massimi sistemi del mondo* (Ed. nazionale VII), p. 129.
[58] Johann Wolfgang Goethe, *Maximen und Reflexionen*, ed. Max Hecker, No. 1346.
[59] Erwin Panofsky, *Idea, Ein Beitrag zur Begriffsgeschichte der älteren Kunsttheorie, Studien der Bibliothek Warburg*, V, ed. Fritz Saxl (Leipzig, 1924), p. 29.
[60] *Il codice Atlantico*, fol. 141ʳ.

law governing phenomena, the *ragioni* that lie at their base, cannot be immediately read through sensory perception of the phenomena; rather, the spontaneity of the mathematical understanding is necessary to discover them. For we do not come to know what is eternal and necessary in things through a mere accumulation and comparison of sensible experiences; rather, the mind must have understood these qualities 'through itself', in order then to find them in the phenomena. Every intellect understands 'by itself' (*da per sè*) the true and necessary things, i.e., those that cannot be other than they are—otherwise, it cannot ever understand them at all.[61] Thus, every experiment, every questioning of experience, presupposes an intellectual 'sketch' of the thought, a *mente concipio*, as Galileo calls it, within which we anticipate a regularity in nature. Then we raise the 'sketch' to certainty by testing it through experience. Objective regularity, i.e., the permanent, basic measurements that determine and govern all natural phenomena, are not simply taken from experience; rather, they are placed at the base of experience as 'hypotheses', to be confirmed or refuted by it. The whole science of nature, according to Galileo, rests upon this new relationship between understanding (*discorso*) and sense, between experience and thought. And it is a relationship which, very clearly, is exactly analogous to the relation that exists in the Renaissance theory of art between the imagination of the painter and the 'objective' reality of things. The power of mind, the power of artistic and of scientific genius does not reside in unfettered arbitrariness but in the ability to teach us to see and to know the 'object' in its truth, in its highest determination. Be it as artist or as thinker, the genius finds the necessity in nature.

Centuries elapsed before this principle was formulated in all its theoretical clarity, i.e., before the 'critique of judgment' could formulate the principle that genius is the gift of nature through which 'nature in the subject' gives the law to art. But the path towards this objective was now clearly indicated.[62] And it was only through this path that the

---

[61] Galilei, loc. cit., p. 183: 'Posso bene insegnarvi delle cose che non son nè vere nè false; ma le vere, cioè le necessarie, cioè quelle che è impossibile ad esser altrimenti, ogni mediocre discorso o le sa da sè o è impossibile che ei le sappia mai.'

[62] I shall not go into the opposition between the 'spontaneity' of genius and the 'objectivity' of rules, as it was formulated in Renaissance poetic theory. There is now considerable new material for an analysis and judgment of this matter in Edgar Zilsel, *Die Entstehung des Geniebegriffs* (Tübingen, 1926); and in a dissertation submitted at the University of Hamburg by Hans Thüme, *Beiträge zur Geschichte des Geniebegriffs in England*. This problem, this controversy between 'imitatio' and 'inventio' was fought out with Politian, the young Pico, and Erasmus on one side, and Cortese and Bembo on the other. To be sure, a clear and distinct definition of principles was never achieved. And yet, Renaissance

Renaissance succeeded in overcoming magic and mysticism as well as the whole complex of 'occult' sciences. The alliance of mathematics and art theory accomplished what had been impossible to achieve through dedication to empirical and sensible observation and through direct immersion of the feelings into the 'inners of nature'.

The new and really modern idea of nature now emerges. As a synthesis of the theoretical and artistic spirit of the Renaissance, it is presented most completely in Kepler's work on the harmony of the world. Kepler himself formulates the relationship in purely Platonic terms: he considers the laws of harmony to be the basic determinations. We find them in the empirical, sensible, and visible world, only because everything visible is created according to the eternal 'archetypes' of order and measure, of arithmetic and geometry. And Galileo, too, the great scientific analyst who always carefully distinguishes the empirical from the metaphysical, the logical from the aesthetic—Galileo, too, is aware that the artistic and the scientific mind have a common root. He considers art and science different ways of giving form. Without hesitation and without envy, he declares that the form-giving power of the great artists is superior to purely theoretical observation. In the same passage wherein he boldly equates the human and the divine intellect, he attempts to prove the nobility of the human mind by referring to the productivity of the creative artist, which is infinitely superior to that of the theoretician. 'When I go through the many wonderful inventions of humanity in the arts and sciences and then think of my own knowledge which is so completely incapable of making anything new,

philosophy anticipated that pregnant formulation which later, passing through English psychology and aesthetics, came to influence Lessing and Kant. Giordano Bruno said it most emphatically when he declared that poetry does not derive from rules but rather that rules are derived from poetry. For there are as many genera and species of genuine rules as there are genera and species of true poets. (Bruno, *Eroici furori* I, *Opere italiane*, ed. Paul de Lagarde, 625.) In any case, Panofsky rightfully emphasized that the 'true Renaissance' knows of no 'conflict between "genius" and "rules", nor between "genius" and "nature".' (Panofsky, op. cit., 38.) The Renaissance concept of the idea 'expressed with particular clarity the compatibility of these opposites which, as a matter of fact, had not yet begun to conflict. The concept of the idea *guarantees* and *limits* the freedom of the artistic spirit against the claims of reality.' This agrees perfectly with the results of our investigation. Only I would not say with Panofsky that Renaissance thought 'empiricized' and 'a-posteriorized' the idea of art in general and the idea of beauty in particular. (Panofsky, op. cit., 56.) What seems to me to be peculiar and decisive in Renaissance thought is that both its theory of nature and its theory of art cling to the 'a priori' character of the idea and nevertheless, through this a priori character itself, place the idea in a new relation to experience. For now, the mathematical idea, the 'a priori' of proportion and of harmony, constitutes the common principle of empirical reality and of artistic beauty. The 'innate' idea of number and the 'innate' idea of beauty led Kepler, as he himself always emphasized, to establish the three basic laws of planetary movements.

or even of only grasping the old, I am overcome with amazement, afflicted with desperation, and almost consider myself unfortunate. When I look at an excellent statue, I say to myself: when will you learn to carve out of a block of marble such an essence; to discover the magnificent form which the marble hid? Or to mix various colours and to spread them on a canvas or on a wall in such a manner that they represent the whole realm of the visible, like Michelangelo, Raphael, Titian?'[63] Once again, we have before us the motif that we encountered earlier in the realm of ethical and religious speculation; but this time it is in connection with the theory of art and the theory of experience. Once again, the mind of man proves to be a second creator, a 'true Prometheus under Jupiter'. From the most various quarters and by the most devious paths, we see the Renaissance always returning to the same image. For the Renaissance, this image is evidently more than a mere allegory; it becomes the symbol of what the Renaissance is and is striving for as a total intellectual movement.

Together with this discovery of the new concept of nature—indeed, as part of the discovery itself—the Renaissance experienced an enrichment and deepening of its *historical consciousness*. For now it has new access to the classical Greek world of thought; it has found the way from the Hellenistic philosophy of late antiquity to Platonic idealism. This process is not concerned merely with making available the genuine Platonic heritage of thought; it is concerned with a real *anamnesis* of Platonic doctrine, i.e., with its renovation in the depths of thought itself. To see this process clearly and distinctly, we need only recall that passage in Plato's Phaedo, in which the deepest motifs of the Platonic doctrine of ideas and their true genesis is revealed to us. Plato believed that the attainment of his basic principle depended upon finding a completely new way of *investigating* being and upon a complete rupture with the whole methodology of pre-Socratic philosophy. He tells us that in his youth, he too felt a prodigious desire for that wisdom called natural science. Its aims had seemed so lofty—to know the causes of everything, to know why everything is, why it is born and decays. And, like the natural philosophers, he too had sought to assuage this desire by letting himself be guided by perception, by trying to immediately grasp things with the eye, the ear, and every other individual sense. But the farther he progressed on this path, the more clearly he became aware that it did not lead to the truth of existing things

---

[63] Galilei, op. cit., p. 118.

(τῶν ὄντων ἡ ἀλήθεια). 'After I had become tired of looking directly at things, it came to me that I ought to beware of having happen to me what often happens to those who gaze upon the sun during an eclipse. Many people spoil their eyes by looking at the sun itself, instead of looking at its image in the water, or in some other place. I noticed something of that sort myself, and I feared that my soul would become completely blind if I directed my eyes immediately upon objects and tried, with all my senses, to apprehend them. It appeared to me that I must have recourse to thoughts, and observe in them the true nature of things. But perhaps the analogy, as I have drawn it, is imperfect. For I should not at all want to admit that whoever contemplates being through thoughts is seeing it more as a reflected image than he who contemplates it in the objects of nature. Well, I moved in that direction, and, using as a basis each time that principle which I considered the strongest, I posited as true whatever seemed to me to agree with it, and as false whatever did not.' In this passage, we can clearly see the core of Plato's new mode of thought and its opposition to the whole of Greek natural philosophy. It is well known that Plato included Anaxagoras in his condemnation of natural philosophers. According to Plato, the νοῦς of Anaxagoras was unworthy of that name, for upon closer observation it proved to be only a moving force and, as such, a mere natural potency. We shall be able to see true being only by turning away from the immediate and sensible perception of things—only through the 'flight into logos'. But to Plato, the flight into logos means flight into mathematics. This is the 'second journey', the δεύτερος πλοῦς, the only one that leads to the shores of the realm of ideas.

If we compare this development with the development of the concept of nature in the Renaissance, we shall observe a startling repetition of the individual phases.[64] The Renaissance also began on the first path, i.e., with the attempt at an immediate and sensible grasping of nature. Telesio's dictum that all knowledge, in the final analysis, can be traced to a *contact* between the Ego and things immediately calls to mind Plato's mockery of those who believed they could seize being 'with their bare hands' (ἀπρὶξ ταῖν χεροῖν). But it was just this attempt that ultimately made the philosophy of nature blind to the

---

[64] On this point and on what follows, cf. the more detailed evidence in my *Erkenntnisproblem*, I, 314ff. Even there, however, the significance of the *aesthetic* factor in the discovery of the modern concept of nature is not sharply enough perceived.

peculiar 'truth' of nature and to its universal regularity, and led it back into the darkness of mysticism and of theosophy. And once again, it was the return to 'logos' that cleared the way for a science of nature. What Plato calls the λόγοι that we must take as a basis, Leonardo calls the *ragioni* that our knowledge must lay bare in experience. And despite the undeniable value he attributes to experience, Leonardo does not hesitate to give the *ragioni* precedence over mere sensible observation. *Nessuno effetto è in natura sanza ragione; intendi la ragione, e non ti bisogna esperienzia.*[65] And Galileo's research is dominated by the same theme. According to him, the basic laws of nature are not laws of immediately given or of factually demonstrable things; rather, they refer completely to ideal cases which in nature can never be quite completely realized. But that does not diminish their truth, their 'objectivity'. That nature never presents us with a body 'completely left to itself' does not constitute an objection against the principle of inertia, just as Archimedes' principle of the spiral is not damaged by the fact that there is no body in nature that moves spirally.

Once we have established this systematic agreement between Leonardo and Galileo on the one hand, and Plato on the other, we need no longer ask how, and by what tortuous paths the knowledge of the true Platonic doctrine was historically transmitted to both of them. One of the miracles of Leonardo's wondrous mind was that he could live in Quattrocento Florence, in the midst of the atmosphere of Neo-Platonism, and yet remain practically untouched by the Neo-Platonic spirit. What led him back to the historical Plato, what made him, as it were, a Platonist *despite* Ficino and the Florentine Academy, was the fact that as an artist, as a theoretician of art, and as a scientific investigator, he agreed thoroughly with the Platonic maxim: μηδεὶς εἰσίτω ἀγεωμέτρητος. He adopted this maxim completely: *non mi legga, chi non è matematico, nelli mia principi.*[66] This new relationship to the Platonic doctrine will emerge with complete consciousness and clarity in Galileo's thought. The Platonic theory of knowledge runs like a red thread throughout his works, especially in his dialogue on the two chief systems of the world. From the Platonic doctrine of ἀνάμνησις he takes his conception of the *a priori* (*da per sè*). This phrase announced the spontaneity of the mind and the autonomy of the theoretical understanding and broke the magic spell that had bound the natural

[65] Leonardo, *Il codice Atlantico*, fol. 147ᵛ.
[66] Richter, op. cit., No. 3.

philosophy of the Renaissance. This phrase brought about the break-through into the open field of objective knowledge of nature and completed the return from Hellenistic to classical antiquity.

In his work on Luther, *Warburg* gives this summary of the astrological ideas in the Renaissance: 'We are in the age of Faust. The modern scientist tries to carve out an intellectual realm for reflection between himself and the·object—a realm located somewhere between magical practice and cosmological mathematics. Athens once again wants to be liberated from Alexandria.'[67] This 'liberation of Athens from Alexandria' was the common objective of the Renaissance theory of art and the theory of science. The 'intellectual realm for reflection' was won back by recalling the Platonic *logos* and the Socratic-Platonic requirement of λόγον διδόναι. Thus, the new conception of nature springs from a new conception of the meaning and aim of knowledge. The natural philosophy of the Renaissance had sought nothing less than an *epistemological* foundation and justification of magic. According to Campanella, the possibility of magic follows from the same principle as the possibility of knowledge. For we could not 're-cognize' anything if subject and object, man and nature, had not originally been one. We know an object only when we fuse with it, when we, as it were, *become* it. *Cognoscere est fieri rem cognitam* is Campanella's definition of the act of knowledge; and according to Patrizzi, *cognoscere est coire cum suo cognobili*. Magic is only a *practical* expression of what is theoretically represented in knowledge. On the basis of the identity of the subject and object, magic shows how the subject not only can grasp but can also dominate the object; it shows how the Ego subjects nature not only to its intellect but also to its will. Thus, magic, construed as 'natural' not as 'demonic' magic, becomes the most noble part of the knowledge of nature and the 'perfection of philosophy'. If we can name a concept by its most perfect representation and embodiment, says Pico della Mirandola, then we may apply the name of magic to the *whole* of science and the whole of philosophy with as much right as we call Rome 'the' city, Virgil 'the' poet, Aristotle 'the' philosopher.[68]

[67] Warburg, 'Heidnisch-antike Weissagung', p. 70.

[68] Pico della Mirandola *Apologia, Opera*, fol. 170: 'Si ergo Magia, idem est quod sapientia, merito hanc practicam scientiae naturalis, quae praesupponit exactam et absolutam cognitionem omnium rerum naturalium, quasi apicem et fastigium totius philosophiae, peculiari et appropriato nomine Magiam, id est sapientiam, sicut Romam urben, Virgilium poetam, Aristotelem philosophum dicimus, appellare voluerunt.'

Neither the theory of art nor the theory of exact science could follow natural philosophy on this path. Unlike the mythical-magical view of nature, both are governed by one and the same intellectual tendency, i.e., by the will to pure *form*. But all form, theoretical or aesthetic, requires delimitation and organization; it requires a definite and clear contour of things. If nature is to be grasped in formed images, or to be thought of as orderly and necessary, pantheism and panentheism of feeling are no longer enough. The tendency towards immersion in nature's all-embracing unity is now opposed by a contrary tendency towards particularization and specificity. Neither art nor mathematics can allow the subject to dissolve in the object and the object to dissolve in the subject. Only by maintaining a *distance* between the two can we possibly have a sphere for the aesthetic image and a sphere for logical-mathematical thoughts.

The collaboration of these two basic intellectual forces of the Renaissance bears still another fruit: it leads to a transformation and a radically new modification of the theoretical conception of 'sensibility'. We have already seen that Leonardo's whole view of nature grew out of the specific, aboriginal force of his own being, out of his exact and sensible fantasy. Pico had considered magic the 'summit of philosophy' (*apex et fastigium totius philosophiae*); but in Leonardo's *Trattato della pittura* painting seems to want to claim this rank for itself. Whoever disregards painting, says Leonardo, loves neither philosophy nor nature.[69] With this conception of the value and meaning of the visual arts, the Renaissance moves away from Plato. For Plato saw in art almost nothing but the 'mimetic' element, the element of imitation of the given; and he therefore excluded it, as art of the idols, from the true vision of ideas.[70] The opposition to Plato's view is deeply rooted in the essence of the Renaissance. Speculative idealism itself takes up the new view and tries to give it a systematic justification. Nicholas Cusanus developed no independent *aesthetic*; but in his theory of knowledge, he gave sensibility a new place and a new value, opposed to the Platonic conception. It is significant and characteristic that whenever Cusanus relies on Plato and directly follows him, he does so precisely in those places where Plato seems to be more friendly than usual to sensory perception, admitting that it has a value for knowledge—though, to be sure, con-

[69] Ravaisson-Mollien, op. cit., A. fol. 20ʳ.
[70] Further details in my lecture, 'Eidos und Eidolon. Das Problem des Schönen und der Kunst in Platons Dialogen', *Vorträge der Bibliothek Warburg* (1922/23), I, 1ff.

ditional and relative. He cites those sentences in Plato's *Republic* which affirm that individual classes of sensory perception indirectly promote the aim of knowledge precisely because of the contradictions they bear within them. For it is just these contradictions that do not permit the soul to rest content with mere perception. They incite thought and become its 'paraclete'. The contradiction in sensibility spurs on the search for genuine and true meaning elsewhere, in the region of the διάνοια.[71]

What Plato conceded only to a particular *species* of sense-perception, Cusanus now extends to the whole *genus*. This animating and awakening power is proper not just to this or that kind of perception but to sense experience as a whole. The intellect cannot attain consciousness of itself and of its capacities unless it be stimulated to its appropriate activity by the forces of sensibility. If, as a result of this stimulus, the intellect turns towards the sensible world, it does not do so to submerge itself there but, rather, so that it may raise the world to itself. Its apparent descent to the sensible actually signifies the ascent of the latter to it. For in the 'otherness' of the sensible world the intellect finds its own indissoluble unity and identity; in giving itself over to what seems to be essentially foreign to it, the intellect finds its own fulfilment, its unfolding and conceiving of itself.[72] In this view, experience is no longer the hostile polar opposite of the basic power of theoretical knowledge and scientific reason; instead, experience becomes the true medium, the field of activity, and the test of theoretical knowledge. Both Leonardo and Galileo look upon the opposition as a purely reciprocal relationship. The difference between reason and experience is only a difference of *direction*. 'My intention,' says Leonardo in one of his investigations of the principle of the lever, 'is first to adduce the experiment, and then to show with reason (*colla ragione dimostrare*) why such an experiment must necessarily operate in this and in no other way. And this is the true way in which those who would investigate the effects of nature must proceed; for although nature begins with reason and ends with experience, we must go the opposite way, i.e., begin with the experiment and with that investigate the reason (*ragione*).'[73] Here, as in Galileo's distinction and correlative union of the 'resolutive' (analytical) and the 'compositive' (synthetic) methods, a truly circular process

[71] Plato *Republic* 523Aff.; cf. Cusanus *Idiota* iii. 4.
[72] Cusanus *De conjecturis* ii. 11, 16. (On the whole, cf. above, p. 43.)
[73] Ravaisson-Mollien, op. cit., E fol. 55ʳ.

takes place. From the phenomena one goes to their 'reasons', and from these back to the phenomena. This erases the sharp dividing line drawn by Plato between the path of the *dialectician* and that of the *mathematician*.[74] The path of the dialectician 'upwards' and that of the mathematician 'downwards' is the same; each of them represents only a different stage in the cyclical process of knowledge. And this also throws new light on the relationship between pure theory and its application. Even Plato's theory of knowledge recognizes an 'applied' mathematics and assigns it a very definite place in the systematically graduated process of knowledge. Indeed, one might well say that Plato was the first to give a completely precise, methodologically significant sense to the concept of 'application' of mathematics to nature. For it was he who assigned the astronomers of his time the famous task of 'saving' the phenomena of the heavens by relating them to and deriving them from strictly uniform movements. Nevertheless, the knowledge of nature, the knowledge of sensible phenomena as such, is not a purpose in itself but must serve only as a preliminary outline of pure theory. The dialectician turns to astronomy not for the sake of its *object* but for the sake of the *problems* it poses to the mathematician and hence to pure thought. He does not want to immerse himself in the observation and admiration of the 'variegated work of the heavens'. Rather, he leaves the things in the heavens alone, for, as a true student of astronomy, he is concerned with making useful instead of useless that which is by nature rational in his soul.[75] The purpose of the true, the philosophical astronomer, is, therefore, propaedeutical, not empirical; he aims not at the sensible world itself, but at that 'reversal' of the soul which leads from the world of the senses to the world of pure thought.

Renaissance thought represents a radical departure from this basic Platonic view. The change is evident even in those cases where Renaissance thought is concerned with the immediate revival of genuinely Platonic motifs. The true independence of the world of experience was really first won by the Renaissance. Empirical content and mathematical form still remain strictly related to one another; but this relationship has now received, so to speak, an opposite sign. The empirical is no longer to be resolved in the ideal, therewith to be stripped of its specific character. On the contrary, the ideal can only be genuinely fulfilled in the empirical, where it is tested and justified. For Plato, the

---

[74] Plato *Republic* 533Cff.
[75] Ibid., 630Aff.

theory of motion was only a 'paradigm', a necessarily incomplete example of abstract mathematical relations; but in the Renaissance, it receives a value in itself, and actually becomes the objective of all pure mathematics. According to Leonardo, mechanics is 'the paradise of all mathematical sciences', because 'the fruits of mathematics' are attained there.[76] Galileo represents the last stage in this development. And he gives it its clearest methodological expression, inasmuch as he considers movement itself an *idea*. It no longer belongs to the shadow realm of becoming, to the Platonic γένεσις; now it is raised to pure being, inasmuch as it possesses a strict regularity, and therewith constancy and necessity. Taken as an object of *knowledge*, movement and even the material mass itself possess ideality. For in both, certain immutable characteristics can be shown which behave in the same way; and in both purely mathematical laws are demonstrable.[77] With this, experience was raised to strict knowledge for the first time. And, as Galileo says at the beginning of his penetrating discussion of local movement in the *Discorsi*, with this was won 'a completely new science of a very old subject'.[78] Both the realistic-empirical and the idealistic tendencies of the Renaissance found their adequate expression in this result. If the Renaissance theory of science was able to assign a new place to sensibility, it was because such a theory was intellectually equal to the task for the first time, i.e., because it had worked out the basic ideal means by which the merely sensible impressions could be transformed into pure intellectual *vision*. The same direction of observation and the same characteristic transition shaped the cosmology of the Renaissance. The new conception of the nature of movement required and created out of itself a new concept of the world. As the problem of movement became more and more the intellectual focal point of research, and as it was ever more precisely understood in its new form, the corresponding need for a radical transformation of the theory of the elements and of the theory of the universe became more and more urgent.

[76] Ravaisson-Mollien, op. cit., E fol. 8ᵛ.

[77] Cf., e.g., Galilei, *Discorsi e dimonstrazioni matematiche intorno a due nuove scienze, I, Opera*, ed. Albèri, XIIII, 7: 'E perchè io suppongo la materia esser inalterabile, cioè sempre l'istessa, è manifesto che di lei come di affezione eterna e necessaria si possono produr dimonstrazioni non meno dell'altre schiette e pure matematiche.' For movement, the same principle is formulated; cf., e.g., Galilei's essay against Vincenzo di Grazia (*Opera*, XII, 507ff.).

[78] Galilei, *Discorsi, Giornata terza, Opera*, XIII, 148.

3

The logical and scientific primacy won by the problem of movement in the philosophy of the Renaissance contains within it the seed and the origin of modern cosmology. At first, this statement seems to present us with a historical paradox. Had not the central place of the concept of movement been assured since antiquity? Did not the *Aristotelian* conception of movement constitute the nucleus and the conceptual centre of the Aristotelian theory of nature? Peripatetic physics was based on the basic distinction it made in the primary forms of movement. Aristotle interprets the concept of κίνησις in a sense so wide that it includes not only change of place but also qualitative change (ἀλλοίωσις), quantitative growth (αὔξησις), and birth and decay (γένεσις καὶ φθορά). Nevertheless, he maintains that *change of place* is first and fundamental compared to the others; it is the genuine πρότερον τῇ φύσει. For change of place brings forth the difference upon which rest the nature and constitution of the subjects that bear this difference within them. The four constitutive elements of the cosmos—the elements of earth, water, air, and fire—show their specific difference by having a specific and peculiar kind of movement proper to each of them. In the constitution of the whole, each of these elements has its natural place, where it can attain its peculiar perfection. And each element, therefore, necessarily strives to return to that place whenever it is separated from it. Out of this basic tendency comes movement in a straight line for the earthly substances, whereas the only form of movement worthy of the indestructible and perfect substance of the heavenly bodies is movement in a perfect circle. Because of its nature, because of its original and absolute gravity, the element of earth strives towards the centre of the world; the element of fire, because of its absolute lightness, strives to flee from that centre. But there is no such struggle in the aether that constitutes the substance of the heavens. There, pure and perfect uniformity reigns. The unity of the divine mover who set the heavenly spheres into orbit must be reflected in the form of this orbit itself; therefore, it can only be completely regular and completely circular.

Thus, for Aristotle, movement becomes the true foundation for a partitioning of the world, a *fundamentum divisionis* in both the physical and metaphysical senses of the word. But movement can only serve as an original moment of the determination of being insofar as it is taken according to its purely qualitative side, as an absolute determination of being. What Aristotle sees in movement, therefore, is no mere ideal *relation* to be defined within both universal *orders* of time and of place. In the Aristotelian view, such a relation would not suffice to assure a real, ontological significance to movement. It would remain mathematically abstract, merely intellectual and thus it would not designate, much less exhaust, the concrete 'whatness', i.e., the essence of the natural object. It is a fact that all our affirmations concerning any concrete 'what' are always accompanied by affirmations concerning its 'where'. And it is also a fact that one cannot make qualitative determinations of physical bodies without basing them on local determinations. These facts must be interpreted by Aristotle in such a way as to confer upon place itself a definite and substantial meaning. Places have their nature and peculiar characteristics, the same as bodies—or, if not the same, at least in an analogous way. And there exists a very definite relationship of community or of conflict, of sympathy or of antipathy between the two natures. The body is by no means indifferent to the place in which it is located and by which it is enclosed; rather, it stands in a real and causal relation to it. Every physical element seeks 'its' place, the place that belongs and corresponds to it, and it flees from any other opposed to it. Thus, with relation to specific elements, place itself seems to be endowed with powers—but they are not definable powers, like those, say, of attraction or repulsion in modern mechanics. The powers of place are not concerned with mathematical and physical *sizes* which could be graduated in relation to each other according to a principle of 'more' or 'less'. Instead of such a relative scale of size values, we have before us absolute values of being.

In expounding his cosmology, Aristotle asks himself whether the tendency by virtue of which a certain element strives towards its natural place is to be thought of as a quantitative and graduatable property, i.e., one which would also change its degree in proportion to the changing distance from its natural place. But, in keeping with the basic assumptions of his physics and his cosmology, he must emphatically answer 'No' to this question. It seems absurd to him that a heavy body should be more strongly drawn to the centre of the earth when it is closer to it. Distance as such is a purely external determination, one which must be left out of consideration when we seek to ascertain the effects that derive from the 'nature', the essence of a thing. This essence, and the tendency of movement determined by it, is proper to all bodies in an absolutely invariable way, and is, therefore, completely independent of such an external and accidental circumstance as greater proximity or distance. τὸ δ' ἀξιοῦν ἄλλην εἶναι φύσιν τῶν ἁπλῶν σωμάτων, ἂν ἀποσχῶσιν ἔλαττον ἢ πλεῖον τῶν οἰκείων τόπων, ἄλογον· τί γὰρ διαφέρει τοσονδὶ φάναι μῆκος ἀποσχεῖν ἢ τοσονδί; διοίσει γὰρ κατὰ λογον, ὅσῳ πλεῖον μᾶλλον, το δ' εἶδος τὸ αὐτό.[79]

These sentences formulate the basic idea of the physics of 'substantial forms' in the most precise and pregnant manner. In modern physics, objective and real meaning is bestowed upon certain immutable *relations*. All the definiteness of physical being and happening is based on these relations as expressions of general *laws of nature*; so that the individual terms of the relations, i.e., the bodies and places, are only definable through these laws. But in Aristotle's thought, we have the completely opposite relationship. The architectonic construction of the cosmos and the form of the activity within it are determined by the nature, i.e., the φύσις and the εἶδος of places 'in themselves' and of bodies and elements 'in themselves'.

Scholastic physics clung to this basic assumption. To be sure, *Duhem* has shown that in the fourteenth century, a new spirit began to awaken even in Scholastic physics. The writings of *Albert of Saxony* in particular formulate certain problems which, if considered purely from the viewpoint of the form in which the *question was formulated*, prepared the way for modern cosmology, i.e., for the theories of Kepler and Newton.[80] But an answer to these questions could only be given after the foundation of Aristotelian physics had been removed—after the groundwork of the doctrine of place and space had been shaken. In speculative philosophy, *De docta ignorantia* represents the first real breach. It attacked the vital centre of the Aristotelian doctrine. In this work, Cusanus resuscitated the ancient—and especially the Pythagorean —theory of the movement of the earth. But the importance of this work for cosmology does not derive primarily from the fact of that resuscitation; rather, it derives from the *principle* that brought the resuscitation about. Here, for the first time, the basic idea of the *relativity of place and of movement* was formulated with true precision. And this idea itself appeared only as a corollary to that more general postulate governing Cusanus' *doctrine of knowledge*. To define the concept of objective truth, Cusanus finds it speculatively and philosophically necessary to embrace the principles of *measurement*, for he considers all know-

[79] Aristotle περὶ οὐρανοῦ A8.   [80] Cf. Duhem, op. cit., II, 82ff., *et passim*.

ledge to be merely a particular case of the univesral function of measuring. *Mens* and *mensura* belong together; whoever has understood the
nature of measurement has also seen the true meaning and depth of the
mind. But this reciprocal relation of the problems brings with it a
further consequence. A genuine doctrine of measurement, a mathematical cosmography and cosmology, are dependent upon the insight into
the fundamental relationship of 'subject' and 'object'. To find the true,
objective measurements of the universe, it is necessary first to consider
the procedure and the basic form of measurement itself, i.e., to have
attained full clarity of the conditions of measurement. But, according to
Cusanus, a basic condition of all measurement, especially of all spatial
and temporal comparisons, consists in the acceptance of certain points
as fixed and invariable. Without *positing* such fixed points, without
determining certain poles or centres, any description of physical movements would be impossible. Indispensable as this positing is, the principle of the *docta ignorantia* requires that we conceive of it precisely as
positing, i.e., that we understand it as a hypothetical and ideal, not as an
absolute and ontological determination. The measuring mind can never
do without fixed points and centres. But the choice of these points is
not prescribed once and for all by the objective nature of things; rather,
it belongs to the freedom proper to the mind. No physical 'place' en-
joys any kind of natural precedence over any other. What is at rest
from the point of view of *one* observer may be seen as moving from the
point of view of *another*, and vice versa. With this, the concept of
absolute place and of absolute movement loses its meaning. If one
observer were situated at the north pole of the earth and another at that
of the heavenly sphere, the former would have the pole and the latter
the Zenith in the centre; and each would be right to consider the place
in which he stands to be the centre and to relate everything else to this
point. It is the task of the *intellect* to relate all these different views to
each other and to assemble them 'complicatively' into a unity. But, in this
process, the world appears to be a wheel within a wheel, a sphere within
a sphere; it does not possess one central point preferable to any other.[81]

---

[81] Cusanus *De docta ignorantia* ii. 11: 'Complica igitur istas diversas imaginationes ut sit
centrum Zenith et e converso; et tunc per intellectum (cui tantum servit docta ignorantia)
vides mundum et ejus motum ac figuram attingi non posse, quoniam apparebit quasi rota
in rota, sphaera in sphaera, nullibi habens centrum vel circumferentiam, ut praefertur.'
For the historical significance and influence of this doctrine cf. especially E. F. Apelt,
Die Reformation der Sternkunde (Jena, 1852), pp. 18ff. For the systematic connection between
Cusanus' metaphysics and his cosmology, I may now refer the reader to a forthcoming
dissertation by Hans Joachim Ritter, at the University of Hamburg.

Contrasted with the Aristotelian world with its fixed places and measurements, this relativism may at first appear to be a complete disintegration. But here, too, the apparent scepticism of the *docta ignorantia* serves only as a preparation and as a vehicle for the conception of a completely new and *positive* task. In Peripatetic physics, we have, so to speak, a reciprocal determination of the fundamental elements: the places are defined by the bodies that belong to them, and the bodies by the places. The realm of space is divided in the same way and according to the same points of view as the world of objects. Just as objects are separated into eternal and mutable, into perfect and imperfect, so, too, an analogous division runs through the spatial world. In the one, properties are not interchangeable; in the other, places are not. An unbridgeable gap separates the 'above' from the 'below', the 'higher' heavenly world from the 'lower' sublunar world. To end this separation would seem also to threaten all definite spatial determinations, all clear and definite delimitations. The ἄπειρον, not only in the sense of the quantitatively infinite but also in the sense of the qualitatively indeterminable, would seem to become again master of the πέρας; chaos would seem to become master over the cosmos.

Just at this point the new, infinitely fruitful, positive requirement makes itself felt. The new principle of knowledge born of Cusanus' philosophy, and the new norm of certainty established by him destroy the Aristotelian image of the world with its fixed central points and its interpenetrating spheres by conceiving of it as a mere image. But precisely because of this destruction, the task of reconstructing a total order of being and happening out of the powers and means proper to the intellect becomes so much the more urgent. The intellect must learn to move in its own medium, in the free aether of thought, without the help and support of the senses, so that it will be able, by virtue of this movement, to master the senses and to raise them up to itself. Thus, compared with Aristotelian-Scholastic physics, the order of problems has been reversed. What had been the starting point there now becomes the end, the objective of cosmological observation. Once the relativity of all local determination is recognized in principle, we may no longer ask how we can establish fixed *points* in the universe; instead, we must ask how fixed *laws* of change may be ascertained in this realm of complete mutual relationship and of limitless variability in which we now stand. The determination of any 'place' now presupposes, and can only be made within, a system of universal *rules* of movement. The unity of the universe as an *universum contractum* is based upon the unity of these rules. For what distinguishes the 'contracted' unity of the world from the absolute unity of God is that in the former, identity is never present as a substantial sameness, but rather is only relative, i.e., it is identity only in relation to 'otherness'. Unity can be grasped only through the medium of multiplicity; and permanence can be understood only through the medium of change. These determinations are not separated in such a way as to be proper to different spheres of the universe, so that change would dominate in the one and unity and uniformity in the other. Such a spatial distinction would conflict with the conceptual principle of *correlativity* as it is now established. In the cosmos of Cusanus there is no longer any individual existence that does not indissolubly unite within itself both determinations: that of 'unity' and that of 'otherness'; duration and constant change. In this cosmos, then, there is no longer any individual part 'outside', 'above', or 'below' any other; the principle of 'everything in everything' (*quodlibet in quodlibet*) prevails. If the universe is recognized to be a totality of movements interacting with each other according to definite laws, there can no longer be any 'above' or 'below'; nor can there be anything eternal and necessary that is separate from the temporal and accidental. Rather, all empirical reality is characterized precisely by the concidence of these opposites. As a qualitative interaction, this coincidence must either be or not be. It cannot be present to a higher degree in one place and to a lower degree in another.

Among the parts of the world there exists that same symbolic relationship which, according to Cusanus, exists between God and the world. Just as the absolute maximum possesses its image in the relative maximum, just as the absolute infinity of God possesses its reflection in the limitlessness of the universe, so, too, the whole of the world is *recognized* in each of its individual parts; and so, too, the *constitution* of this whole reflects itself in its every particular determination, and in its every individual state. No part is any longer the whole, no part can embrace the completeness and perfection of the whole; but every part has the same right to *represent* this perfection. Out of this basic metaphysical conception Cusanus develops the new cosmological concept of *uniformity*. Using the principle of the *docta ignorantia*, he attains the insight into uniformity by enlarging to infinity the distance between the empirical world and the world of 'absolute' form, and, at the same time, resolving and making relative the differences *within* the world of conditioned, sensible and empirical reality. Every part of the cosmos is what it is only in connection with the whole; but this connection itself is now understood in such a way that no part can be dispensed with without destroying the function of the whole. The *movement* of the cosmos is also based on the inner mutual relationship of all its parts and not upon some push received from without. As soon as one has seen that what manifests itself in movement is only this mutual relationship of things, their own immanent 'reality', there ceases to be any need for an impulse from without, for a divine mover. In the totality, in the infinite variety of the individual movements, and in the universal law that embraces them as a unifying principle, the concept of nature is defined and exhausted. 'Nature' is nothing but the 'complication' of everything that happens in and through movement.

With this the foundation was laid for a new theory of dynamics. But certainly Cusanus' speculative thought, which had understood the problem with amazing clarity, could not solve it by its own means alone. From a distance he saw and pointed out the goal. But before it could be attained, the means corresponding to it and the thought forms adequate to it had to be created step by step. Through his concrete interpretation of the laws of planetary movement, and even more through their foundation in method and principle, *Kepler*, more than anyone else, proves to be the creator of a new concept of science. Place, he emphasizes, is not something given and definite; rather, the determination of place is the work of the mind: *omnis locatio est mentis seu mavis sensus communis opus.*[82] This fundamental proposition dominates Kepler's theoretical astronomy, his optics, and his theory of perception, fusing all three of them into an intellectual unity. Only from this standpoint can we completely understand what services the insight into the relativity of place and of movement performed for modern thought. Through this principle, a new basic relationship emerges between 'nature' and 'mind', between 'object' and 'subject'. Now, we can see clearly the *ideal* element that exists in every positing of an object and even in every spatial objectification. Since place is no longer seen as an immediately given objective element, and since it is interpreted as pure relationship, the task arises of assigning to this relationship its definite place in the whole science of nature and of conceiving of it in its peculiar and characteristic 'context'.

Even the relationship of the individual 'place' to 'space' undergoes an

[82] Kepler *Opera*, ed. Frisch. ii. 55.

essential transformation. Aristotle considers all individual determinations of place to be united in one whole space; but he conceives of the
relationship in physical rather than in mathematical terms. The connection is viewed not as ideal but as entitative; the one, all-embracing
space contains the particular places within it as contituent parts. Between the place a body occupies and the body itself there is a relationship of thing to thing. Aristotle compares this to the relationship that
exists between a vessel and the fluid poured into it. Just as the same jug
or wine-skin can contain wine or water, so, too, the same place can
contain this or that object. What we call space is neither the stuff of the
body nor the body itself. Both of these are the enclosed, whereas in the
concept of space, we think not of the enclosed but of that which encloses. But the latter does not mean the body's own boundaries, or its
configuration; for the configuration of the body is movable together
with it, so that if we took that to be an expression of space, the body
would not move *in* space, but *with* it. Thus, space can only be defined
as the boundary between the enclosing body and the enclosed. The
place of every individual body is determined by the internal boundaries
of the body next to it that encloses it, whereas space as a whole is to be
thought of as the boundary of the outermost heavenly sphere.[83] Of
course, boundary is to be understood as a geometrical line and not as
something material. Nevertheless, the totality of all these geometrical
determinations is more like a mere *aggregate* than like a *system*. The
πόπος κοινός, 'general' space, does not signify the *condition* for the
poisiting of individual spaces; as that which is sensible and which encloses, it stands in an analogous relation to particular places as these
stand to the individual bodies. Every particular 'place', every ἴδιος
τόπος, wraps itself around the particular body that it encloses, like a
pod, so to speak; and in this interrelationship, in this continuous encapsulization, general space only signifies the last, most external shell,
beyond which there can be neither space nor bodies.

In the system of Peripatetic physics, the concept of 'empty space' is
completely without meaning. Since space is conceived of only as a
determination *of* the body, as its boundary, it must necessarily adhere
to it, so that where there is no body there is also no possibility of space.
An empty space, as something which encloses, but encloses nothing,
would be a *contradictio in adjecto*. Accordingly, the continuity of space
is transformed from a geometrical and ideal determination to a kind of

83 Cf. Aristotle *Physics* iv. 5–7; *De coelo* iv. 3, *et passim*.

objective determination. We call the world of things continuous because next to every body we always find another body with no gaps
anywhere; so, too, there can be no *hiatus* in the connection of individual
places and the whole of space. The continuity of space is not, as in the
idealistic theories of space, founded in its 'form' and in its 'principle';
rather, it follows from what space is as a substantial and objective
entity, as a sub-stratum.

One of the most important tasks of Renaissance philosophy and
mathematics was the creation, step by step, of the conditions for a new
concept of space. The task was to replace *aggregate space* by *system space*,
i.e., to replace space as a *substratum* by space as a *function*. Space had to
be stripped of its objectivity, of its substantial nature, and had to be
discovered as a free, ideal complex of lines.[84] The first step on this path
consisted in establishing the general principle of the homogeneity of
space. In the system of Aristotelian physics, space could not be homogeneous because the difference between 'places' was as essential as the
difference between physical elements. If a certain element naturally
strives upwards, and another naturally strives downwards, it means that
the 'up' and the 'down' possess their own, fixed constitutions, their
own specific φύσις. But if space is to be conceived of not as com-
prising these given constitutions but, rather, as a systematic whole to
be synthetically constructed, the first requirement must be that the
form of this construction obey a strictly unitary law. In principle, the
same constructions must be possible from all points in space. Each point
must be conceivable as the point of departure and the objective for
every possible geometrical *operation*. Cusanus had already grasped this
postulate in its generality, but it found its first truly concrete fulfilment
in Galileo's theory of motion. We can now understand why Galileo
always comes back to this central problem in his criticism of Peripatetic
philosophy and physics. For the solution to the problem brings about
nothing less than a complete reversal of the hitherto accepted *concept* of
nature. 'Nature' no longer means the world of substantial forms; nor is
it the grounds for the movement and rest of the elements. Rather, it
designates that universal *regularity of movement* which no particular being
can escape, no matter how it is constituted, because only through it and

---

[84] Panofsky has shown that this discovery was made not only in mathematics and in
cosmology but in the plastic arts and in the art theory of the Renaissance as well; and, in
fact, that the theory of perspective anticipated the results of modern mathematics and
cosmology. Cf. his lecture 'Die Perspektive als symbolische Form', *Vorträge der Bibliothek
Warburg*, IV (1924/25).

by virtue of it can being be fitted into the universal *order* of occurrences. By conceiving of this order as ideal and mathematical and then comparing and testing it with the data of sensible experience, an intimate relationship arises between mathematics and sense experience. In principle, this relationship is bound by no limitations. In Galileo's world, there is no barrier to impede the full applicability of the 'ideal' to the 'real', nor to obstruct the complete validity of the 'abstract' for the 'concrete'. For Galileo, the homogeneity of the world follows from the necessary homogeneity of geometrical space. Movement ceases being a peculiar *quale*, to be found in the variously constituted bodies in varying modes; it now becomes definable through one and the same universally valid law of measure and size. The unification and synthesis of movements now follows no principle other than the synthesis of pure numbers, or the constructive summarizing of various geometrical operations. So long as one clung to the basic assumptions of Aristotelian physics, such a summary was impossible; for in that physics there existed both a real and a logical opposition among the various forms of movement. To be sure, in addition to the two opposite basic forms of movement, the rectilinear and the circular, Aristotle recognized a 'mixed' movement, which partook of both. But such a mixture, according to him, is only conceivable where we are not dealing with a unitary *subject* of movement, i.e., where the thing that moves is not a simple body but one made up of various constituent parts. But if we go back to the truly simple, we find that one and only one movement corresponds to the 'nature' of every element. To attribute several to it would mean to deny the simple determinateness proper to it. From the standpoint of Aristotelian physics, a 'simple' body to which were proper circular as well as rectilinear movement, movement towards as well as away from the centre, would, indeed, be a monstrosity. For such a body to exist one would have to conceive of the union of two substantial forms opposed to each other.

At this point, Galileo reverses the Aristotelian-Scholastic rule embodied in the proposition *operari sequitur esse*. Instead of deriving the form of activity from the dogmatic assumption of a form of being, he begins with the empirical laws of activity, and through these indirectly gains the point of departure for the determination of being.[85] And his view of the form of *activity* is, in turn, determined and carried by his basic view of the form of *knowledge*. For Galileo, the unity of nature,

[85] For details cf. my *Erkenntnisproblem*, I, 401ff.

the unity of *physis*, follows from the unity of physics which, in turn, is guaranteed by the unity of geometry and mathematics. Because there are general axioms for measurement and for the exact and empirical determination of quantities, the world of the measurable contains no oppositions that cannot be resolved. We must understand the fall of a stone and the movements of the stars by the same basic norms; and by these same norms we must define both heaven and earth. Both from the systematic and from the historical point of view we can see in this reversal the decisive importance of the problem of method for the problem of being. In the Middle Ages, methodological dualism, the opposition between theology and physics, reflects itself in a dualistic concept of matter. Indeed, Thomas Aquinas emphasizes that the essences of earthly and heavenly matter have nothing in common whatsoever except the *name*. The modern view, based on the assumption of the unity of the intellect and on the idea of a *mathesis universalis* as established by Descartes, draws the opposite conclusion: the *substance* of the physical world must be one because and inasmuch as empirical and rational knowledge is always subject to the same rules and principles, no matter how different its object may be.

Here, the ideal norms of mathematical knowledge exercise a decisive influence upon the form of empirical physics and upon the interpretation of the concept of movement; but the reverse process may also be observed. The new unity achieved between physics and geometry immediately has the effect of making movement, considered as a mathematical idea, enter into the treatment of geometry. This step signifies one of the most important stages on the path from ancient to modern mathematics, from the 'synthetic' geometry of the Greeks to analytical geometry and to the analysis of the infinite. This step makes it possible to attain a clear distinction between the intution of space and that of empirical things—i.e., to transform the 'space of entities' into a purely 'systematic space'. In Aristotelian physics, space is defined as the boundary of the enclosing body around the enclosed body. And precisely this definition shows that space remains attached to bodies, and that it is merely a determination through and of bodies. In that kind of space, there can be no true freedom of movement or of thought. No line may be extended to infinity in the true sense, for the actually infinite contains a contradiction. Nor is it possible to think of movement continued without limitation in any direction whatsoever, since the specific character of the *movable* immediately sets rigid limits upon this continuance. Certain places and certain directions are proper and natural to certain elements, whereas others would conflict with their nature.

Modern dynamics reverses this state of affairs in that it makes of movement, understood in its complete universality and breadth, a vehicle of spatial knowledge and a determination of geometrical forms. This reversal is most clearly visible in Kepler's stereometric investigations. Kepler ascertains the quantitative relationship between complicated corporeal figures not by juxtaposing them as finished and given entities but by considering, instead of the figures themselves, the rule by which their genesis may be understood. Every corporeal figure now appears as a total of the infinitely many particular determinations of positions through which the figure passes in its genetic process of formation; and it is the task of mathematical thought to find a unitary concept of measurement for this total. From this point of view, the circle appears as the sum total of infinitely many and infinitely small isosceles triangles whose apices meet at its centre; and, analogously, the sphere is thought of and calculated as a whole consisting of an infinite number of cones. Nor do Kepler's investigations extend only to such well-known basic geometrical forms. From the movement of various spherical and conical surfaces around certain axes, diameters, and ordinates, he makes a vast number of new figures emerge, and he tries to determine their volume by general methods.[86] In this way, the concept of infinity proves to be not only a legitimate but actually a necessary *means* for mathematical knowledge; and with that, both the concept of the world and the concept of the *object* of mathematical knowledge receive a new form.

Kepler's method consists precisely in conceiving of and reducing geometrical figures to 'definite integrals'; and every 'definite integral' includes within it the intimate union of two moments that had hitherto seemed irreconcilable. As the ἄπειρον, the infinite had seemed to be the contradiction of limit (πέρας). But in the new form of mathematical analysis, the infinite is placed in the service of quantitative determination, and indeed, proves to be one of its most important tools. The metaphysical transcendence of infinity transforms itself into logical immanence. The concept of space strips itself of the last vestiges of

---

[86] Details about the method of Kepler's 'Stereometria doliorum', in Hieronymus Georg Zeuthen, *Geschichte der Mathematik im 16. und 17. Jahrhundert,* and in Carl Immanuel Gerhardt, *Die Entdeckung der höheren Analysis* (Halle, 1855), 15ff.

materiality and becomes a purely ordinative complex. This transformation is most clearly evident in the *concept of co-ordinates* introduced by Fermat and Descartes. Descartes' analytical geometry is based upon a logical and geometrical basic principle similar to Kepler's *stereometria doliorum*. Descartes also does not deal with curves simply as sensible and visual data but, rather, lets them emerge from an ordered complex of movements. The form of the curve is analytically reduced to the law of these movements. The insight into the relative character of all movement further leads to the possibility of reducing, in principle, any movement, no matter how complex, into elementary movements. These elementary movements take on the most simple form when we think of them as extending along two axes perpendicular to each other. The different relation of velocity that exists between these two movements—the one running along the abscissa and the other along the ordinate axis—determines in an unequivocal way the geometrical form of the resulting curve and makes all its properties completely knowable. And at the same time, in a space thought of purely as relation and system, as is now the case, mathematical thought is perfectly free to determine *which* points will be considered at rest, and which moving. We can move from any given system of co-ordinates to any other, in accordance with a simple rule of transformation, without having the laws of movement and the equations by which specific curves are expressed undergo any but a purely formal change.

Herein lies one of the most important advances of modern analytical geometry beyond Greek mathematics. In the latter, too, there are some very definite beginnings of the use of the concept of co-ordinates. But they are always concerned solely with an individual figure, given in each instance. The notion never raises itself to a truly general principle. The starting point of the co-ordinates had to belong to the figure under consideration itself, or be immediately related to it and to its basic geometrical properties. It was *Fermat* who first created a method that was free of all such limitations and that permitted the centre of the relational system to be located anywhere in the plane of the curve. The direction of the abscissa and ordinate axes also allows all sorts of translations and rotations. Instead of perpendicular co-ordinates one can also use obliquely intersecting axes—in short, the system of co-ordinates is completely independent of the curve itself. In his work, *Ad locos planos et solidos isagoge*, Fermat expressly pointed out the methodological advantage of his procedure as compared to that of the ancients. His central task, he said, was 'to subject this branch of knowledge to an analysis proper and fitting to it, so that in the future there will be universal access to [the concept of] locus'.[87] Pure mathematics would not have been able to conquer this universality in its view of space, if the Aristotelian-Scholastic concept of space had not first been weakened and broken down by attacks from other quarters—especially from cosmology and natural philosophy.

Indeed, long before this change becomes visible in the methodology of the exact sciences, it announces itself in what might be called the new attitude and the new tone of the whole way of *feeling the world*. Giordano Bruno is the typical witness to this change of orientation. The infinite as an instrument of exact scientific knowledge is still alien to him; indeed, in his doctrine of the minimum, he expressly fought against it and denied that the infinite had such a function. But although he fails to see the logical structure of the new mathematical infinity, he nevertheless embraces the infinite universe with all the ardour of a passionate emotion. This heroic fervour now wages battle against the *ne plus ultra* of the medieval dogmatic doctrines of faith and against the Aristotelian cosmology. The free flight of fantasy must never be obstructed by rigid spatial and material limits. Time after time, Bruno attacks the conception of space as 'that which encloses', the σῶμα περιέχον of Peripatetic physics. For Bruno, the space in which the universe exists is not the farthest boundary in which, so to speak, the universe is embedded and wrapped; rather, space is the free medium of movement, extending unhindered beyond every finite border and in all directions. This movement cannot and may not find any obstacle in the 'nature' of any individual thing, or in the general constitution of the cosmos. For movement itself, in its universality and in its limitlessness, constitutes nature as such. Infinite *space* is required as the vehicle of infinite *power*; and this, in turn, is nothing but an expression of the infinite *life* of the universe. In Bruno's thought, these three moments are never sharply distinguished. As in the Stoic and the Neo-Platonic physics, upon which he leans, the concept of space merges with that of the aether, and this, in turn, with the concept of a world soul. Here again, a dynamic motif breaks through, and overcomes, the rigidity of the Aristotelian-Scholastic cosmos. But, this time, the scales are turned by a dynamic *feeling* for the world, not, as with Kepler and Galileo, by

---

[87] Cf. Heinrich Karl Wieleitner, *Die Geburt der modernen Mathematik, Historisches und Grundsätzliches*, vol. I: *Die analytische Geometrie* (Karlsruhe, 1924), 36ff.

the form of the new *science* of dynamics. Even in Copernicus, Bruno
sees not so much the computing astronomer as the hero of this feeling
for the world. 'Who can fully evaluate the magnanimity of this German
who, impervious to the judgments of the stupid masses and against the
current of a contrary belief, first helped the true view to conquer—the
view that liberated our knowledge from a narrow prison, from which
it could only see the stars through tiny openings . . . that view which
traversed the air, penetrated the heavens, and broke down the imaginary
walls of the first, the eighth, ninth, and tenth spheres?'[88]

Sentences such as these make it clear that Giordano Bruno did not
look upon the problem of space as exclusively or even primarily a
problem of cosmology or natural philosophy, but, rather, as a question
of *ethics*. The reason for this curious view may be seen if we recall that
Bruno never affirms the infinity of space by basing himself on the
simple testimony of empirical or mathematical vision. He considers
sense and intuition as such to be incapable of leading to the true concept
of infinity. Rather, we grasp the infinite with the same organ with
which we grasp our own spiritual being and essence: the principle of
its knowledge is to be sought nowhere but in the Ego, in the principle
of self-consciousness.[89] If we want to penetrate the true essence of the
infinite, we must not stop at passive observation or at mere sensible or
aesthetic contemplation. Instead, we must perform a free act and a free
upward movement of the mind to raise ourselves to it. Through this
act the Ego assures itself of its own inner freedom. This act also gives
birth to the vision of the infinite universe which represents, so to speak,
the polar opposite to the Ego's intellectual vision of itself. The knowledge of subject and object are here inextricably intertwined. Whoever
does not find within himself the heroic fervour of self-assertion and of
limitless unfolding will always remain blind to the cosmos and its

[88] Giordano Bruno, *La cena de le ceneri, Opere italiane*, ed. Lagarde, pp. 124ff.; cf. *De
Immenso et Innumerabilibus* i. 1, *Opera latina* i. 1. 201:

> 'Intrepidus spatium immensum sic findere pennis
> Exorior, neque fama facit me impingere in orbes,
> Quos falso statuit verus de principio error,
> Ut sub conficto reprimamur carcere vere,
> Tamquam adamanteis concludatur moenibus totum.
> Nam mihi mens melior . . .'

[89] Giordano Bruno, *De l'infinito, universo e mondi*. Dial. I, *Opere italiane*, 307: 'Non è
senso che vegga l'infinito, non è senso da cui si richieda questa conclusione, perchè l'infinito
non può essere oggetto del senso: et però chi dimanda di conoscere questo per via di senso,
e simile a colui che volesse veder con gl'occhi la sustanza e l'essenza: et chi negasse per
questo la cosa, perchè non è sensibile, o visibile, verebe a negar la propria sustanza et
essere.'

infinity. Throughout Bruno's dialogue *Degli eroici furori*, the form of Renaissance psychology and the form of Renaissance ethics prove to be the decisive motif of the new cosmology. The vision of the infinite is described as an act of the Ego and *required* as an act of the Ego.

The idea of a plurality of worlds, even of an infinity of worlds, was not unknown to medieval speculation. It examined the theoretical *possibility* of this idea from all sides, but generally decided against it, agreeing with the evidence for the unity of the cosmos cited by Aristotle in his *De coelo*.[90] Here again, the form of the refutation reveals that ethical and religious rather than intellectual motifs are operative in it. The sacrifice of the oneness of the world seemed to imply sacrificing the idea of the unique *value* of man, and, furthermore, seemed to deprive the religious process of its proper and unitary centre. This basic attitude was still present in the leading minds of the early Renaissance. In his *De sui ipsius et aliorum ignorantia*, Petrarch emphatically characterized the thesis of the infinity of worlds as the 'peak of insanity', and branded it as philosophical heresy. For Bruno, instead, the intellectual and moral dignity of the Ego, the concept of *person*, requires a new concept of the world. In the entire presentation of his cosmological views, one senses this subjective pathos. He always puts the real emphasis not so much on the universe as on the Ego that must produce the vision of the universe within itself. The new view of the world represents itself in the form of a new, urgent, and swelling impulse. Man finds his true Ego by drawing the infinite universe into himself, and, conversely, by extending himself to it. The boundary between life and death is also blurred; for in death, in the surrender of the individual form of existence, the real truth and universality of life itself is first grasped. It was surely not as a philosopher but as a poet that Bruno—in the sonnets woven into the dialogue *Degli eroici furori*—gave the purest and strongest expression of this basic conception.

> Poi che spiegat' ho l'ali al bel desio
> Quanto più sott' il piè l'aria mi scorgo,
> Più le veloci penne al vento porgo,
> E spreggio il mondo, e verso il ciel m'invio.

[90] For further details on the treatment of this problem in Scholastic physics of the twelfth and thirteenth centuries, cf. Duhem, 'Léonard de Vinci et les deux Infinis', *Études sur Léonard de Vinci*, II.

Nè del figliuol di Dedalo il fin rio
Fa che giù pieghi, anzi via più risorgo.
Ch'i cadrò morto a terra, ben m'accorgo;
Ma qual vita pareggia al morir mio?

La voce del mio cor per l'aria sento:
Ove mi porti, temerario? China,
Chè raro è senza duol tropp'ardimento.—

Non temer, respond' io, l'alta ruina.
Fendi sicur le nubi, e muor contento.
S'il ciel sí illustre morte ne destina.*[91]

Here, the problem of space again flows into the general and basic philosophical problem of the Renaissance, i.e., the relation between 'subject' and 'object'. And with this emerges again the dialectic with which Renaissance philosophy constantly wrestled. Indeed, inasmuch as it is now presented to us in its most concrete form, in the language of spatial vision, the dialectic now seems to have attained its most precise expression. Man, the Ego, appears to the universe, the world, at once as the enclosing and the enclosed. Both determinations are equally indispensable to express his relationship to the cosmos. And thus a continuous mutual reaction and a continuous interaction takes place between them. The infinity of the cosmos threatens not only to limit the Ego, but even to annihilate it completely; but the same infinity seems also to be the source of the Ego's constant self-elevation, for the mind is like the world that it conceives. The philosophy of the Renaissance seizes upon this basic motif from the most diverse points of view and varies it continually. In a dialogue between God and the soul, which Ficino composed on Augustine's model, God says: 'I fill and penetrate and contain heaven and earth; I fill and am not filled because I am fullness itself. I penetrate and am not penetrated, because I am the power

---

* Now that I have given wings to that beautiful desire/ the more I see the air under my feet/ the more do I set my speedy feathers to the wind/ and, disdaining the world, move toward the heavens.// Nor does the cruel end of the son of Deadalus/ induce me to come down; in fact, I climb higher./ I know full well that I shall fall dead to the earth/ But what life compares with this death.// I hear the voice of my heart in the air./ Where are you taking me, temerarious one? Bow,/ for great ardour rarely is not accompanied by pain// Fear not exalted ruin I answer,/ Cleave with certainty the clouds, and die content./ If heaven destines such illustrious death for us.// Though included in Bruno's *Eroici furori*, the sonnet is by Luigi Tansillo, one of the interlocutors in the dialogue. Cf. Francesco Fiorentino, *Poesie liriche edite ed inedite di Luigi Tansillo* (Napoli 1882), pp. 214–17. (M.D.)

[91] *Eroici furori*, Dial. III, *Opere italiane*, 648.

of penetration. I contain and yet am not contained, because I myself
am the faculty of containing.'[92] But all these predicates claimed by the
divinity are now equally attributable to the human *soul*. As the subject
of knowledge, it, too, contains objective reality instead of being contained by it. Its primacy over mere things is assured once and for all.
The Ego can face the infinite cosmos inasmuch as it finds within itself
the principles by which it *knows* that the cosmos is infinite. But this
knowledge itself is not of a merely abstract or of a purely discursive
kind. It is an intuitive certainty that springs, and continuously rushes
forth, not from the logical intellect but from the specific and vital
principle of the Ego. Like Goethe's Ganymede, the man of the Renaissance confronts the divinity and the infinite universe as both 'captor and
captive'. The philosophy of the Renaissance never resolved the dialectical antinomy that is enclosed in this double relationship. But it has
the indisputable merit of having determined the problem and handed
it down in a new form to the following centuries, the centuries of exact
science and systematic philosophy.

[92] Ficino 'Dialogus inter Deum et animam Theologicus', *Epistolae* i, *Opera* fol. 610.

INDEX

Abraham, 30
absolute, the, 8, 10f., 14, 20, 26, 28, 32, 39,
    68f., 127, 132f., 179
abstraction, 158f.
Academy, Platonic, of Florence, 2, 4, 61ff.,
    64, 66f., 69, 77, 83, 88, 98, 114, 130, 131,
    135, 140, 141, 168
Accademia dei Secreti, 152
acedia, 90
acting/action, 84f., 115, 155, 183
Adam, 85, 92, 94, 95
aesthetics, 51, 61, 63f., 66f., 134, 142, 152,
    159, 163, 165f., 169f.
Aggsbach, Vincent von, 13
Aindorffer, Gaspar, 13, 38
Albert of Saxony, 34, 176
Alberti, Leon Battista, 50, 77, 161; works:
    Intercoenales, 77; *Della tranquillità
    dell'animo libri*, 77; *Trattato della Pittura*,
    161
Albertus Magnus, 8
Alexander of Aphrodisias, 81; work: περὶ
    εἱμαρμεύης, 81
Alexandrists, 4
allegory, 73f., 80, 89, 94
analogy, 88, 149
anamnesis (ἀνάμνεσις), 58, 124, 166, 168
Anaxagoras, 26, 167
Andreas, John, bishop of Aleria, 34
angels, 104
Apelt, E. F., 177
Apollo, 80
appearance, 16f., 132
a priori, concept of, 168
Aquinas, Thomas, 8, 54; 127, 138, 139, 184;
    work: *De unitate intellectus contra Aver-
    roistas*, 127
Arabs, 30; Arabic philosophy, 126–27
Archimedes, 35, 168
Aristotelianism (-ists), 1, 2, 19, 84, 88,
    102f., 124, 127, 138, 155; world scheme,
    25f., 102f., 178
Aristotle, 1, 2, 3, 12, 15–18, 24, 26, 59, 81,
    116, 119, 126, 136, 138, 139, 140, 147,
    148, 156, 174, 175, 176, 181, 182, 183;
    works: *De anima*, 140; *Physics*, 181; *De
    coelo*, 181, 189
art, 61, 66ff., 90f., 134, 157, 165, 170

arts, seven liberal, 99f.
Ascoli, Cecco d', 107
astrology, 82, 99–107, 109–19, 121, 147,
    169
astronomy, 7, 27, 111, 117
Augustine, 15, 37, 43, 54, 65, 69f., 95, 98,
    100, 128, 129, 190; works: *Confessions*,
    144; *De civitate Dei*, 71; *De trinitate*,
    128; *De vera religione*, 128, 144
autonomy, ideal of, 98
Averroes/Averroists, 4, 103, 127, 128, 130,
    136, 138, 160

Bacon, Francis, 145
Barbaro, Ermolao, 2
Basle, Council of, 15, 60
Battle between Fortune and Hercules, 73
Bayle, Pierre, 78
beauty, beautiful, the, 61, 63f., 67, 135f.,
    159, 163
becoming, 17, 25, 70, 83, 85, 90, 108, 125,
    132, 173
being, 9f., 14, 17f., 20–22, 25, 28f., 31,
    42f., 52, 58, 64, 68, 80, 84, 89f., 95, 107,
    110, 114, 118, 119, 125, 128, 132–36,
    138f., 142, 151, 156, 166, 173ff., 182ff.
Bembo, Pietro, 164
Benivieni, Girolamo, 131; work: *Canzone
    dell'amor celeste e divino*, 131
Bessarion, 15, 16, 46
Beyond, the, 116
Boccaccio, 95; work: *De genealogia deorum*,
    95
body, the, 114, 126, 130, 133, 136–40
Boll, Franz, 115
bonum: see good, the
Borgia, Lucrezia, 73
Borinski, Karl, 6, 159, 160
Bovillus, Carolus, 88ff.; work: *De sapiente*,
    88, 89, 90ff., 96
Brahe, Tycho, 117, 121
Brothers of the Common Life, 33, 49
Bruni, Leonardo, 1, 2, 5
Bruno, Giordano, 37, 46, 47, 69, 73, 74, 77,
    83, 97, 99, 102, 121, 122, 135, 147f., 165,
    187, 188, 189; works: *La cena de le
    ceneri*, 188; *Degli eroici furori*, 77, 97, 98,
    165, 189, 190; *De immenso et innumerabiliis*,

193

Pennsylvania Paperbacks

Pennsylvania Paperbacks continued